Pretty from the Outside

Pretty from the Outside

The Autobiography of Miss England
1955

Margaret Rowe

© Margaret Rowe, 2025

The right of Margaret Rowe to be identified as the author of this work has been asserted in accordance with the Copyright, Design and Patents Act 1988.

All rights reserved. Except for the quotation of short passages for the purposes of criticism and review, no part of this publication may be reproduced, stored in a retrieval system, or transmitted, in any form or by any means, electronic, mechanical, photocopying, or recording or otherwise, without prior permission of the publisher.

First published by Arena Books in 2025
www.arenabooks.co.uk

Pretty from the Outside
Margaret Rowe

ISBN: 978-1-914390-41-8 Paperback
ISBN: 978-1-914390-42-5 Ebook

A Catalogue record for this book is available from the British Library.

Thema: DNBA; DNBF1; DNBH1; KNSX; JBCC3.

Cover design by Arena Books

~ Contents ~

Chapter 1	~	Early Days	1
Chapter 2	~	Longfords Mill	7
Chapter 3	~	London	21
Chapter 4	~	Hankins Farm	31
Chapter 5	~	Anerley	61
Chapter 6	~	Cwmcarn	79
Chapter 7	~	Lee, South East London	93
Chapter 8	~	Bromley	119
Chapter 9	~	Berkhamsted	159
Chapter 10	~	London	197
Chapter 11	~	Saunton Sands	219
Chapter 12	~	London	225
Chapter 13	~	Monaco	257
Chapter 14	~	Côte d'Azur	263
Chapter 15	~	London	281

1

Early Days

'I couldn't be the father of that! Someone's mixed the babies up,' were my father's first words upon my entrance into the world, on the morning of 13 November 1935 in a nursing home in West Norwood, South East London.

My mother was crying, and the other mothers in the ward were unsettled by the rumpus, so it was decided to send for Matron. Matters did not improve when Matron, taking one look at me, declared, 'But Mr Rowe, she's the image of you.' I was three weeks overdue, weighing 4lbs, with long black hair, fingernails so overgrown they had to be dug out of my palms, my head resembling a shrivelled monkey.

Dad was a hard-working man and tried his hand at all kinds of jobs. When he was courting my mother, he worked as a window cleaner, and after work he would pick her up from her place of work on his immaculate motorbike, his pride and joy. One afternoon, he told her he wouldn't be able to see her again, as he couldn't afford both a motorbike and a girlfriend – one of them had to go. A few days later, she found him waiting outside her workplace, as if nothing had changed.

Their on-off romance continued until they unwisely married.

Pretty from the Outside

After the wedding service they had a falling-out, which saw my mother spend the first afternoon of married life alone, watching a matinee performance at the local cinema.

Dad was a handsome but vain man. A fastidious dandy, he wore the latest fashions of the day. Like the film star Errol Flynn, his moustache was finely trimmed, his Brylcreemed hair always sleek and shining. He fancied himself as a George Raft lookalike. George, a tough American film star, was famed for the white spats he wore in his roles as a ruthless gangster. Spats were usually seen on men of eminence, such as doctors and lawyers, rather than working-class men, but Dad wore white spats as he liked to stand out from the crowd.

Dad's saving grace was his fine sense of humour, providing the joke wasn't on him. Unfortunately, a marked stammer caused him to be self-conscious, detracting from his image of himself as a suave man about town.

Dad's grandmother was a variety artist when she was young, appearing on stage with musical stars, including the great Marie Lloyd who was much loved for the risqué nature of her act. His mother was the exquisite Virginia, whose name I was given. Yearning for a life of fun and frivolity, she had married a studious man who was devoted to serious music and literature. Eventually, she left him and her four children for Mr Percy, a wealthy man with a successful furniture business in Brixton High Street, in South East London. She might have walked out on her husband but she didn't neglect her children, and made sure they were always immaculately dressed and well fed. Every day the four children walked to her house, where she cooked them a nourishing hot meal. Sadly, Mr Percy died in his early fifties, leaving Virginia desolate. Unable to recover from his death, she lost the will to live and, within two years at the age of fifty-two, she succeeded in killing herself with the aid of alcohol.

My mother came from Elephant and Castle, in South London. Her father, an unreliable man, was far too fond of the pub, and her mother died following a backstreet abortion, leaving four children. As the eldest, my mother took over the running of the house, at the age of twelve.

One day when I was a toddler, a strange man came to the house and took my mummy away. I remember Dad telling me, 'Your Mummy doesn't love you any more, so she's gone away.' Dad's sister, my Aunty Vivian, looked after me with her own little boy, Stan, while Dad was at work. I learned many years later that Aunty Viv had wanted to adopt me, but Dad wouldn't hear of it.

It was 1939, and by now the whole country was jittery. It was almost certain we would soon be at war with Germany. I was sent to a nearby children's home, Miss Berryman's Home for Children.

With the declaration of war on 1 September 1939, Miss Berryman and her charges were evacuated to Gloucestershire. Clutching our Mickey Mouse gas masks, we children piled into a noisy train at Paddington Station, where, huddled together, we hurtled through the English countryside for what seemed like an eternity, before pulling into Stroud Station. I was to live in this part of the Cotswolds for the following five years. Exhausted but excited, we youngsters clambered up the steep steps of a charabanc waiting to take us to our new home, me staring intently out of the window, not wanting to miss a moment of this exciting adventure. Woollen mills worked at full pace, their tall chimneys billowing dark smoke high into the clouds. I marvelled at the sight of rolling hills of the greenest green to the right and left, and cows, the colour of rich amber, indolently munching the verdant grass without a care in the world.

On leaving the main road, we made our way through tall white gates, where a long curving drive eventually deposited us at the entrance of a country mansion, our new home. Delightful Holcombe House was set in the beautiful surroundings of Gloucestershire, a mile or so from the nearest town of Nailsworth.

I grew to love the beautiful Cotswolds, with the steep, sloping hills that were tough to climb but crazy to race down. I relished the biting winds of winter when I could barely feel my frozen face but as soon as I was back in the warmth of the house my cheeks became burning fireballs.

In summer, contented cows spent long, lazy days grazing the hills, their luminous eyes gazing, unblinking into mine, with curiosity, never in fear. Glorious autumn rolled in with languid, golden days of heat and colour, bringing forth a thousand and one wasps, spiteful little things ready to attack given half a chance. Hazel trees laden with shining nuts, plopping wherever they happened to fall. Squirrels digging frantically as their winter rations tumbled to the ground, signalling the season's impending arrival.

The first sign of spring was the birdsong in the woods, as longer, warmer days set in and shoots pushed through the dank, decaying matter of winter. Masses of nodding snowdrops, and golden aconites, were the first to show their heads, followed by clusters of dark woodland anemones, their snow-white blooms penetrating the gloom. Clumps of yellow primroses among carpets of tiny violets burst forth in natural order, wherever the warming sun could search them out, bringing new life to a country at war.

The woollen mills in this part of Gloucestershire were working flat out for the war effort, spinning cloth for urgently needed blankets and soldiers' uniforms. I adored the hustle and bustle of the mills. We rascals from Holcombe House became well known for being a menace. We used to press our noses against the windowpanes of the spinning shed, convinced that we were an absolute hoot, and pull comical faces, but not once did those workers so much as glance our way as they sang along to the latest popular songs blaring from the loudspeaker. As much as we persevered in our attempt to get their attention, not once did we succeed.

One sunny afternoon while playing in the garden with other children, we watched as a motorbike with sidecar made its way along the drive, eventually coming to a stop near the front door. A man clambered from the motorbike, before walking with great difficulty towards the rear to open the sidecar. One of the man's legs was rigid, and much shorter than the other one. He wore a heavy, invalid boot, which he swung in a full circle as he slowly made his unwieldy way. I felt sorry for him, but found his fixed grin somewhat disconcerting. It took some effort to free his passenger from the cramped sidecar, but eventually a woman managed to unfold herself from the tiny prison while supporting a small baby wrapped in a white shawl. Two years had passed since I'd last seen her, but there was no mistaking the petite woman with the unforgettable face –my mother. Initially shy, I soon recovered, entranced as I was by the presents they'd brought for me.

My favourite was Rosie, a china baby doll, who became my closest friend throughout the years ahead. I loved her more than Golliwog, more than beloved Teddy, even with the blob of green paint on the tip of her nose she'd picked up somewhere along the way.

The man with the wonky leg was very jolly, scrambling around taking endless photographs of me, whereas my mother seemed worryingly sad and pensive. When I look at those photos today, they depict a giggling, prancing girl, madly overacting, without a care in the world. The truth is, that day I felt lost and bewildered, on the verge of tears. Whose baby was it? Who was the man with the big boot? When their visit was over, I sat on a wall and watched the motorbike disappear round a bend, thinking, 'She's taken that baby, and left me here.'

In our Garden of Eden, it was easy to forget the conflict of war, but we residents of Holcombe House found ourselves guided into the garden at dusk, weather permitting, as the last rays of sun slipped slowly below the horizon, where we listened intently for the distant hum of convoys of bomber aeroplanes making their slow orderly way through the twilight skies towards the English Channel on their nightly mission to drop bombs on Germany. We stood in awe, waiting with bated breath for the deafening drone above our heads, the earth trembling beneath our feet, as we recited, parrot-fashion, 'they're going over,' ignorant of the significance of our words until we were somewhat older.

Sometimes, in the late morning, I would hear the sound of a lone, damaged plane spluttering its way back to base, like a wounded bird of prey seeking the security of its nest.

~ 2 ~
Longfords Mill

During my time at Holcombe House, Dad visited whenever he could. Never certain when he could get away, he would turn up unexpectedly. He tried telling me that he was a conscientious objector. I say 'tried', because at the age of four, I had no idea what he was talking about. The only thing I understood was that he didn't like people fighting each other, which made me proud to have such a kind man as my father.

Kind or not, he was obliged to do his duty for his country in its hour of need. Ernest Bevin, the Minister of Labour throughout the war years, decreed that anyone refusing to fight, had to either be a firefighter in the London Blitz or go down the coal mines in South Wales, as what was known as a Bevin Boy. Dad chose the former.

At the age of five, I had to leave Miss Berryman's care to live with a local family as an evacuee. I was sent to The Clockhouse, at Longfords Woollen Mill, a short stroll from Holcombe House. The family consisted of Mr and Mrs Hopes, Kenneth, a boy of seven, and Barbara, a girl of almost my age. I was to live with them until the war ended, five years later.

On the day I left Holcombe House, Mrs Hopes and Barbara

came to collect me. Unhappy to be leaving everything familiar, my heart sank as I set out with these strangers, with their funny way of talking. We walked a short distance along the main Nailsworth to Tetbury road, then turned sharply down Tabrams Pitch, leading directly to the mill. As we rounded a bend, I perked up considerably. The valley opened up before us, a picture-perfect scene, the powerful elegant mill, central to a cluster of pretty workers' cottages. Swirling smoke curled high from a towering chimney into a clear blue sky, the light Cotswold stone of mill and cottages reflecting a warm, peachy glow, cast by the reflection of the afternoon sun.

The mill was alive with activity, workers rushing here and there, pushing heavy-wheeled containers, piled high with urgently needed cloth for our fighting armies. Turning into our lane, we passed the busy spinning shed, pausing to watch the women at work, singing their hearts out to the latest hit songs as they spun, their cheerful sounds pouring forth at full volume from a loudspeaker blasting into the lane. The Clockhouse stood next to the spinning shed. Chickens pecked leisurely at the grass verges. I spotted what I took to be baby chicks among the large birds, but the bigger ones were a dull brown, whereas the smaller birds' plumage was scarlet, turquoise and gold. Noticing how taken I was with the little ones, Mrs Hopes explained that the little beauties were Bantam Hens. Those little birds were to keep us supplied with tiny fresh eggs throughout the harsh times ahead.

Among the family we were known as Our Dad, Our Mum, Our Ken, Our Barb, with me becoming Our Marg. Our Mum was a skinny, wiry, outspoken little woman in her mid-forties, with greying hair kept in order by a sensible perm, forthright, a spade was a spade, Our Mum took no nonsense from anyone.

Longfords Mill

Not given to kind words, she was hard-working and caring but was darned if she'd let anyone know that. Working non-stop, she kept set days for different chores. From day one, I was treated the same as Our Ken and Our Barb. Right from the start, we girls were dressed identically, but in different colours. I loved my clothes, but loathed the haircut I was forced to have. The slightest hint of shaggy and we were packed off to the barber and given a short back and sides. The barber took delight in shearing us like sheep, but I was miserable as I hated looking like a boy. With time, my hair grew back and I loved letting it blow freely in the breeze, until the day arrived when Our Mum pounced again.

It was just as well Our Dad liked a quiet life, as it was clear who wore the trousers in that house. Tall and fit, with thick dark hair, a gentle presence, setting about his work with no fuss, the smooth running of the mill dependent on him. During the five years I lived at The Clockhouse, I never once saw him lose his temper, or get rattled. Knowing how important my dolls were to me, when he came upon a discarded doll's pram, he rescued it, slowly working away to repair it and meticulously giving it a coat of bright green paint. It looked brand-new when he kindly presented it to me, because that's the kind of person he was. It made me happy, knowing my little family were snuggled together, cosy and safe, inside their pram.

Our Ken, being older than us, did his best to annoy us, especially me, who he considered to be a softy. We girls decided from the off to give him a wide berth, and it was the best thing we ever did.

Our Barb was a tomboy, not the least bit interested in dolls, preferring to climb trees, and that sort of thing, but we formed an easy truce and never fell out.

Pretty from the Outside

Both Our Mum and Our Dad were enthusiastic members of a cycling club. Every Saturday morning, from early spring to late autumn, they were up with the larks, lunches packed, wearing the shortest of shorts, hefty shoes, with thick socks, astride their prized tandem, off to join their fellow cyclists at the local clubhouse. Left to our own devices, we were free until evening.

You had to be tough to live at The Clockhouse. Our only fresh water was carried by bucket from a tap in the garden, then ladled out as needed in the kitchen, before being refilled.

With no gas or electricity, our only heat came from a coal fire, part of an iron range including the oven, the heat of which, being most unreliable, was responsible for the many soggy, pale yellow cakes I tackled. Artificial light came from a single gas globe above the centre of the family table, lit by taking a paper spill from the fire as soon as dusk set in. The gas exploded with a loud pop, before settling to a soothing hum, guaranteed to make us drowsy as the evening wore on. During the long winter evenings we spaced ourselves beneath its feeble glow making rag rugs, or knitting. Needing the lavatory meant a bothersome trip to the end of the garden. On a dark wet night, I'd hang on until I was fit to burst, then grab a torch and make a mad dash for the shed at the end of the garden. Toilet paper was last week's newspaper, torn into squares.

The wireless was our main link with the outside world. Lighthearted variety shows, music, and comedy throughout the day kept our spirits high, but every evening, come nine o'clock, families in every corner of the country gathered around the wireless to hear the latest news bulletin of the day, sometimes encouraging, often grave. Now and then, the voice of the newsreader announced in his voice of doom, 'Following the nine o'clock news, the prime

Longfords Mill

minister will address the nation.' Anxiety filled the hearts of the listeners, dreading bad news, but no matter how worrying the news might be, Mr Churchill had the power to lift us, as his powerful tones travelled over the airwaves: 'We shall never surrender, we will overcome.' The next morning, a discernible lift could be spotted in the demeanour of the workers; those who'd been flagging now set about their tasks with a cheery smile and renewed energy.

As soon as the news bulletin ended, we girls took a lighted candle, and a hot stone water bottle wrapped in a towel, before climbing up the stairs to the attic we shared with the ancient clock, which took up half the room. We would leap into bed, enveloping ourselves in our cosy eiderdown, the hot water bottle between us as we snuggled down back-to-back for the night. Minutes later we'd hear Our Dad's clumping footsteps mounting the stairs on his way to wind the clock, with its hefty handle, so heavy even he found it took all his strength. I grew to love the never-ceasing tick-tock of my never-ceasing friendly clock.

On winter mornings, we woke to icicles hanging inside the window, Our Barb, couldn't resist snapping them off, before heading down for breakfast, where Our Mum would already have a hot fire blazing. We three kids dived in to whatever cereal was on offer, which the other two smothered with sugar. I worried about Our Mum being so scrawny and would tell her I didn't like sugar in hot drinks, hoping she would get my ration. I noticed my ruse didn't work as I had hoped, but I unwittingly did myself a favour, never taking sugar to this day.

The most popular programme of the week, *Workers' Playtime*, aired at 12 pm, Monday to Friday, when workers stopped for lunch. Heavy factory machinery fell silent at 12 pm on the dot, followed by moments of eerie silence, after hours of incessant din.

The workers gathered themselves together, before making their way to the canteen, where they could take it easy for an hour, eat their home-made sandwiches and bite into the wife's home-made apple pie while enjoying their favourite programme.

Over the airwaves came the golden tones of much-loved singers such as the Forces' 'Sweetheart,' Vera Lynn, Gracie Fields, known as 'the lass from Lancashire,' and Anne Shelton's much-loved 'I'll be seeing you.' All over the country, listeners delighted in nostalgic longing, conveyed by the message in the lyrics, 'Everything will be alright, when you come home again,' which reached the heart of every person present, living with the same fears and longings.

My favourite song was 'I'll be with you in Apple Blossom Time.' I loved to imagine lovers taking it easy in fields of glorious trees, their white blossoms waving in the breezy sunshine, too young to recognise my own fears, with Dad fighting fires in the London Blitz, day after day.

Leading names in all fields of entertainment worked ceaselessly for the war effort, at home and in any part of the world where needed, frequently putting themselves in danger, keeping up the spirits of our men and women, at home and at the front, often staying in the most basic conditions.

Monday was washing day – always a hard day at The Clockhouse. Our Mum rose at dawn, keen to set about getting things under way. Her first task was to fill the copper in the wash house with buckets of water, then get a good fire going under the copper. The sooner she had boiling water, the sooner she could get on.

Mr Hankins, the local farmer, arrived at dawn, dragging a trailer of gleaming churns and doling out the day's milk allowance into Our Mum's jug, which she kept in our cool, stone larder. Having already been up for hours, Mr Hankins was up to date with the very latest war news, passing it on to his eagerly awaiting customers. Our Mum enjoyed their daily chats as not only was he a valuable source of news from the front, but he was the first to pass on any local intrigue.

When the water reached the desired temperature, Our Mum could deal with her orderly piles. Bed linen was the first to endure the scalding cauldron, poked about with a heavy wooden pole to Our Mum's satisfaction, then hauled out by the pole and pushed through a wringer several times, before being hung to dry on the washing line in the garden. Our Dad's working overalls, heavily stained with oil, had to undergo an extra boil, because you could never be too careful. The family's daily clothing was subjected to its own punishment when a vicious scrubbing board came into its own. Taking a block of sunlight soap, our best clothes suffered on the board's rough surface to within an inch of survival.

Fearing for my 'delicates', from time to time I plucked up the courage to watch them being sandwiched, again and yet again, by the wringer, before being pegged to the washing line to get a good airing. Our Mum was without a doubt gifted; not once did I know her washing to be less than pristine.

The copper came into its own again on Friday evenings, bath night. A tin bath was taken from the wall of the wash house and filled with hot water. We took it in turns to be painfully scrubbed from head to toe, ahead of our hair being washed with a smelly carbolic soap. I soon realised that it was imperative to get the first bath, meaning hotter, clean water, and thereby avoiding the thick, grimy layer of scum that built up as the evening wore on. A towel hastily wrapped about me, I made a mad dash through the garden to throw myself in front of a blazing fire, thankful to have that ordeal behind me for another week.

We children attended school in the historic small town of Minchinhampton, about two miles from Longfords, set at the highest peak of two miles of horrendous hills, the likes of which I have never had to endure since. We kept well clear of 'Our Ken,' an absolute pest with his bullying and never-ending cruel tricks, mainly aimed at me.

No matter the weather, we proceeded at a snail's pace to try to delay for as long as possible the misery that awaited. Leaving the mill behind us, we passed a charming house, set well back from the road. In the shelter of a porch, wrapped snugly in blankets from head to toe, a teenaged boy sat watching the world go by from a wheelchair. We looked out for him every morning, giving him a cheerful wave, which he always returned with a smile. One day he wasn't in his usual spot, and we learned that he'd died during the night from tuberculosis, a common disease in those days. His name was John Allway, and his death had a profound effect on me, not only because this was the first time someone I knew had died, but also because I'd always believed that you didn't die until you were very old, and worn out. About sixty years later on a visit to Longfords, I walked past the house. A nameplate on the gate read, 'John Allway Cottage.'

In the summer we took to the fields, first crossing Mr Hankins' land, before facing slopes which were too steep to climb straight up. Over the centuries, grazing cattle had worn zigzagging pathways, leading eventually to the top. We followed these paths in the company of slow, trundling cows, their calves at heel with one thought in mind: munching the fresh grass. Now and again, it was necessary to heave a heavyweight animal from our path.

Longfords Mill

Bearing no grudge, and not even looking at the human being who had the temerity to yank her aside, she and her offspring calmly resumed munching.

These pastures once belonged to us children, but today they form part of Princess Anne's estate, and are therefore strictly out of bounds. I wonder if the Princess enjoys these riches any more today than we did as children in the 1940s.

Winters at Longfords were tough. After a warm breakfast, 'Our Mum,' packed us off to school, swaddled from head to toe against the cold. Aimlessly, with no sense of urgency, we took to the roads. We trudged up icy hills in the face of brutal winds and snowdrifts until we reached a fast-running stream, where, without fail, I would plunge my numbed hands into its fast, freezing flow, knowing that in a fleeting moment they would be tingling with heat. Small wonder I suffered with chilblains. Exhausted, hardly able to put one foot in front of the other, we kept going, urged onwards by the penny in our pocket, put there by Our Mum for us to buy a Chelsea bun at the bakers, raked from a blazing oven as we looked on. We always looked forward to this treat as it made our last quarter mile bearable.

On the way home from school, meandering down the hills which had been such a devil earlier in the day, we dilly-dallied to our hearts' content, made even more enjoyable, by the company of my friend Mary, daughter of Mr Hankins the farmer and his wife Lucy. Mary was a delicate, quiet girl, with long dark hair, a pale complexion, with a hint of mauve shadows beneath her eyes. A gentle person, she loved dolls as much as I did and had no desire to climb trees, unlike my raucous housemates. Following our steep descent, we took a shortcut over Mr Hankins' high field to the farmhouse, where, tumbling, muddy wellies cluttered the hallway, leading to a bright, friendly living room, next to the ancient kitchen, whose white stone flagstones had been worn into permanent hollows from years of hefty boots being inflicted on them.

The kitchen was where I would find Mrs Hankins, the lady I revered above all others. Lucy Hankins fitted my ideal of a lady of the manor to perfection. With pale golden hair framing her gentle face with soft curls, she was tall and slender, softly spoken, a warm, caring person reflected in the serenity of her lovely face. She used to call me Margie, which I appreciated. It was so much nicer than Our Marg. I was to spend many long, perfect days on the farm.

During the war years, we had no bananas. I'd seen illustrations and photographs of them at school, but could only dream of the day I might taste one. Anyone at school who'd been lucky enough to have tasted one was looked on with awe by the rest of us.

Turning up at the farm one morning, I sensed an air of excitement. Mrs Hankins had somehow or other come by a banana. What's more, she'd given instructions that no one touch it until Margie arrived. At teatime, we gathered in the kitchen for the ceremony of slicing and tasting the banana. After everything I'd heard about bananas, I had at last tasted one, but even more thrilling than tasting a banana, Mrs Hankins had waited for me.

Happy at home and at school, the only cloud hanging over me was my constant worry about Dad. Listening to the news and overhearing grown-ups talk, I knew the dangers he faced daily as a firefighter. Whenever he left at the end of a visit, his parting words were, 'See you in a fortnight.' At the end of two weeks, I'd make my way to the bus stop at Tabrams Pitch, where I'd sit on the iron railings, waiting for the 8 pm bus from Nailsworth. Several weeks might pass before he appeared. If he wasn't on the 8 pm bus, I took

Longfords Mill

myself off home to bed, fighting to stay awake until the last bus at 10 pm was due. The 'ting' of a bell, echoing across the valley, told me the bus had stopped. At that hour, it was always Dad, so I could go back my sleep relieved.

One night I had a vivid dream, whereby a devil brutally took out all my teeth. Try as I may to push the dream from my mind, it haunted me. While chatting to my friend Danny in the playground, I told him about my dream. 'I know all about dreams,' he boasted, saying that when you dream of losing your teeth, it means that someone close to you has died. At this, I screamed hysterically, certain that Dad had been killed, which would explain why he'd not come to see me for such a long time.

Hearing my anguished cries, our teacher, Miss Natress, raced to the playground, demanding to know who was responsible for causing Margaret's outburst. Danny was severely reprimanded, but the poor little chap must have wondered what he'd done to deserve such a scolding. After all, he'd only interpreted a dream.

From my usual position on the railings, I waited week after week for Dad, almost without hope, but when I saw him alight from the bus, there was no mistake, he was alive after all. Jumping down from the railings, I ran towards him. As delighted to see me as I was him, he would sweep me into his arms, covering my face with enthusiastic kisses. In spite of my fears, he hadn't forgotten me. Having Dad back in The Clockhouse made everything all right again. Our Ken, as always, found himself turfed out of his little room, but I slept peacefully that night knowing Dad was just on the other side of the wall.

Over the weekend, the two of us would walk for miles, holding hands as we sang the latest hit songs. My favourite, 'The Umbrella Man,' sung by comedy double act Bud Flanagan and

Pretty from the Outside

Chesney Allen, reached number one on the hit parade and was played incessantly on the wireless. During the war, umbrella menders plied their trade on the streets of busy markets, repairing umbrellas and parasols while the customer waited.

Bud Flanagan was one of the 'Crazy Gang,' possibly the most idolised group of comedians in the country, performing well into their nineties, until, one by one, each toppled from his perch.

The Umbrella Man, Bud Flanagan and Chesney Allen:

Toodle-luma-luma
Toodle-luma-luma
Toodle-lai-ai

Any umbrellas, any umbrellas to mend today
Bring your parasol, it may be small, it may be big,
He repairs them all with what you call a thingamajig

Pitter patter patter,
Pitter patter patter
Here comes the rain

Let it pitter patter
Let it pitter patter
Don't mind the rain

He'll mend your umbrellas
Then go on his way singing
Toodle-luma-luma toodle-lai
Toodle-luma-luma toodle-lai

Any umbrellas to mend today?

Longfords Mill

Famished and exhausted from our travels, we always ended up at our local pub, The Weighbridge, directly opposite my old home, Holcombe House. As children weren't allowed in the bar, I'd take my place on a bench in the garden and wait for Dad to join me with a pint or two of Stroud Brewery's best bitter. Of major importance were the cigarette cards he saved for me. I adored these cards and would spend hours looking at the glamorous ladies, with their radiant complexions, the blondest hair, in alluring, peekaboo styles, wearing shimmering, slinky gowns, and exquisite high-heeled shoes, leaning languidly against Hollywood pillars, sensuously drawing on the longest cigarette holder you've ever seen. Then there were the male stars, handsome men staring invitingly at the camera from beneath furrowed brows, while drawing deeply on a cigarette. Only one man could hold a candle to these handsome hunks, my dad.

A group of keen card collectors operated at school where I could swap my doubles for those I was short of. Dad, being a heavy smoker, combined with the cards his fellow firemen saved for him, made me a popular member of the group.

Directly opposite the Hankins Farm stood a distinguished mansion, once the home of the owner of Longfords Mill, at the time a home for naughty girls. Every Sunday, around midday, it was my job to fetch the Sunday newspaper from The Weighbridge pub. Often a group of girls from the home would be sitting on the railings at the top of Tabrams Pitch, chatting to a couple of soldiers. The girls weren't six, like me and Our Barb, but teenagers, more like film stars, all polished and grown up, with the latest pageboy hairstyles, wearing lipstick and smoking cigarettes.

One afternoon, we girls were sauntering home from school when a threatening crack of thunder rolled overhead and heavy drops of rain plopped around us. Racing for the only tree in the middle of the field we made it, just moments before a mighty deluge set in. After a while I noticed a soldier in uniform sheltering behind the tree. It wasn't long before he made his presence known to us by enquiring if we girls liked sweets, as he had some in his pocket. Our love of sweets got the better of us. Imagine, a bounty of barley sugar, sherbet lemons, and, with luck, a bar or two of chocolate. The soldier suggested we each put a hand in a trouser pocket, which we hastened to do. However, the bounty we'd been dreaming of was not what our greedy fingers grasped. Instead we felt something hot, hard, and without doubt, dangerous.

Glancing at each other, hands hastily withdrawn, we took off as fast as our legs would carry us. Lightening flashed, the earth trembled, blinding, torrential rain drenched us to the skin, but we kept going. We ran through squelchy cowpats and heavy mud, and never looked back until we reached the safety of the farm kitchen.

Sent on an errand a few days later, I passed the bus stop where a group of girls were sitting on the railings, enjoying a smoke and making small talk to that soldier.

My head held proudly, I showed no sign of recognition, although on reflection, I wouldn't have thought those older girls would be interested in sweets.

~ 3 ~
London

In May 1941, the Blitz suddenly came to a halt. After eight months of being pounded day and night, London and other major cities fell silent. Londoners, unaccustomed to the quiet, were wary at first, fearing it might be a trick, but over time they relaxed, enjoying the respite, no matter how brief. Dad felt it a good time to visit London, to stay with some old friends who were keen to see me at the ripe old age of six. I believe they'd once been close friends of my mother.

On the morning of our departure, we took a bus from Nailsworth, to Stroud. Entering the town, I couldn't help but notice a pervasive unpleasant odour, which seemed to grow stronger as we neared the station.

Waiting excitedly on the platform, holding Dad's hand, a grand old building directly beyond the railway track caught my eye. High on the wall engraved in large, fancy letters, Dad read aloud, 'Stroud Brewery.' Stroud beer was the county's favourite beer, highly esteemed and widely advertised. I must say, I was chuffed to have solved the riddle of the 'Stroud Pong,' and to learn where the famous beer was brewed.

Suddenly the charging train powered in, screeching to a halt alongside the crowded platform. Whistles blew, clouds of steam gushed from the hissing engine when I momentarily caught a glimpse of a fireman shovelling coal into a blazing, red-hot, cavernous mouth. Everything happened so fast, amid so much noise, that I was quite scared, but I didn't let on. Passengers gathered their luggage together, rushing to be first through the carriage doors to grab the best seats.

Slamming doors, shrieking whistles, there was such a carry-on, until an official waved a green flag from the rear of the train, signalling the off, and the train slowly chugged out of the station.

Settling into my corner next to Dad, I found myself following the rhythm of the train, musing silently. *Clackety-clack* along the track, *clackety-clack* along the track, building up speed, faster and faster, always more insistent, the carriage rolling wildly from side to side. Slightly unnerved, fearing the train was about to overturn, I fleetingly caught sight of the name 'Didcot' on a passing platform. On we hurtled, alongside lush green countryside, *clackety-clack* along the track, *clackety-clack* along the track, until, noticeably losing speed, the train approached Reading Station.

Reading Station heaved with activity as the train pulled in. Stroud Station had been hectic, but compared to the scrum at Reading, it was a haven of peace.

The need to stretch our legs while battling against more incoming passengers all anxious to secure their favoured seats demanded considerable resilience. All quite a shock for a girl from Longfords, but exciting all the same.

A magnificent building took pride of place that overpowered the station's frontage. Huntley & Palmers. Even more impressive was the Coat of Arms of our king, displayed high above the station's imposing entrance, declaring, 'By Royal Appointment to his Majesty King George VI.' I would have thought the king preferred royal biscuits, not ordinary ones like normal folks, such as the Hopes. From now on, I shall treat Huntley & Palmers with more respect, knowing they are good enough for our king.

Leaving Reading behind, we resumed our journey through the English countryside, until slowly but surely the landscape merged into suburbia, where green fields had been converted into orderly parkland settings, where locals socialised, and mothers pushed their youngsters on swings and roundabouts. Row upon row of identical terraced houses stretched into the distance, each with its own square of front garden, and a fair-sized strip behind, some well looked after and awash with colour, some neglected, and others just somewhere to hang the washing. Here and there were small parades of shops, where the locals could buy the essentials to eke out the main weekly shop. The roads were almost devoid of cars, as they were viewed as a luxury few could afford at this time of hardship. London Transport ran an excellent bus service, popular and well supported, as was the London Underground Service, covering suburbs far from the centre of London, well within the reach of suburbanites, many dependent on public transport to get them to work.

As we drew closer to the centre of London, the houses changed character. They were generally tall terraces, elegant in their day, but today they were shabby, most of them rented out as bedsits. Nearing Paddington, these bedsits towered over the railway line, which meant no light entered the rooms and the occupants had to have the electric lights on as they went about their daily life, seemingly oblivious to being stared at by nosy folk like me. I knew it was rude to stare, but try as I may I couldn't help myself.

On arriving at Paddington Station, our carriage was charged

with commotion, as those who'd fought to be first on now fought to be first off. We stayed put, waiting for the crowds to disperse, before making our way to an ABC café, one of Dad's favourite calling places when visiting Longfords, where we tucked into a hot meal, before facing the next stage of our journey.

The bus service was nearby, so, feeling refreshed and energised, we mounted the steep stairs of the Red London Bus, taking us across London, all the way to West Norwood. We chose the front seats, knowing we'd get the best views. This was really important to me, as I was to see the place where I was born, and to which I'd return as soon as the war ended, because Dad had promised. I secretly tried to catch sight of my mother out shopping among the crowds. I didn't mention this to Dad, knowing it was a sore point.

The bus took us along Edgware Road towards Marble Arch, where whole buildings had been demolished by the Blitz, leaving gaping craters where shops had just a few weeks ago been thriving businesses. I spotted the common weed, Rosebay willowherb, its tall emerald green leaves and bright pink blossoms already flourishing in the disturbed soil, alongside piles of rubble. All along Park Lane, debris was stacked in orderly heaps. Dad said that as there'd been no recent bombs, they'd had time to get things shipshape, as it was important to keep the traffic moving.

Heading towards Hyde Park Corner, traffic merged into a frightening free-for-all, coming at us from all directions. Black taxis, hurtling at breakneck speed, took on crazy motorbikes, zooming in and out of slower traffic. Red buses swayed in their haste to take corners at speed, lorries used their size to intimidate smaller vehicles. Our driver, well used to such a scrummage, kept well clear, continuing calmly, at a steady pace.

It was not until we crossed the River Thames and were in

London

South London, that I fully appreciated the scale of the devastation. Mutilated streets, with one house left standing in miles of wastelands stretching far into the distance. Strewn among the debris, now and then I caught sight of a child's smashed bicycle, a broken pram, everyday reminders that real families had lived here. I wondered where they lived now.

Later, we passed grand houses, where one side of the road was completely flattened, trees from their beautiful gardens sawn into sections, then pushed to one side, allowing the traffic to keep moving, while homes opposite stood untouched. At one bleak point, I spotted in the distance a group of houses with their outside walls decorated with wallpapers of vibrant, floral designs, some with fashionable stripes, or painted in simple rainbow tints.

I wondered why more people didn't choose wallpaper for their outside walls. It was so much prettier than plain bricks. As we continued on, I sensed things were not all they appeared to be. Lavatories hung precariously from the pretty walls. I noticed a number of large baths suspended in mid-air, hanging on by one foot, certain to crash to the garden below should a strong wind blow. Heavy pictures, mirrors and family portraits clung to their given positions, upstairs and down.

'Why are the walls hanging out, Daddy?' I asked.

'It's because of the bombs,' he replied, leaving me none the wiser.

Trundling on, accustomed now, to the never-ending scenes of desolation, we passed parades of shops, badly damaged, a few open for business. Here and there I spotted a shopkeeper trying his best to retrieve what he could of his damaged wares as he struggled to regain some kind of order.

We got off the bus at West Norwood, where it was obvious

it too had taken its fair share of punishment – the now familiar sight of immaculate buildings alternating with gaping black holes. Feeling tired and dispirited, we walked on, passing damage to the left and right of us, but I cheered up no end, when on turning a corner, we found ourselves in Cheviot Road, a surprisingly quiet, welcoming tree-lined road of stylish houses, each with a well-tended front garden behind its own small gate, a peaceful corner in war-torn London.

As we made our way through the gate of one such house, the front door flew open and Dad's friends, the two Aunties, rushed to welcome us. Aunty Minnie and Aunty Elsie were sisters, in their late thirties, I should think. Similar in every way, with identical short haircuts, they were attractive women, stylish, both wearing lipstick, and pink rouge on their cheeks. Clearly great friends, they joked and giggled between themselves from the moment we arrived until the day we left.

After a much-needed, welcoming meal, I faced a barrage of presents, a tall doll, dressed top to toe in pink, with blonde curls. I called her Molly. I fell in love with her the moment I saw her. A party dress, the likes of which I'd never imagined owning, red velvet, with diamonds sprinkled round the sleeves and round the hem of the skirt, perfect for Farmer Hankins' Christmas party.

The inside of the house was an eye-opener, with the softest creamy carpet everywhere, even up the stairs. It struck me they must have lots of money to afford carpet on the stairs.

Splendid curtains hung at the bay window of the front room, patterned all over with pale pink roses and green leaves. There was the softest green velvety settee, so long it could seat three people at the same time.

Upstairs, there was a bathroom with shining silver taps, one for hot water – fancy having hot water inside a house – and one for cold. Above the bath was a fitted heater, so I could have a really warm soak, every day if I wanted to. Not like The Clockhouse, only on Fridays, in the wash house so cold I'd be in and out of that tin bath in no time at all.

Next to the bathroom, there was a tiny room with a lavatory which meant there'd be no more frantic dashes through the garden every time you needed to wee. Above the lavatory was a chain you pulled yourself, then, like magic, water rushed down, leaving everything fresh and nice for the next person.

I must say, the Aunties quite wore me out with their fussing and giggling, trying to make me laugh at some childish trick or other, never serious for a minute. I wonder if they'd have found things so funny if I'd messed the place up, everything being so polished and new.

Naturally, Dad was constantly running out of cigarettes, a good reason for us to take lots of walks. He took me to what used to be the hospital on Knights Hill, where I was born, now turned into a fire station. Much more sensible than lots of ladies coming in and having babies, especially when there was a war going on.

We stood outside the house where we'd lived with my mother in Saint Julian's Farm Road, before she ran away with the man with the big boot. We were lucky to see it because the opposite side of the road was no more, having been hit by a bomb, but I couldn't remember living there. Dad took me to see the tiny terraced cottage where his mother, my grandmother, Virginia, was born. It gave me a lovely warm feeling knowing that once upon a time, I'd been a part of my own family. Dad said my mother couldn't be bothered to give me a name, so he had chosen Margaret Virginia. Although he didn't have anything good to say about my mother I knew how much he missed her, and would do anything to get her back, but he'd burned his bridges as far as she was concerned. She had to live with the man with the boot, look after their two little boys and do the cooking.

The Aunties' jokes were wearing thin and making me tired, as much as I'd loved staying in their lovely home, and being spoiled rotten, with the best cooking ever, much tastier than Our Mum's efforts. With all her good points, bless her, she was no cook.

The day came for us to leave. To my surprise, I felt a tingle of excitement run through me, thinking of The Clockhouse, the farm and being back with everyone again.

Following enthusiastic hugs and kisses, Dad and I headed along streets of now familiar scenes of desolation. I thought kindly of the Aunties, how lucky I'd been to share their warm paradise for a while, safe from all the bomb damage.

Throughout the long journey to Paddington, I silently took in poor, broken London. How could it possibly be put back together again? Passing mile after mile of barren waste, I tried to make some sense of it all. I was too young to fully comprehend but old enough to know it was wrong, and to realise the danger that Dad, and his workmates, were in every single day, putting out fires as bombs fell all around them.

Forty or so years later, finding myself in South East London, I drove past the Aunties' house. Cheviot Road had escaped the bombs and I was able to spot their house. In many ways the road looked exactly as I remembered it. The trees still grew on the pavement, tall but naked, their branches sawn off. The road was still upmarket, but the front gardens had been paved, providing parking for cars and vans. That's progress for you, the serenity gone, never to return. I hastened away, lucky to have known it

London

back in 1941.

Over the years, my memories of the Aunties have faded somewhat, but I've never forgotten the houses that were 'pretty on the outside.'

~ 4 ~
Hankins Farm

As spring turned into summer I spent much of my free time at the farm. Early morning saw me heading for the spotless cow shed in good time for the morning ritual of milking the herd. The shed was pristine, all the brass utensils were highly polished, even the milking pails looked brand-new. I believe Mr Hankins even polished the cows! Every item on the farm was cared for by him, a lone farmer without assistance. The cows were named after flowers, Daisy, Cowslip, Primrose, and Bluebell, among others, all sweet-natured and gentle, more like pets than farm animals. One day, Mr Hankins let me have a go at milking Bluebell, who welcomed me, but try as I may, I failed. My hands were just not strong enough to give the good hard jerk that was required. She was very nice about it, though, and never resented my feeble efforts.

One morning I was up in the high field when a dreadful fight broke out between two cows. Fearing one might kill the other, I raced to find Mr Hankins, breathlessly insisting he come right away to avoid a fight to the death. Smiling benevolently, and quite relaxed about the whole thing, he said, 'Don't you worry your pretty little head, Margie, you leave-um be.' Well, I tried. If he wasn't concerned that his cows were fighting to the death, he would have to deal with the consequences.

A steep slope ran from the Hankins' front garden down to a fast-running stream below. A few disused chicken sheds were dotted about the slope, and we children wondered if we could make our own hideaway in the shed nearest the stream, so we could take a paddle before having a picnic outside our shed. Mr Hankins agreed, so we set about cleaning out the messy droppings left by the last inhabitants. Mrs Hankins rescued an outdoor table and chairs from somewhere or other, and we stashed away personal bits and pieces on the well-scrubbed shelves, and cosied up safely inside. It was particularly comforting to be inside the shed when heavy rain pummelled the roof. Unfortunately, we were unable to eat our lunch inside. As much as we scrubbed and scrubbed, it was impossible to rid our haven of ancient chicken waste, but we enjoyed many outdoor picnics in the midday sun. A few yards beyond The Clockhouse lay magical Longfords Lake, today, Gatcombe Lake. This was part of Princess Anne's estate, but in the 1940s the lake belonged to us. We spent many happy hours fighting our way through choking undergrowth, our aim being to get to the boathouse on the opposite side. A lovelier sight you couldn't imagine, but it was a vast lake, and we never quite made it.

The lake was neglected; all the strong men were away fighting, those left behind were too old, or had better things to do than tend our lake. Messing about at the water's edge one day, gingerly making my way over slimy, mossy stones, that menace, Our Ken, pushed me into the water. Soaked and ice-cold, my shrieks could be heard for miles as I raced the short distance to The Clockhouse, where Our Mum soon sorted me out.

At wild strawberry time, I wandered the woodlands high

above the mill, feasting my eyes on the scarlet carpet set against dark soil, stretching as far as the eye could see, against a backdrop of bright summer green. Throughout the season we girls gathered bowl upon bowl of these tiny fruits for Our Mum to turn into jam. The jam was then stored in saved jam jars, before being stacked away in the larder to see us through the coming winter.

Saturdays being a free day, we often made our way into Nailsworth to visit Our Gramp and Our Gran Wilson, Our Mum's parents, both born in the 1860s, so quite ancient, but there were no flies on them. Their home, a solid brick house, was set right in the centre of town, with all the shops they needed on their doorstep.

Our Gran was a tiny creature, her face a map of tiny wrinkles, her pure white hair cut sensibly and kept in order with a hair grip, ensuring no straying forelock interfered with her busy day. Fiercely independent, always with a wraparound apron to protect her dress, she did all the cooking and cleaning. Our Gramp, always to be found pottering in his shed out in the back yard, was a tall, skinny old man, with a curling handlebar moustache stretching from ear to ear. He was never seen without a stinking pipe between his teeth, which he sucked on constantly, his flat cap, a permanent fixture, both indoors and out, and the tightest waistcoat housing his pocket watch on a silver chain. Many a happy hour I spent watching him silently working at his vice, making or mending something or other, lost in a world of his own, as he sucked and puffed.

Whenever we turned up, Our Gran produced a supply of sweets, chocolate, and home-made cakes, packed and ready for us to take home, plus a selection for Our Ken. Should a younger pair of legs be needed to collect something from some distance, I would always volunteer, happy to be of use in some way, because I loved them both dearly.

Aunty Betty, Our Mum's unmarried sister, lived with Our Gran and Our Gramp. She was seemingly a quaint, timid lady in her mid-forties, quietly spoken, with permanently rounded shoulders, a soft perm controlling her fair hair, sure to be wearing a cardigan, buttoned up to her chin, a typical spinster. Whenever I visited, she invited me upstairs to her bedroom, where she regaled me with the latest beauty hints devoured from the latest fashionable women's magazines. One day, she confided in me that she rinsed her face in the wee in her chamber pot every morning. It seemed that a leading expert in the field of beauty had discovered that human urine contained miraculous beautifying properties, fortifying the delicate skin of a lady's complexion considerably. Suggesting I take a closer look at her face, I duly peered at it but couldn't see that it had done much for her. However, I may have been wrong as Aunty Betty went on to marry not once but twice, outliving both husbands, and eventually passing away, aged ninety-six.

Early evening, we girls made our way home, laden with delicacies, our pockets jingling with coins. Without fail, we called at the fish and chip stall, parked in front of the Nailsworth Bus Station, where we ordered two servings of 'Burn your mouth chips,' doused with vinegar, before being wrapped in newspaper, ready to be devoured on the way home.

The summer of 1941 was a happy one, the warm weather making our hike to school a pleasure. During the war, all school children were assigned a free pint of milk at mid-morning, and any child considered malnourished, or in danger of developing rickets, was also made to swallow a tablespoon of malt extract, the strange thing being, the ones in need of the toffee-like extract

Hankins Farm

loathed it, complaining the texture made them feel sick, going to any lengths to avoid swallowing it, including bribery, whereas the fittest of us relished the sticky toffeelike stuff. I have to admit to helping out in a few emergencies.

We all hated it when the dentist visited. Well, I remember being dragged kicking and screaming to the dentist's chair where I was held down, still fighting, by several adults, as a soft cushion with a peculiar odour was pressed to my face, then waking up to find bloody gaps where teeth had once been, leaving me with not only fewer teeth, but with a lifelong terror of dentists.

More enjoyable was the annual visit from the school photographer. We'd take turns to stand before a traditional Cotswold wall, while our head and shoulders were photographed for the sake of posterity, as we beamed from ear to ear. I have before me now the image of a laughing girl without a care in the world, an immaculate ribbon in my hair, specially ironed for the occasion by Our Mum.

One day, Brian, a real know-it-all, took it upon himself to tell a group of we girls where babies came from. I didn't believe him for a minute, laughingly assuring the girls, 'That's a load of nonsense, it can't be true. I know my Dad would never do anything like that.'

Not long afterwards, I was in the farmhouse kitchen with my idol, hanging onto her every word as usual, when she completely took the wind out of my sails. She was going to have a new baby, a little brother or sister for Mary. In a flash, it struck me, Brian had been telling the truth. Hard as it was for me to face, Mrs Hankins was guilty. How could someone I idolised let me down so badly? After putting my complete trust in her, I had been betrayed. Shaken to my very core, I brooded for some time, but the pain of finding out the most wonderful human being in the world was imperfect eased when she came home from the hospital with Baby John, with his tiny wriggling toes, and his strong fingers tightly gripping my own, as his blue eyes gazed into mine.

Completely smitten by the baby, he became mine. Wielding the heavy pram around various nooks or crannies was hard work, but thankfully the pram was soon replaced by a sensible pushchair. This made it possible to zigzag around the bends of the steep slope to our hideaway where Baby John joined us in our daily picnics beside the stream, before making our way to the opposite bank by way of sturdy stepping stones, then cooling our feet in its clear, fast-flowing water.

Above the farmhouse lay Mr Hankins' dairy, which, like his cowshed, was always immaculate. He could be found every morning pasteurising that morning's milk yield, making sure his customers didn't catch any germs. Baby John loved to watch his Daddy working, while I could only marvel at the spotlessness of the place. Glinting in the morning sunlight streaming through long, narrow windows set high on the tall walls, even the ancient flagstones on the floor were snowy white. Mr Hankins went quietly about his business, cleaning every corner of the farm himself. Not once in five years did I see anything grubby or out of place. From time to time, I would catch sight of him quietly working in a far field repairing something or other, always working at his own steady pace. As Our Mum was fond of saying, 'You could eat your dinner off the floor of Mr Hankins' cowshed.' Sixty years later, I was in the area and called in at the farm. The door was opened by none other than Baby John, now an elderly man. He greeted me with, 'It's Margaret, isn't it?'

Autumn crept in, teasing everyone with lazy days of sweet, sunny stillness, and not a hint of a hostile winter skulking around

Hankins Farm

every corner, waiting to catch us out. I celebrated my seventh birthday in November 1942. Dad thought it was time to have a proper photograph taken of me. At the time, all sizeable towns were in possession of a professional photographer, with his own studio, set in the most exclusive part of town. The Brownie was the only camera available to the general public, fine for snapshots, but for true excellence you needed a professional. Dad thought Cheltenham would be the ideal town, so after a thorough going-over by Our Mum, wearing a recently knitted green cardigan, and a freshly ironed pink hair ribbon, that's where we headed by bus one Saturday morning.

After strolling to the end of the promenade, we somehow or other found ourselves in the exclusive region of Montpellier, with its dazzling selection of fashionable shops, clearly aimed at the well-to-do. It was here we came upon a quality photographic studio, just the place Dad had in mind.

Expertly displayed in the front window was a selection of the loveliest photographs I'd ever seen, including stunning brides, group shots of families sitting in front of a welcoming fire with many including a much-loved pet taking prime position in the foreground. Scenes of the landed gentry dressed to the hilt in their hunting pinks just before the off were especially popular, as were images of young men and women posing in their service uniforms.

Plucking up the courage to enter such a chic establishment, in we dived, to the sound of a loudly clanging bell. In a flash, a dapper, middle-aged man, sporting a well-tended, greying beard, clad in a casual tan-coloured corduroy jacket, typical of these parts, sprang from behind the scene, inviting us to take a seat in the lush reception where we could make ourselves at home as we discussed our requirements.

Pretty from the Outside

My eyes were drawn to several tall easels, each displaying samples of the highest-quality portraits, all his own work, the gentleman informed us. After explaining what he had in mind, Dad was assured it would be an honour to take the young lady's photograph, whereupon he escorted me to a small dressing room and advised me to adjust my clothing and put the finishing touches to my hair.

The spacious studio resembled a scene in a country garden, with a small tree I thought was real, but on closer inspection proved to be artificial. Potted plants were scattered casually around the set, effectively bringing the outdoors inside. Instructed to sit on a wooden stool in the foreground, the cheery photographer arranged my skirt neatly about my knees.

We aim for perfection at all times, he expounded, the bulging hankie hastily stuffed up my sleeve, escaping his perfectionist's eye. To this day, the bulge in my sleeve jars my orderly mind. Special lights were carefully lined up at varying heights in order to enhance my best features, and we were ready to go. Just as he was about to take the first shot, I completely froze. It wasn't in my nature to play up, but I was adamant, I had no intention of smiling. The poor man, no longer dapper but frenzied, nearing the end of his tether, telling every joke in the book, squeaking every squeaky toy in the place, all to no avail, no smile was forthcoming, until, after an absolute age, for one unguarded moment my concentration slipped and I relaxed my frown, producing an involuntary half-smile. In that split second the poor fellow seized the moment and got his shot.

Relieved that was behind me, I cheered up no end, remembering Dad had tickets for a matinee performance of the pantomime 'Little Red Riding Hood,' playing at the terribly grand, Everyman Theatre near the town centre. We joined the long queue that led from the doors of the theatre, slowly inching forward with excited family groups, their exuberant offspring hardly able to contain themselves, desperate for the show to get going. On reaching the foyer, I stared with unbelieving eyes at the glories surrounding me. Surely, this must be like the king's palace. From our seats in the stalls I stared behind me at three balconies rising upwards, all with row upon row of richly covered crimson seats lit by soft overhead lights, guiding the excited audience to their seats. High above our heads was a domed ceiling, adorned by paintings of exquisite handmaidens wearing floating gowns of pastel shades, their golden hair piled high like goddesses, but most impressive of all was the beauty of the largest, magnificent chandelier imaginable, its glittering beams shooting throughout the vast auditorium, lighting up the whole theatre.

Without warning, the orchestra started up, taking everyone off guard. Heavy velvet red curtains slowly parted, revealing, mid-stage, a radiant Fairy Queen. And so began an afternoon of enchantment.

Shimmering in her white gown, a crown encrusted with diamonds placed on her long golden hair, and sparkling with every turn of her head, as did the magic wand she waved when performing amazing magic tricks. Melodious tones flowed from her throat as she trilled from songs of melancholy to happiness, depending on the scene.

It must have been an awful shock for Little Red Riding Hood finding a dreadful wolf in her grandmother's bed. She was lucky to get away with it. It's just as well there happened to be a kindly woodsman nearby to save her life.

I especially loved two comical fellows, because they made me laugh as they pleaded with the audience to help them sing along to a special song. The silence that followed made me think they were out of luck, but eventually we were worn down. I begged Dad to sing along with me. 'I'm not making a fool of myself in front of a load of strangers,' was all he said. I think he was a bit shy. The title, 'The Banana Song,' flashed up on a big screen, and before long, the whole lot of us were cheerfully singing along to:

> *When can I have a banana again*
> *tell me, Mother, do*
> *when can I have a banana again*
> *like I used to do*
> *I like them for breakfast*
> *I like them for lunch*
> *I don't mind them single*
> *or in a bunch.*
> *when can I have a banana again*
> *tell me, Mother, do.*

Completely relaxed, troubles forgotten for the time being, the comics had their work cut out to quieten us down after they'd made us so happy. There was no doubt about it: they were the highlight of the afternoon. Eventually, things ended happily ever after for Little Red Riding Hood. I hope she learned her lesson and was more careful about who she trusted in the future. The unforgettable afternoon eventually came to its happy conclusion, the crimson velvet curtains slowly drew to a close and the orchestra started up as I stumbled, entranced, from the theatre.

The following morning, I took Dad a cup of tea in his bedroom. He greeted me with, 'Here's my own Little Red Riding

Hankins Farm

Hood.' At that moment, my life was perfect.

As Christmas 1942 neared, excitement grew, when our class was selected to present the school's seasonal play. Christmas was always a jolly time, a break from the routine bringing about an early holiday mood, our concentration gone to pot, as our time was taken up making frivolous Christmas presents. Pretty containers were a favourite gift, used to keep topped up with spills on the mantlepiece over the fireplace, which was always handy when you wanted to get a light from the fire.

Our teacher, Miss Natress, found it easy to cast the Prince and Princess in our play, but was having difficulty finding a Wicked Witch. 'I'll be the witch,' I volunteered. Delighted to have filled the notoriously unpopular role, Miss Natress jumped at the idea. I quite fancied myself dressed all in black, wearing a pointed witch's hat, playing a hag with warts and long hairs growing out of her chin. I would stand out from the crowd, that's for sure.

On the evening of the play, Dad took an earlier train than usual, not wanting to miss a moment of my leading role. Everything was going well, until I, relishing every moment of my devilish power, stepped into view. At my big moment, Dad leapt to his feet, interrupting the performance, before turning on Miss Natress in a most unpleasant manner.

'How dare you make my daughter the witch!' he shrieked viciously, right in her face.

I was afraid he would hit her, so quickly could he turn, that I rushed forward, desperately grabbing him by the arm, trying to make him understand it was all my fault, I was the one who'd wanted to play the part. Hurling me aside, he continued baiting my poor teacher, now red-faced with embarrassment and terror. Mortified by his treatment of the kindest of teachers, I retreated in shocked disbelief.

Christmas of 1942 was a bleak time for everyone, with seasonal fare almost impossible to get hold of. If we'd managed to get hold of a chicken, Our Mum would have ruined it anyway, so it was no hardship. A meander alongside the lake before the king's speech found us returning to The Clockhouse, laden with scarlet-berried holly, ivy and mistletoe, all of which we draped around the house and hung from the garden gate. Huddling together by the blazing fire in the evenings, making coloured paper chains, adding to the festive mood, we enjoyed seasonal variety shows over the wireless, until it was time for bed.

If Dad could get away from work, he would just turn up, making everything that bit nicer. One Friday evening, Dad arrived out of the blue, with the news we were to meet my mother in Gloucester the following afternoon. She had moved away from London, and now lived somewhere in the Cotswolds. Our Mum, as always, worked her magic to make me look my best, anxious that I should look clean and tidy so I wouldn't show her up.

The pain of the meeting is a little blurred, but I remember feeling sick with nerves waiting for her to appear. I hadn't seen her since that afternoon at Holcombe House when she gave me Rosie. Today, walking towards me, I looked on a stylish 'Pocket Venus,' wearing an up-to-the-minute, grey tailored suit, her long dark hair softly coiled into in a chignon, secured on the nape of her neck, under a large brimmed navy blue 'Greta Garbo' hat. Her pretty face was lightly made-up, and tastefully finished off with a cheery coral red lipstick, very much the look of the 1940s. Feeling gauche and clumsy by comparison with this superior lady, when she reached for my hand, I fled to the far side of Dad, clinging to him for safety, I hadn't forgotten all those nasty things he'd told me. By the end of the afternoon, she remained an enigma to me. Bewildered by the experience, I returned to Longfords, secretly proud that such a beauty could be my mother.

On his next visit, Dad shocked us by telling us he was moving to South Wales to work as a coal miner at Cwmcarn Colliery, Cwmcarn being a small mining town in the Rhondda Valley. He gave no reason for this move, but his visits carried on as before, with him turning up from the west rather than the east, most Friday nights, leaving early on Sunday evenings.

One morning, Our Mum surprised us with wonderful news: we would be going on holiday to the seaside in the long summer break from school. I was in heaven just thinking about the marvel ahead of me. Having only seen pictures of the sea, I spent hours imagining the real sea, where tiny curling waves starting at the shallow sea's edge began their never-ending voyage towards the distant horizon, perhaps to flow on for ever and ever. We children couldn't swim, as war children were not taught; all outdoor pools were emptied for safety reasons in 1939, remaining so until the end of the war.

I remember a magnificent open-air swimming pool we visited near Stroud when the weather allowed, set in lovely grounds, its pale blue tiles now clogged and discoloured with rotting leaves, but without the clamour of excited children hurtling down the rusted slide, a dispiriting silence reigned. Never mind, soon we'd be splashing about in the salty sea.

Meanwhile, my ownership of Baby John continued happily but was now hard work. The little fellow always needed to be rescued from some near catastrophe or other. I needed to keep my wits about me, I can tell you. The war dragged on and on, with the whole country hanging on to the latest news bulletins, families worried sick about their loved ones fighting overseas. But for heedless children such as we, romping about the fields before picnicking outside our hideaway, then cooling off in the fast-flowing steam, these truly were halcyon days.

August arrived, and along with the day of our longed-for departure came the exciting news that Dad would be joining us later, at the boarding house. We were to spend a whole week on the popular Barry Island, in the Welsh county of Glamorganshire, a two-hour train journey from Gloucester Station.

As the train pulled into Barry Island Station on this sunny afternoon, I thrust my nose out of the open window of our carriage, breathing in the salt fresh air, which I found both invigorating and pungent.

Aching to see the beach, we each gathered our suitcases and as fast as we could headed for our boarding house on the seafront. Too early to be allowed into our rooms, an austere woman in a black lacey frock permitted us to pile our cases in a corner of the hall. 'Well out of everyone's way,' she brusquely said, before adding, 'And don't forget, supper is at 6.30 pm. Sharp.'

In no time at all, we raced across the seafront to the beach, cast off our sandals and raced to the water's edge, where we had to content ourselves with a cooling paddle in the ebb and flow of the wash, our swimming costumes being locked away in our cases.

Never mind, there was always tomorrow. As luck would have it, that very afternoon we made an exciting discovery: the wonderful world of candy floss. While exploring the many distractions of the seafront, I noticed adults, as well as children, munching their way through bales of finely spun clouds of the softest pink, each floating on the end of a long, thin stick. Made and sold from a whirring machine, operating from morning to night on the seafront, candy floss was a hit with sugar-deprived, English holidaymakers. Coupons were needed for our meagre monthly sweet ration, but no such law applied to this newly discovered delight. Our Mum rationed us to one each a day, but somehow or other we managed to sneak in at least one more. The wonder of candy floss proved to be the highlight of our holiday.

Most days turned into beach days, which we spent splashing about in the warmth of the waves until exhausted, then renewing our energy by gorging on hot sausage sandwiches, always with a smidgen of sand, followed by fizzy drinks.

Not permitted to return to the boarding house until late afternoon was no problem for we youngsters. Always on the point of starvation, we became experts at cadging an extra candy floss, or the odd currant bun, in spite of there being a top-rate evening meal awaiting us. One issue I had throughout my years with the Hope family was my problem with scorten, and Our Mum's problem with me and scorten, scorten meaning kicking about in loose gravel. I can still hear Our Mum's never-ending cry of, 'Stop that scorten, Our Marg, you gonna ruin them shoes.'

On the afternoon of our last full day, Dad suggested the two of us take a stroll along the seafront. I liked it best when it was just the two of us, so off we set. I must have been scorten again, not looking where I was going, when I crashed full speed into an iron lamp post, hitting one side of my face with such force, I wasn't sure if I was going to faint, or be sick.

Somehow, I heaved myself away from gaping passers-by, towards a small group of evergreen bushes, where I took refuge among the sheltering clumps, hiding myself away, feeling too poorly to face the world again, when I heard Dad's voice ring out sneeringly to all and sundry. 'She's so stupid, she walked straight into the lamp post.'

Emerging warily from my hiding place, he pointed at me, repeating the tale of my stupidity with contempt to anyone who'd listen. Somehow, I managed to make the long slog back to our lodgings, all the while Dad regaling the tale to anyone who'd listen. My father never said a kind word to me again.

Years later, I was walking my little dachshund Jake in Regent's Park in London. It had been raining earlier and the park benches were still sodden. When Jake jumped onto a bench, he soon slid off the far side. Making a supreme effort to appear nonchalant (dachshunds are renowned for their pride), I noticed he was walking with a limp. At that moment, my mind went back to the afternoon on the seafront. I ran to pick him up, to comfort him. He snuggled his whimpering head into my neck, his kisses coming thick and fast, thankful that I'd come to his rescue. Duly fussed over, he then raced off, having more important things to attend to.

Following my encounter with the lamp post, I woke on the morning of our departure to a swollen, closed eye, made up of various shades of mauve to purple above an angry, burning cheek. At breakfast, Dad found this amusing. He didn't like me any more. It was like a bad dream I was desperate to wake up from, but I knew this was no dream.

I'd watched as he made ladies look foolish in the past. Witnessing their discomfort had always made me squirm, but this was the first time he'd shown this side of himself to me. I longed to return to Longfords, where I could lick my wounds behind closed doors, away from the fickle frivolity of the funfair, and the glossy world of candy floss.

While working down the coal mine, Dad had formed a close friendship with a fellow miner, Brother John Roberts. With little in the way of entertainment in the Welsh Valleys, the locals turned to either the Welsh Chapel or the Pentecostal Church for their social lives.

Brother John, a born-again Christian, was an Elder of some eminence, at the Elim Pentecostal Church in Crosskeys, a small town approximately two miles from Cwmcarn. He'd invited Dad to a meeting at the church, which led to Dad 'seeing the light,' and becoming a full-fledged, born-again Christian.

On his next visit to Longfords, we were faced with a completely different dad. No more happy rambles, holding hands as we sang along to our favourite songs, no visits to The Weighbridge pub. Cigarettes being the Devil's poison meant the end of cigarette cards. Certainly no pantomimes; watching those evil sinners dancing before you. It seemed that anything enjoyable was the work of the Devil, to be avoided at all costs. Every time he visited, he would insist I was a sinner. No matter how often I tried to assure him that I'd done nothing wrong, his reply was always, 'You were born in sin.' One day, unable to take it anymore, I pointed out politely that my birth had more to do with him than me. He gave me a sharp clip round the ear for answering back.

Finding a suitable church where Dad could worship when visiting Longfords was of prime importance. After much searching, he was forced to accept there were no Pentecostal Churches in Gloucestershire and he had no choice but to settle for a different brand. This was seen as a major setback, but with time he had to accept a Methodist Church, despite strongly disagreeing with many of their teachings.

Sunday mornings now meant a reverential walk into Nailsworth, Bibles tucked firmly under our arms, to attend morning service in a spacious, high-ceilinged building, an ice-block, in winter and summer. It wasn't my cup of tea, and quite frankly I was bored stiff. I learned to amuse myself by watching elderly members, huddled in their designated pews, dewdrops plopping intermittently from their poor old purple noses. A stuffy old lot on the whole, and such tedious sermons, I took to pressing wild flowers in certain pages of my Bible, together with the pretty texts handed to me at the door on our arrival, which was quite fun really once boredom set in. In spite of my grumblings, I grew to love the teachings of the Bible, as I do today, but everything in moderation. That same Bible sits in my bookcase beside me, complete with the flowers I pressed into it all those years ago.

I'm afraid to say that Dad's visits had become tedious, to say the least. Quite worn out by the endless tales of Brother John's numerous merits, I do believe Brother John meant more to Dad than the Lord Jesus.

Our Mum had taken a job at Nailsworth Woollen Mill. During the long summer school holidays, we girls spent the mornings on the farm, helping out in the cow shed, or messing about with Baby John. Most of all, I enjoyed the time I spent chatting with Mrs Hankins in the kitchen. I enjoyed our serious discussions. One day I told her Dad had called me stupid, and she said he must be pulling my leg, I was anything but stupid. On cloud nine, after spending time with my favourite lady, come late morning, we girls were off, trekking through deep woods, above my old home, Holcombe House, where we took the Nailsworth road, leading to Our Mum's works canteen to join her for sandwiches and the buttered spicy buns she'd prepared before leaving the house that morning. Nearing the factory gates, we could tell we were on time by the sound of the machines suddenly cutting out, followed by an eerie silence, much welcomed by the exhausted workers. As always, *Workers' Playtime* was great company for those who managed to stay awake. I enjoyed the company of both the younger and older women as I listened to their female chatter, at times learning more than might be considered good for a girl of my age. The starting up of the machines was the signal for we girls to be on our way. An orchard laden with the sweetest apples right next to The Weighbridge meant a quick hop over the wall for a bit of scrumping.

News from the front had been heartening of late, with the overwhelming success of the Battle of Stalingrad, fought by Britain's Allies, and the Battle of El Alamein, fought by the Eighth Army, led by General Montgomery, nicknamed fondly by his men as 'Monty', who, by the end of the war, had proved himself to be a supreme leader. Mr Churchill, speaking on the news, referred to, El Alamein as, 'This is not the end. It is not even the beginning of the end. But it is, perhaps, the end of the beginning.'

Hearing genuine good news perked everyone up no end. With heads held high, lines of worry smoothed away, and smiles appeared on faces. After years of intense worry, a small light of hope glimmered on the horizon.

We children, blissfully unaware of the drama unfolding the world over, lived each carefree moment with nothing to worry our heads about, safe from the horror of war, in what I see in hindsight was a childhood paradise.

Hot summer days drifted lazily on, but I wasn't about to let the cruel onslaught of winter catch me out again. Our Barb and me, with help from Our Mum, herself a skilled knitter, whiled away long summer evenings, knitting needles clicking away, frantically creating sections of fashionable jumpers, by selecting wools and patterns with written instructions from the Nailsworth

Wool Shop. Patiently stitching each section into place, to my surprise I produced two jumpers, one heavy, in cheerful, bright red for the bitter cold, and one in a fine lacy design, which took an age to complete, but proved to be well worth the trouble, in readiness for the odd day when winter chose to be kind. My jumpers were as fine as those expensive ones in top-class women's shops. It bucked me up no end to find I was capable of making something not only attractive, but useful.

Early morning mists hovering over Longfords Lake signalled the late arrival of autumn, eventually lifting to give way to perfect days of late summer heat, revealing the boat house on the far side of the lake, its pleasing lines framed against a mass of scarlet and gold seasonal shades, a true artist's impression of a fleeting moment of perfection.

Devilish winter swept in without warning. As usual, forced to abandon the fields, we girls had no choice but to stick to the steep hills, where foolishly, I courted chilblains yet again, by plunging my numbed hands into the icy flow of my favourite stream, until my stomach's complaining rumble reminded me of the scrumptious hot Chelsea bun, which right this minute would be entering the roaring red-hot oven.

The steepest part of our journey began with the cruellest hill, leading up to the centre of the town with its selection of shops. Tired as we were, we passed little old ladies from the terraced cottages on that same hill, coping with the long grind upwards, shopping basket in one hand, walking stick in the other, slowly working their way to the corner shop at the top, their tiny worn heads bent low, focusing on the ground, as they mounted, at a snail's pace, this unforgiving hill. Small wonder they lived to be ancient.

Hankins Farm

Christmas of 1943 rolled in, and an unusual peace descended over Longfords Mill, as the machines were silenced for a few hours. Even Our Dad took it easy for a day or two.

Never having known anything but hard times, we children thought of Christmas as party time. My yearly present of a book was guaranteed to keep me engrossed for weeks on end, unlike a single orange; a couple of quick swallows, then gone forever, as were the Christmas bits and pieces sent by various relatives of the Hope family, many of whom I'd never met. Our Mum made Christmas dinner, which usually consisted of a tough cut of beef, with boiled potatoes and soggy cabbage. Our Mum had many skills, cooking not being one of them, although her Christmas pudding wasn't too bad, if a little indigestible. The most important event of the day was the King's speech, when families settled down after their Christmas dinner to listen to King George VI address the nation. His stammer could be disconcerting when lengthy silences took over, making me hold my breath for him, but, to give him his due, he never gave in, painfully seeing it through to the end, drawing respect from all his subjects.

My favourite place to spend Christmas afternoon was the farmhouse. Along with Our Barb, we took the familiar walk to spend time with quiet Mary and lively Little John. It was most agreeable to be treated with respect by the adults, who discussed serious matters with me, as if I was a grown up. Dad was included in the invitation, but I didn't encourage it, him being poor company these days, always singing the praises of the Great Brother John, ruining any spirit of Christmas. Mrs Hankins was a first-rate cook, spending weeks before the big day labouring in the kitchen, making Christmas cakes and trifles to die for, and there was sure to be jelly and blancmange, which meant everyone indulged in a good spread, even with a war going on.

Life at Longfords in 1944 followed the usual pattern, we children contending with the icy hazards of winter, before the eagerly awaited arrival of spring, with its fresh delights.

I enjoyed nothing more than taking off alone, wandering at leisure among my favourite haunts, my thoughts my sole companion. Setting off from the mill, I'd take the familiar road towards Nailsworth, pass by my old home, Holcombe House, and nip over the first stile I came to, leading to a number of uncut fields of long green grasses which had been left to their own devices, the workers occupied with serving their country in one way or another. The only residents, the gentle cows, lifted their heads lazily, peering at me with unblinking interest for a moment until, realising I was of no importance, returned to the serious matter of munching grass, while I took to watching the antics of tits, of all varieties, darting here and there, ready to pounce on any crawling creature foolhardy enough to emerge from the security of home, whose fate was to be gobbled whole by the squawking mouths of nestlings, tucked away safely in the overhanging boughs.

Reaching the woodlands, I stood, sole witness to the return of England's loveliest annual offering: golden aconites, their smiles beaming from the tiniest cranny, coaxed out by the warmth of the sun. Snow-white woodland anemones lifted the darkness of dank coverts, together with tiny wild cyclamen in shades of pink, red or white, all at one with the world. After time spent in a favourite nook, I wended my way through the high woods, above Holcombe House, forked right at Minchinhampton Road, where I turned down the steep hill, arriving at my favourite place, the farm, in good time for what the Hankins termed lunch, but in the Hope household was called dinner. Lunch behind us, I stayed close to Mr Hankins, helping him clear up the never-ending mess of the farmyard while absorbing his every word. I enjoyed these afternoons. I don't suppose I was of much use, but he said I made the time fly by.

It was late afternoon and time to return to The Clockhouse. When I got to a certain point, I glanced above the work sheds towards my mate the clock, urging me to speed up, or find myself late for tea. Please let it not be baked beans day. Usually Tuesday was the day when Our Mum opened a tin of baked beans, poured them into a large saucepan topped to the brim with water, making a watery gruel, where, if you were lucky, you might discover a bean or two in the depths of your bowl. Although a favourite with everyone else, I detested the filthy stuff and for the life of me couldn't keep it down, the outcome being every Tuesday night I was sent to bed on an empty stomach.

We children had recently joined a Saturday morning film club for young people in Stroud, showing the latest war newsreels from all around the world. Seeing scenes of the war was an eye-opener, ships being shelled to smithereens, people being blown up in their own homes, and all for real. I preferred to see the reality of war for myself, to know the truth rather than watch John Wayne winning wars right left and centre, although I admit to being badly shaken by some of the footage. After all, I was growing up, no longer a mere child. I would discuss what I'd seen with Mr and Mrs Hankins as it was a waste of time trying to talk to Dad. His reply was always the same, 'The end is nigh, we're living in the last days. The book of Revelation warns us, in the latter days, there will be wars, and rumours of wars, those days are come upon us. Soon it will be too late, Judgement Day, is at hand. Repent all your sins, while there is time, only the righteous may enter the kingdom of

Pretty from the Outside

God.' I'd heard it so many times, I knew it by heart. He's been proved wrong anyway, because I'm still standing, in 2021.

Saturdays were still devoted to Our Gran and Our Gramp Wilson. The battle scenes and bombings we'd recently been so immersed in at the Saturday morning film club took on a lesser importance when we clapped our eyes on Gran's home-made cake, sure to contain a month's allowance of dried fruits. Naturally I paid my usual visit to Aunty Betty's boudoir to hear the very latest in her quest for perfection. It seems there was no end to improving on nature, but to give the lady her due, she never stopped trying.

Our leisurely summer came and went, one long, happy holiday. Our Dad, due some time off from the mill, reckoned it was a good time to visit some places of interest. One such place was Bristol Zoo, the main attraction being Alfred, the world-famous gorilla whose human-like personality made everyone fall in love with him.

Alfred arrived at the zoo in 1930. He died in 1948, rumour has it, killed by his detested enemy, the sound of overhead aeroplanes. To this day, Alfred reigns supreme, stuffed and positioned, in a place of honour.

The River Severn Bore, according to Our Dad, was something every child should see, especially with us living within reasonable reach of the river. The Bore is a tidal wave occurring daily on the River Severn, at a point where too much water meets too narrow a space, causing a wall of water to rush upstream, sometimes to a height of fifteen metres. Our Dad had really done his homework and knew the exact spot to get the best view. We ventured forth one morning in August, with Granny and Gramp Wilson, and Aunty Betty in tow, taking an early bus to Gloucester, as it was vital we arrive at the best viewpoint at the right time, before

Hankins Farm

which we dawdled the mile or so to Minsterworth, a village on the river with a choice of several pretty cafés and a pub. Today the Severn Bore, as the second highest bore in the world, is famous for competitive surfboarding and canoeing, both hazardous and challenging, but in 1944, there were no surfers, only we onlookers, nervously watching, until the overwhelming wall of dark water roared upstream in our direction, threatening to devour anything in its path, only to pass on a moment later, leaving behind an eerie stillness, as silent as the grave.

After such an other-worldly experience, we were happy to retreat to the family pub, where we enjoyed scrumptious sausages and home-made chips, which we smothered with tomato ketchup.

Come September, with the start of a new term, and glorious weather, a number of us took to wandering onto Minchinhampton Common after school, for no particular reason, other than for something to do.

We children were aware that things were reaching a critical stage in the war, nevertheless, we were taken aback to find the common overrun by American soldiers, their tents dominating every blade of grass. I can't imagine what the poor cows, who'd owned the common for centuries, thought of being so rudely turfed out of their own territory.

Every afternoon, as soon as we were free, we gravitated towards the common, where the friendly soldiers, sounding like American film stars, kept us well supplied with candy and our pockets stuffed with packets of chewing gum. The soldiers were smitten by our accents, trying their hardest to copy us, but they weren't very good at Gloucestershire talk. We kids were equally tickled pink by their American twang, but never quite got the hang of it. There were a number of black soldiers. I'd never seen a black man before, but they were as friendly as the other soldiers, except for having the blackest skin, the tightest curly hair, and pearly white teeth, shown off by the widest grins I had ever seen.

We visited our new friends every day, until one day, the cows were back, munching what was left of their grass, as if they'd never gone away. Overnight, our American friends had flown away, taking their candy and chewing gum with them.

We were aware from the 9 pm news bulletins how desperate the situation had become, with Mr Churchill regaling us every evening with tales of battles won by the Allies as they swept across Europe from Russia, while General Montgomery and The Eighth Army made their way through Italy, liberating Rome in June, the ultimate aim being for our armies to meet up and drive Hitler out of Germany.

Self-absorbed, we children didn't fully comprehend the extent of the turmoil we were living through, although it was impossible not to pick up on the pervasive tense energy.

The same restlessness hung over me. As happy as I was in my life at The Clockhouse and as much as I loved the family, I had never felt I belonged there. Instinctively, I was aware that the time was approaching when I had to move on, but move on to what? I had no idea. My thoughts flew constantly to my new life with Dad. Hopefully, when back in his own surroundings, he would revert to being the old dad I loved, and stop going on about Jesus and repenting sins the whole time.

Dad's visits continued, but he was completely in awe of Brother John. It was 'Brother John says this,' 'Brother John says that.' The Nailsworth Methodist Church held sway whenever Dad visited, the ancient regulars perched in their usual seats, except for those who had gone on to a better place, having frozen to death in their personal pew. As members of such a highly revered place of worship, I'm sure they were assured a grand send-off with all the trimmings.

By autumn of 1944, reports from the war were encouraging on the whole. The Allies lost a major battle now and again, but it seemed, Hitler was well and truly on the run. The blackout, which had been in force from the start of the war, was demoted to the dim-out, as it seemed unlikely we would be invaded again.

Everyone flourished during this radiant autumn. The frenetic energy previously displayed by the women working at their looms had given way to an easy demeanour. Even the songs from the hit parade made for easier listening.

Making our way to school, we chose the fields and steep hills, criss-crossing the slopes in the company of docile cows, knowing we would have no choice but to take to the roads as soon as winter set in.

Throughout this spell of clement weather, I took to my favourite hideaways whenever I found the time. Only recently, I'd sussed out a secret spot, right under my nose, tucked away behind Tabrams Pitch. It was here I'd spend my time, amused by bundles of ever-active squirrels preparing their food supplies in readiness for a hard winter. Dodging here and there, never pausing, forever retrieving, then burying full-blown hazelnuts, as they fell incessantly from branches overhead. Clever little chaps, completely indifferent to my presence, their bums stuck in the air, heads down, crazily digging, their grubby little forelegs well set up for any tempest heading their way. The bane of my life were the teams of hovering wasps, odious, bad-tempered little savages. They'd give you a nasty nip as soon as look at you.

My favourites, the knowing blackbirds, greedily attacked

the seasonal glut of juicy hawthorn berries, ignoring my shout of, 'Take it easy, boys, you'll be starving when winter hits home.' Wily winter did hit home, sooner than expected. The shock of its sudden arrival meant we were unprepared.

Overnight our pretty summer clothes were packed away, making space for sensible items such as a liberty bodice, with its rubber buttons. I never learned what the rubber buttons were for, they just hung there without a purpose as the seasons came and went. Heavy items like winter boots were dug out, as were all our knitted jumpers, anything to avoid getting pneumonia, because, in spite of our best intentions, we girls never gave up loitering during our hikes up to Minchinhampton. Once upon a time, I saw those never-ending treks to school as divine punishment from above; today I remember them as benevolent treasures.

Nothing got in the way of the Saturday film club, neither the early start, nor the grim weather. It was there we saw for ourselves the war as it happened. We wanted to be kept in the picture; after all, it was our war, even if we were young. Mr Churchill spoke to us over the BBC most nights during this time, always cheering us on with his natural optimism, not like the regular newsreader. Just the tone of his glum, posh accent was enough to put the fear of God into you, no matter if the news was good or bad.

Winter at Longfords trudged by in a repeat performance of the previous winter, the highlight as always being King George VI's speech to the nation, which he delivered manfully, God bless him. It must have been an ordeal for the poor man, with his stammer, having to face the whole of his kingdom on Christmas Day. In those days there wasn't the ability to record a speech in advance, like today. Poor King George VI, trapped like Daniel in the Lions' Den. I bet he felt relieved when it was behind him and he could move on to a nice glass of sherry before his well-earned Christmas dinner.

As the days lengthened, I strode the woodlands searching for any signs of new life. Burgeoning bulbs, almost imperceptible, began their yearly process, bulging through the black earth, baby shoots of spring easing their way through wintry branches. Here and there a pure white anemone on the point of opening caused my spirits to soar, anticipating what lay ahead, spring, summer, autumn, the end of the war, then back to London to live with my dad.

There was no doubt something major was going on. Things were very hush-hush, but there could be no mistaking the signs of tense urgency, both on the ground and in the air. It was only later that we learned that some of the greatest battles of the war were being fought at this time, as the Allies liberated Eastern countries, scuttling the Germans, on route to driving Hitler out of Germany.

It was Mr Hankins on his morning round who spread the news that the war was over, on 8 May 1945. Unable to face the consequences of his actions, both Hitler and his lady friend had committed suicide on 30 April 1945 in his private quarters in Berlin.

Our Mum, blunt as ever, broached the subject of adopting me as soon as Dad next turned up. He was adamant: under no circumstances would he consider such a thing. Our Mum had no choice but to insist that it was only right to get me settled into my new home as soon as possible, for my sake. At last I was to get my long-held wish. I was going back where I belonged, to live with my father.

Britain celebrated the end of the war, as did the rest of Europe. Crazed with happiness, after five years of worry and hardship, thousands headed for London. The Royal Family appeared on Buckingham Palace balcony throughout the day, joined eventually by Mr Churchill, much to the joy of the exhilarated crowds. The centre of London had never experienced such celebrations. Young people climbed to the top of any building or balcony they could reach, and good-natured young men hung from street lights. People did anything they could think of to express the sheer joy of the day. Street parties were held all over the country, in every city, town and village, and bonfires were lit in every market square. Both young and old had waited so long for this day.

Minchinhampton built its own bonfire in the marketplace, on top of which was placed a limp effigy of Hitler, his notorious black moustache flying, alight, into the black sky, before his undignified descent into purgatory.

On the day I left The Clockhouse, so immersed was I in my own happiness that I omitted to tell Our Mum and Our Dad how much I loved them, but I'm sure they knew. I was to return the following year for a holiday.

~ 5 ~
Anerley

Once again, Dad and I were on our way to Stroud Station. Ever the optimist, I was so excited at what lay ahead. We were to lodge with an elderly couple at 31 Thicket Road, Anerley, in South East London.

We'd no sooner settled into our seats than Dad announced he needed to have a serious talk with me. No one wanted me living in their house, children were more trouble than they were worth, only adults needed apply for vacancies, so having found a place willing to accept me, I'd better behave myself. He had no choice but to put up with me, but at the first sign of my putting a foot wrong, he would send me to a children's home. I'd learned to withstand his sneering taunts, careful never to reveal how much they hurt me, but the threat of another children's home threw me into such a state of terror, I couldn't hide my feelings This was to be his favourite way of putting the fear of God in me.

Rather deflated and somewhat scared after Dad's lecture, I settled into my seat, where I soon recovered my equilibrium. We took what was fast becoming a routine trip across London, although the destruction was ever more apparent with each visit. Poor London wore an air of abandonment and defeat. I imagined the city's warriors limping away to recover from everything they'd gone through, much as a wounded animal returns to the safety of its lair to lick its wounds and recover before once again setting out to face the world.

Thicket Road was undoubtedly one of the longest roads I'd ever come across, running from Anerley High Road through to Penge in the next borough. It had its share of decimated properties with overrun wastelands, which was all that remained of once opulent homes.

At first sight, 31 Thicket Road appeared to be a decaying mansion. A four-storey corner house surrounded by neglected gardens with a flight of steep steps leading up to the front door. Owned by Grandad and Nanny Oldfield, the first floor was the only one in use, the remainder of the house dingy, dusty and forbidding.

It was late afternoon by the time we rang the doorbell of 31 Thicket Road, having hauled our worldly belongings up the steps. After some time, Nanny Oldfield made her way to the front door, with difficulty. Pausing to get her breath, she signalled to us to enter, while pointing to the heavy balustrade. An obese elderly lady, it was clear she didn't enjoy the best of health. She huffed and puffed her way up the stairs behind us, clinging to the balustrade and pausing to rest midway, at which point I took the opportunity to take in her face. Her complexion was an unhealthy yellow with a perpetual damp sheen, no matter the weather. Grandad Oldfield, on the other hand, was a spritely old chap, forever protecting me from the wrath of Nanny, I can still hear his perpetual, 'Leave the girl alone, can't you?'

The heavy, curving balustrade led from the ground floor to the first, where there were two immense rooms, one the Oldfields' bedroom, the other running from the front of the house all the way to the back, overlooking both the front and back gardens. This other room was the sitting room, but I never knew anyone to sit in it; it was far too cold in winter or summer to remove your coat.

Dad had a single bed tucked away in a far corner, surrounded by a screen, far from any potential visitors. A chest of drawers stood next to his bed, on which was placed a large stylishly framed studio photograph of himself, looking like Clark Gable, next to a smaller copy of my Cheltenham portrait, with Our Mum's perfect bow of ribbon, and my hanky bulging up my sleeve in a most unladylike manner.

My room was a small box room, sandwiched between the two main rooms, directly over the front door. Here, I was in luck as it was without doubt the prettiest room in this spooky house, decorated with floral wallpaper of pastel pink roses, floating on a background of palest blue, with the added bonus of catching any morning sunshine. This little room was to be my refuge, where nobody could get at me, a personal hideaway far away from Nanny's endless complaining.

Across the landing was the room used for everything, with the exception of sleeping. It was a long back room overlooking the garden, with a combined kitchen and dining room at the far end, a cosy lounge area, where a roaring coal fire blazed every evening, as we all snuggled into our regular positions to listen to the wireless. It was the only time of day that Nanny wasn't hostile towards me.

Nanny had one redeeming quality, her cooking, which was second to none. Hearts of beef stuffed with her own recipe excelled, in spite of food rationing, which would continue for several more years. Nanny's cooking kept me going, which was just as well, as she was to turn me into an exhausted slave.

Two luxuries at Thicket Road were an indoor bathroom and a separate lavatory with a flush system. It was forever ice-cold in the bathroom, the water heated by a geyser fixed to the wall. The moment I turned on the hot water tap, the thing exploded with a terrifying whoosh, making me jump out of my skin. I never came to terms with this modern invention. Nanny insisted on staying with me at bath time, she said, to wash my back. One bath night, she caught me looking in the mirror at my developing breasts, out of curiosity, noting with interest the changes I saw. 'Stop admiring yourself,' she snapped. 'You're nothing special.'

I settled into a busy local secondary school, two minutes from Thicket Road, where I soon felt at home once I'd adjusted to the new routines following the years spent at homely Minchinhampton school. The other pupils were friendly, but I missed my special buddies. I tried to keep my life secret, fearing as I did the threat of a children's home, because you could never be too careful.

Dad had searched out a Pentecostal Church suitable for his needs, all the way over at Lee Green, in the borough of Lewisham. This meant changing buses three times, but having attended several meetings, he'd been made welcome and felt at home with the Brothers and Sisters there. Up early on Sundays, we walked to the end of Thicket Road, into Penge, where we waited for our first bus. On that first Sunday, it so happened that as we stood at the bus stop, a small bird perched on a branch above us and chose to deposit something nasty on Dad's head. I found this hilarious, telling him it was a sign of good luck. However, unable see the funny side of things, he landed me a sharp clip on my ear for finding his confusion so funny.

We changed buses at Forest Hill, where, without fail, Dad

allowed plenty of time to gaze longingly into the window of a motorbike showroom that specialised in the his beloved 'Norton Motor Bikes,' the perfection of these shining machines having been well drilled into me over the years. On we journeyed, through New Cross, Catford, Lewisham, then on to Lee High Road. At this point we got off the bus to take the short walk up Boone Street, where Emmanuel Pentecostal Church, an old traditional Church Hall, stood, the one surviving building among a mass of pre-fabs, hastily built to replace dozens of terraced homes which had been recently flattened by bombs.

A group of people were gathered outside Emmanuel Church that Sunday morning, mainly made up of matronly ladies, long and skinny, or short and skinny, a fat person being a rare sight during these hard times. There were married couples of all ages, as well as elderly widows and widowers.

A number of young men and women, some in couples, more often alone, rejoiced in being beloved Brothers and Sisters of the House of the Lord. Dad became Brother Fred.

Brother Fred was without doubt the most handsome man in the place. At the age of thirty-seven, he prided himself on his good looks, remaining a committed follower of the latest fashions. I stood shyly among this band of worshippers with whom I had nothing in common. I was well used to elderly ladies remarking on first meeting me, 'My word, she's a big girl,' as if I was being fattened for Christmas, making me feel more ungainly and lumpy than I already felt, my hair sticking out in two stiff plaits giving me a headache, long grey socks reaching to my footballer's knees, and sensible schoolgirl shoes, with not a hint of finesse about them.

Soon it was time for the morning service. The first thing I saw on entering the 'Lord's House,' was a grotesque painting of Christ on the Cross, a crown of thorns pressed on his bleeding head, a sword thrust into his side, blood dripping from his wounds, with the words, 'Washed in the blood of the Lamb.'

I couldn't imagine anything more disgusting than being washed in blood. Unfortunately, the painting hung directly above Pastor Barnes' head, meaning that whenever he addressed the congregation, from his personal balcony, I had no choice but to reflect on the sufferings of the Lord.

Dad and I sat in what would become our regular seats, among a packed house. Three eminent Elders of the Church, two old and rather infirm, the other a wimp of a chap in his thirties, took their seats on the balcony with the pastor. The congregation rose to its feet as one, cheerfully embracing a rousing hymn, 'What a friend we have in Jesus, all our sins to bear.' Everyone enthusiastically embraced the happy mood until it was time for Pastor Barnes' sermon. The mood changed, silence descending as we settled down and prepared to drink in his words of wisdom.

Of course, I'd heard it all before, not put as eloquently as Pastor Barnes, but it all boiled down to the same thing Dad had been going on about for yonks. The congregation sat quietly, dwelling on the words of the Lord: Repent your sins, only then can ye enter the Kingdom of Heaven. I couldn't think of any sins I'd committed, except perhaps not being too keen on Nanny Oldfield.

As we sat in quiet contemplation, dwelling on the recent guidance we'd been granted – though I wasn't contemplating, I was sorting out the pressed flowers in my Bible – I almost jumped out of my skin as a Brother, with no warning, leapt to his feet, breaking the silence with a charged outpouring in a foreign language that seemed to go on forever. On the conclusion of his passionate oration, he returned to his seat, his deliverance followed by a Sister of middle years offering a forthright translation of the outpouring in English, causing much jubilation and praising of the Lord on hearing God's message. Afterwards, a kind Brother sitting next to me explained the gift of speaking in tongues, a precious gift given by God to a select few Brothers and Sisters. I turned to glance at the chosen one, finding it hard to believe God would select an insignificant little fellow like that to pass on his important message. As Dad was fond of quoting, 'God moves in mysterious ways.'

Once the service was over, the congregation started to disperse and we stood in line at the door, waiting for a blessing from Pastor Barnes. When it was my turn, he offered a firm handshake, welcoming me into the fold. Then it was off to the bus stop, for the first stage of our journey back to Nanny.

My new life, so completely different from the life I'd so recently led, affected me badly. The worst part was the way Dad treated me in public. Waiting at bus stops was one of this favourites. He would approach any amiable-looking couple waiting for a bus, then proceed to bombard them with tales of my stupidity and many failings, 'Ask her what eight and six are, she'll tell you fifteen. Go on, ask her.' I watched these sitting targets growing ever more ill at ease, anxious for their bus to arrive and take them away from this madman. In all the years of accosting these innocents, not once did anyone speak up for me.

As I gradually became used to this constant in my life, it didn't take me long to recognise his cowardice as well as his cruelty. He never showed this side of himself to anyone who was of importance to him, only ships passing in the night. With time I learned to isolate myself from his taunts and jibes, determined never to give him a weapon with which to harm me.

There was one teacher at school who was intent on taking me under her wing. I never knew why she took such an interest in me. A young married woman, Mrs Peel stood out from the other teachers, in that she was very pretty and slender, her dark hair cut in the cheekiest short hairstyle, and a youthful way of dressing.

It so happened that Mrs Peel and her husband lived around the corner from Thicket Road, on the side of Lillington Road, which had been partly flattened in the war. It soon became a regular thing for me to join her at her home for lunch most Saturdays. I enjoyed going there, it being warm and welcoming, and bright – as if the sun was always shining, even on the darkest day. Mrs Peel told me she'd made all her own curtains and painted the whole flat herself. She was also an excellent cook, preferring the latest healthy style of nutrition, all natural, with lots of raw vegetables and salads, not a bit like Nanny's rich roasts. Sometimes we had the company of Mr Peel, if he could manage it. I loved it when he joined us, as he would discuss serious subjects with me, as if I had a brain. Although it was kind of them to invite me, I'd be exhausted by the time I left, having to be careful what I might inadvertently let drop. The threat of the children's home was always hanging over me.

I didn't mention the Pentecostal Church and all those carryings-on, not like Dad, who, given half a chance, would tell anyone they were sinners, whether they were interested or not. It was so embarrassing. I was surprised he didn't get a punch on his perfectly aquiline nose. Lovely Mrs Peel never questioned me, for which I was grateful, and I was always made to feel at home when I visited, until the day I left Anerley.

The moment I got home from school I'd set about my daily

duties. First, I'd boil a kettle to wash up that morning's breakfast things, including the porridge saucepan, a devil to clean what with non-stick not yet invented, clean out yesterday's fireplace, lay another fire for the current evening, down the stairs and front steps, round to the back of the house, before descending to the spooky coal cellar. One day I picked up a slimy cold toad, causing me an acute attack of the heebie-jeebies. From that day, I made sure to always carry a torch with me. Two trips meant enough coal to see us through the evening. Next, a quick trip over the wastelands, not forgetting the ration book, or lists of the day's needs. Shopping accomplished, back to Number 31, where Nanny would be preparing the evening's meal, and Grandad, whose first task on getting home was to get a good fire going, would now be settled in his chair, a blanket over his knees to ward off the slightest draught while puffing on his smelly old pipe. Nanny kept me on the go until Dad was due home. At that point she made certain the moment the door opened I was to be seen taking things easy in front of the fire.

With the end of war, there was no need to be glued to the wireless for the latest news bulletin, so instead, we waited with bated breath for *Dick Barton: Special Agent*. At 6.45 pm, every weekday evening, families everywhere gathered round the wireless to learn the outcome of the latest exploits of Dick and his assistant, Snowey. As soon as we'd finished our evening meal, and I'd done the washing-up, we'd gather around the blazing fire, eagerly awaiting the ominous undertones heralding the arrival of Dick and Snowey, as usual, finding themselves in desperate straits, outnumbered by villainous criminals in full cry, intent on fighting to the death. After fifteen minutes of nail-biting tension, the thunderous tones started up again, leaving the whole nation on tenterhooks until the next evening. Will Dick and Snowey solve the dastardly deed? Or have they perished?

Nanny's daughter, Aunty Doll, lived in the basement flat of a house directly opposite us, with her husband, and three children, two girls, Gill and Josey, both slightly younger than me, and a young boy, Bill. I liked Aunty Doll, she treated me kindly, not like the old harridan over the road. It was Aunty Doll who shattered my belief in Father Christmas, when she entered my little room late one Christmas Eve and I distinctly saw her leave a pile of wrapped gifts by my bed.

Sometimes, if Aunty Doll had something important to deal with, Nanny would take care of the children, cooking them a meal. On such occasions, she used me as a servant, waiting on the children, clearing each course in turn, before washing the used dishes and putting them away. When I'd completed all the chores, I was allowed to eat my meal at a small table tucked away in a corner. I found this embarrassing and hurtful, as did the children, who, unable to meet my eyes, found it upsetting. As the eldest, it had been taken for granted I was the leader of our group, and that's how it stayed, in spite of Nanny.

Cleaning and polishing verged on being a form of punishment. On Thursdays I rose extra early, as Nanny demanded the linoleum in the sitting room was polished, from the front of the house to the back wall, before school. If I was running late, I had to finish the job as soon as I got home. I knew Dad was paying well for us to live here. Nanny wasn't paying me to clean the house. I tried telling him how hard I was being made to work, but his response was simply, 'It won't hurt you.' The only other person that knew what was going on was Grandad, with his constant plea, 'For crying out loud, leave the girl alone'

Anerley

One Saturday evening, Dad took me to Kingsway Hall, Holborn, in Central London, to hear a revolutionary Pentecostal preacher from the United States. Billy Graham, already revered in his country, as yet unknown over here, with the exception of Wales where he was worshipped as the Lord's greatest ambassador of all time. We arrived at a splendid hall which was already packed to the rafters with worshippers. We managed to find seats towards the rear among other curious worshippers.

Taking his place before the huge gathering, I vividly recall a tall man with blond hair and film star looks, in his mid-thirties, his most arresting features being his mesmeric blue eyes, which I found impossible to look into, and a rich American voice of such conviction I could see why almost the whole audience, when asked to come forward, to give their hearts to Jesus, clamoured to get close to him, until most seats in the hall stood empty. Worshippers crowded to get as close to him as possible. Having heard it all before, I was not impressed. Dad dragged me to several of Billy Graham's gatherings throughout his long campaign, which was to lead to a series of Pentecostal Crusades that swept the country throughout the 1950s, the promise of salvation bringing hope and happiness to millions.

One evening, as we were finishing our evening meal, Dad came up with the strangest notion. He'd long held the dream that I would play the piano at Emmanuel Church. It was the first I'd heard about it. I had no interest in playing the piano, and what's more, I had no intention of playing the piano anywhere.

Lessons were arranged with a highly accomplished teacher, a pocket-sized little old lady with the tiniest wizened face held together by a maze of wrinkles. Off I went one Saturday morning, my journey halved by a series of steep wastelands, until I arrived at the high point of busy Crystal Palace, once a real palace, built by Prince Albert, husband of Queen Victoria, destroyed in a horrendous fire in 1936, watched by the whole of London, including my mother, living in nearby West Norwood, while holding me in her arms.

Miss Bailey lived in a small row of working men's cottages, unscathed by bombs and quite different from the huge houses of nearby Anerley. We pursued my lessons for some weeks, but it didn't take either of us long to realise my heart wasn't in it. One day I was taken aback when, quite unexpectedly, Miss Bailey presented me with a gift, the score of Walt Disney's *Snow White and the Seven Dwarfs*, with the words, 'I'm sure you'll enjoy this, please accept it as a gift.'

Provided I'd finished my chores, Nanny allowed me to practise on her piano in the sitting room, where it was so cold I could hardly feel my fingers or toes. I soon forgot the cold as Miss Bailey's gift came into its own, and I fell madly in love with, 'Whistle While You Work,' and 'Someday My Prince Will Come.' Memories of the pantomime, so long ago in Cheltenham, came flooding back. Each day I lost myself in my music. It was just as well we had no neighbours as I'd have driven them out of their minds while waiting for my prince to arrive. Miss Bailey opened my eyes that day. The piano lessons faded with time, but I've never forgotten that wise, little old lady who taught me that I had the right to make my own music.

One Sunday evening, as Dad and I were on the last stage of our journey back from church, something amazing happened. We were walking along Thicket Road when something different caught my eye. In a flash, I'd caught sight of an opening in the broken-down fence. Quickly turning my head, I glimpsed what

Anerley

appeared to be woodlands, among a tangled mass of overgrown greenery behind what had once been a handsome pair of wrought-iron gates, now rusted and pushed aside. I said nothing to Dad, but vowed to return as soon as possible.

The following day, as soon as school ended, I raced to the abandoned gate. After crawling through dense undergrowth for some time, I raised my head and found myself in a vast open green space, surrounded by trees. I paused to catch my breath. Being springtime, the gently swaying trees were full of sprouting young leaves, shimmering in the light breeze. Even the choking undergrowth gleamed with health, suffocating what should have been footpaths. Fighting my way forwards, with no idea where I was heading, dodging any object daring to hinder my progress, I came face to face with a gigantic dinosaur blocking my path, luckily for me not alive. Somehow, I managed to get through the surrounding wilderness by pressing myself against his enormous scaly body until, on reaching the tip of his curving tail, I noticed a nearby hillock, where, after crawling to the top, and finding a clear view, I realised that my dinosaur was not alone. There were a number of these magnificent creatures, each with a thousand pearly grey scales, glinting in the dappled sunshine, their proud heads rearing high above the strangled mess of unkempt trees and rampant plant growth. After scraping away handfuls of wandering shoots, I managed to perch myself on the rear end of one of my new acquaintances, to look around and get my bearings. I'd discovered my own secret paradise, a haven, where I could flee Nanny's relentless nagging and Dad's disapproval.

Unwittingly, I'd come across the famous Crystal Palace Dinosaurs, located in Crystal Palace Park, where they'd been abandoned since the start of the recent war. At home, nobody ever asked where I was spending so much time, and nor did I see another living soul during my many happy sojourns in Crystal Palace Park.

On Saturday evenings, Grandad and Nanny took themselves off for an evening of revelling. In the early hours of Sunday, they rambled home, noisy and giggling like a couple of naughty kids. Later that morning, as Dad and I set of for church, the house was as silent as the grave. Why shouldn't they have a touch of brightness in their lives? Whose business was it where they took their pleasure, be it in a pub or a church? Dad never said a word about such sinning, but I bet he thought it.

With the joy of finding my personal sanctuary and the company of my new friends, my life took on a new joy. Simply knowing I could slip away, whenever time lent itself, to regain my inner peace, where the only sounds in this vast city were the movement of the wind brushing through massed, neglected trees, and the enchanting sound of birdsong.

One Monday morning I woke up feeling poorly. I followed my usual routine, expecting to feel better as the day wore on. I knew what the consequence would be if I became a nuisance. As the week went by, I dragged myself about my duties before going to join my dinosaur friends. By Friday, unable to face school, I hauled my aching body to my place of refuge, snuggling into the welcoming curve of a friendly tail before falling into a deep sleep in the warmth of the sun. Waking hours later, panic-stricken, with no idea of the time, I rushed home to start my duties before I was caught out. The next morning being Saturday, we all breakfasted together, but I couldn't hide how ill I was. Bathed in perspiration and unable to swallow, I passed out. Dad, realising something was amiss, took me by bus to the nearest doctor. As I entered the

Anerley

doctor's surgery, I passed out again.

As I came round, I realised I'd been placed on a couch. The kindly doctor demanded to know of Dad what was going on, couldn't he see I should be in hospital? Dad explained that I had told no one I was feeling ill. As for finding a hospital to take me, that was out of the question, as only a handful were still standing after the bombing, so the doctor insisted on driving me home. On seeing my lovely little room, he tucked me into bed, then gave instructions for my care and medication, saying he would be back the next day. 'Don't worry, little one' was to be his regular farewell. I felt comforted, knowing someone was on my side.

As soon as the doctor departed, I overheard Nanny shrieking on the landing outside my room, 'Get her out of here, I don't want anyone sick in my house.' Dad pleaded with her not to turn us out. With time, she calmed down, and I was allowed to stay. After all, where else would she find a free servant?

During the week, when everyone was out, the front door was left ajar for the doctor. He always greeted me cheerfully, with the words, 'How are we today, little one?'

I was suffering from quinsy, an infection of the throat, which, before the arrival of antibiotics, was treated by regular gargling with hot water and crushed aspirin. One morning the doctor told me he was concerned, as the quinsy should have burst by now. If it hadn't done so by tomorrow, he would be forced to lance it. When Dad came home from work, he asked how I was. I told him what was planned for the following morning. With that, he leaned over me, his face almost touching mine, staring wildly into my eyes, spittle flying in all directions as he hissed, 'I knew a man who had the same thing. The doctor had to lance his throat, but the knife slipped, cutting an artery. Blood spurted on to the ceiling, and the man was dead in three minutes. But you'll go to live with Jesus, and be happy forever.'

'I don't want to live with Jesus,' I yelled feebly.

Luck was with me. During the night, the disgusting thing burst. Within moments, I felt strength flooding through my body, and for the first time in ages I quite fancied breakfast. My heroic doctor gave strict instructions not to overdo things, to take it easy for a few days. I spent those days sleeping and musing on the pretty blue and pink roses covering the walls from top to bottom. How lucky I'd been to have my kindly doctor turning up at the right time, together with my good fortune in having the only happy room in the house.

My happiness was short-lived as trouble soon reared its ugly head. Nanny was planning to visit her sister the coming weekend, in the pretty village of Downe, in Kent. Hearing I'd been poorly, Nanny's sister suggested she bring me with her, as the country air would be healing. Broaching the subject with Dad, he almost had a fit. 'I know my daughter would prefer to go to church, to thank the Lord for saving her life.'

After much haggling, the final choice was to be left to me. I immediately opted for the country. Dad's endless nagging went on all week. How could I be so ungrateful to the Lord, who'd restored life to a sinner such as me? Feeling completely defeated, it was surprising I didn't fall ill again. Why wouldn't he shut up about the darned church? Wearing me down until I was on the verge of tears, I found myself pleading to be allowed to go to church. The outcome of this wrangle was that I went to the country and had a lovely time, after promising to give thanks to the Lord the following Sunday.

At church a week later, Pastor Barnes made an announcement.

Anerley

'Our prayers have been answered. The Lord in his goodness has chosen to spare the life of Sister Margaret. Would she come forward and take a seat in the front row.'

It appeared that the whole congregation had been praying for my survival. We would give thanks to the Lord for his mercy, by the laying of hands. With this, the three eminent beings from the balcony on high descended, each of them placing a trembling hand on my head, while at the same time offering heartfelt thanks to Our Saviour for healing his servant.

As we left the church, Brothers and Sisters offered their blessing, together with much praising of the Lord for his merciful benevolence in saving me. I felt like the most important person in the church, but the whole experience had been embarrassing, and I was glad to put the day behind me. Passing my special gate, I sent a silent message to the dinosaurs, 'Back to normal, tomorrow.'

A quiet sunny day, everything back as it should be, tall birches showing the first signs of autumn, an oasis of calm in poor shattered London, a secret haven shared by me and the dinosaurs.

Just as things were running smoothly, Dad told me we were leaving London, to live in Cwmcarn. Sensing this must be connected with Brother John Roberts, his mentor who had first directed him to the Lord, I was thoroughly fed up, having grown used to London, and my dinosaur friends. When the day came for our departure, the pain of leaving them was unbearable. I couldn't face them.

It would be thirty years or more before I returned to see how my old friends had fared; the dinosaur section of the huge park had become unrecognisable. Now an open waterpark, a number of my friends had been dropped into sullied water while others were now on parched, dusty grassland, ill at ease in the baking sun. No longer reigning supreme, masters of their kingdom, their proud heads rearing over refreshing woodlands. The woodlands were now a tarmacked car park with parking meters and ice cream vans. One thing of which I was certain, my friends and I had known it at its best, my place of refuge at a time of need.

Nanny and Grandad saw us off. Making my way along the road, I paused to change hands, my suitcase being heavy. Glancing behind me, I felt sad; Nanny looked tired and vulnerable. I don't think she was long for this world. Who would she find to do the cleaning? What a pity she had to be so nasty. Did the sun catch a tear running down her cheek, as I looked back? I wouldn't bet on it, but I was pretty sure I was right.

~6~
Cwmcarn

Once again, we found ourselves travelling westward, transported by a now familiar steam train, not to beloved Stroud, but this time to Newport in Wales. From there, a bus would take us through the lengthy Rhondda Valley into the heart of Welsh Coal Mining Country, which had played such a major part during the recent war and would continue to do for many years to come.

Throughout the tedious journey, I was eager to take in the scene, so different from anything I'd previously encountered, but after mile upon mile with nothing but bleakness in view, my spirits plummeted. With no sign of beauty, I tired of overbearing darkness, endless mountains of black slagheaps, and wondered how I would survive in these surroundings.

I heard a true story. During the war, a serving American officer based in Italy asked a British war photographer to which part of Britain he would send his worst enemy. 'Cwmcarn,' came the reply.

On arrival at the small town, Dad decided we'd go straight to Brother John's house, a small terraced miner's cottage, identical to a thousand others in this drab town. We knocked on the door and

Pretty from the Outside

waited for quite some time before Brother John's sister opened it. She was a woman of larger size. She moved carefully through the narrow hall to the living room, where she settled into a well-worn armchair that fit snugly around her. A beaming smile never left her chubby face, but she didn't say a word, and nor did she offer us so much as a cup of tea, which would have been very welcome after our long journey. I perched myself on the edge of a well-worn settee, where I noticed bunched strands of black straw protruding from a gaping black hole. I dared to peep into the hole, where I was horrified to see a mass of small wriggling creatures heaving themselves about. I noticed a similar cavity towards the far end of the settee. Keeping as far from the holes as possible, I couldn't help thinking, 'Cleanliness is next to godliness.' Who was I to question the integrity of a great man such as Brother John?

Before long, Brother John returned from his shift in the mine, looking exhausted and haggard. A man in his forties, I spotted numerous specks of coal dust embedded in his complexion and noticed a marked rattle in his chest.

It took him some effort to ease himself into a seat at the far end of the dining table, where a place had been set for one. Since his arrival, he'd hardly said a word, only grunting to acknowledge Dad, and nodding to me. His sister reluctantly eased herself from the depths of her armchair to make her listless way to a small kitchen, eventually returning with his hot meal.

Brother John removed his false teeth and placed them on the table. Within seconds, a small black and white female cat sprung lightly onto his shoulder, made herself comfortable, and leaning forward with ladylike manners daintily shared Brother John's meal, before leaping down to commence a thorough grooming session. There were no airs and graces in this house. Brother John replaced his teeth, cheering up no end with a good meal inside him. Now, happy in each other's company, he joined Dad in an intense bout of setting the world to rights. Finding myself excluded from such an important discussion, I glanced about me. John's sister never uttered a word. If she didn't want to talk to me, that was up to her. Brother John obviously had breathing difficulties, his crackling chest causing him to cough up an amount of revolting green stuff into his handkerchief. Chest problems were an everyday part of being a coal miner, the common name being, 'Black Lung,' or the medical term, 'pneumoconiosis', an inevitable illness that afflicted coal miners, turning young men into invalids, often leading to an early death, as was to befall Brother John.

Late afternoon found us outside the door of our new lodgings, a neat, traditional, three-bedroom, mid-terrace house in the middle of town. Mr and Mrs Davies were a nice enough elderly couple, not particularly memorable, but I've no complaints. However, I well remember Deaf Danny, their white cat, who took to sleeping under my eiderdown, soon becoming my close, and warming, pal. Unforgettable too was the stench of the lavatory at the end of the garden, particularly in summer when it was not the place to stop to smell the roses.

Our meals were taken together at set times, otherwise we didn't mix, except on special occasions, such as Christmas, when the front room was opened, and a coal fire lit.

Christmas of 1946 found us with the largest pork joint I had ever seen. Unable to buy such a luxurious chunk from the butcher, it arrived by way of the black market, very hush-hush, it being imperative that we didn't tell a soul how we had come by such a feast. Almost impossible to lift, the pork was displayed for some days in a position of honour, on the proper dining table in the freezing front room. Although our Christmas dinner was not strictly legal, a few trusted friends and neighbours were allowed in to view this hot property.

Just before the big day, I happened to be standing with Mrs Davis admiring our Christmas dinner, when to my surprise she became weepy, confiding in me that just before my arrival, her Mother's open coffin had lain on this very table for visitors to pay their last respects in the run-up to the funeral. Naturally I was sorry for her recent loss, but I hoped against hope that the thought of a dead body lying where my dinner was soon to reside wouldn't put me off my pork.

On our first morning in Cwmcarn, I thought I'd take a walk around the town to get my bearings. There was little of interest, other than a few shops selling food or home essentials. For anything special, the locals took a bus to the nearest town of Risca, or went further afield to the city of Newport.

While meandering along a narrow back street I turned a sharp corner, where, much to my surprise, I found myself facing a quaint fish and chip shop. Of more interest was the old-fashioned picture house next to it. A brilliantly coloured poster announced they were showing a film called *Down to Earth*, starring an exquisite girl called Rita Hayworth, playing the role of the Goddess of Dance in 'glorious technicolour.'

Rita is seen flying through the air in a shimmering gown, her luxurious mane of auburn hair streaming out behind her, as she descends from heaven to earth. Who would have believed I'd find something so impossibly glamorous in Cwmcarn, of all places? I knew Dad would never let me go to the pictures, but there was a new film every week, so I could always look out for the change of posters. Dad reckoned the cinema was the house of the Devil,

Cwmcarn

and anyone seen to frequent such places were encouraging those lost souls dancing before them to partake in his evil work. The posters reminded me of happier times, when at The Weighbridge pub Dad would give me his saved cigarette cards to add to my collection, but that was a long time ago, before he saw the light. After discovering my wonderful secret, I made a point of passing the picture house whenever possible. A glance at the current week's poster was enough to keep my dreams alive.

One morning I was wandering about town for no particular reason. I had checked my poster of the week, which this week featured the Forces' sweetheart, Betty Grable, whose fabulous legs were considered to be the most beautiful in the world. Photos of Betty in a body-hugging swimsuit adorned American fighter planes, cheering on the young men who flew them. On I strolled, lost in a world of film stars, before realising I'd reached the highest point of the town where, taking advantage of someone's garden wall, I stopped for a rest, while familiarising myself with the layout of the town. From my position, I had a bird's-eye view of the coalface directly below me, where a never-ending stream of cranes, transporting heavy containers piled high with freshly dug coal, deposited their loads at the workface, before repeating their never-ending round trip. The miners were taken from the coalface in an iron cage and delivered to the very bowels of the earth. At the end of their working day, the cage returned them to ground level. Day after day, these men crawled through miles of cramped tunnels, unable to stand upright, chiselling out the coal which had lain undisturbed for centuries, now to be brought from the depths to the earth's surface.

Small ponies were used to assist the miners in their work. Many of these animals were blind from living permanently in total darkness. Those who could see would never get to see daylight, which upset me no end, but I took some comfort from hearing they were well loved by the miners, who did all they could to improve their tragic lives.

I took to leaning on the wall by the exit, waiting for Dad at the end of his shift, watching groups of men dispiritedly making their way home through the gloom. Not once, during my days of loitering, did I see a miner, young or old, who wasn't silent, gaunt and far too thin.

On Sundays, we walked the two miles or so to Elim Pentecostal Church in Crosskeys to attend morning service. Brother John was a changed man at the church, where he was revered as a man of standing by the congregation. Dressed in his Sunday suit, his poor face still bore the marks of deeply embedded soot, and his chest was as before, but all in all he brushed up nicely.

The children clearly adored him, hanging on his every word. It was surprising to see how he came into his own in his chosen setting, with his irascible teasing and endless storytelling. The sermon, offered with great passion by Pastor Evans, was not my cup of tea. Instead, I immersed myself in tales of Christ's miracles, or re-arranged the pressed flowers in my Bible.

My visit to Brother John's home was never repeated, and nor did I see his sister again as she wasn't a believer. The Welsh were avid churchgoers; the church provided stability, a place to make new friends and enjoy an agreeable social life. Aside from family life and the church, in my day there wasn't much more to fill our lives in Crosskeys. We had the fish and chip shop, the pub, and the picture palace, which of course was out of bounds to me. Dad would have had a fit if he had the slightest idea how drawn I was to the cinema, especially if he thought there might be the slightest hint of any kissing or ladies' breasts on show.

Quite often, come Saturday afternoon, the two of us would take the bus to Newport. Being Londoners, we never tired of the buzz of a city, and a good mooch round the shops. On my first visit, I was horrified by the devastation everywhere I looked, which was on a par with poor old London. We made our way through vast bomb damage to the city centre, which had been spruced up and was pretty lively, with many distractions laid on, where we amused ourselves, before meandering through the best store in town, checking out the latest fashions. We always ending up separated, as Dad could never resist indulging in his swanky tastes. Since the end of war nothing new had permeated the world of ladies' fashions; sensible utility outerwear still ruled the racks of dull grey suits and sensible warm brown coats, along with sturdy lace-up shoes guaranteed to provide long service if treated with respect, and certain to see you out.

With luck, Dad would be in a good mood, having searched out a colourful pullover to lift his spirits. This usually culminated in a couple of Eldorado choc ices for him and at least one for me, sold on the streets from ice cream carts, devoured by us in a friendly small park, where we could rest while enjoying the cheering sound of a rowdy brass band in the background.

Late afternoon saw us homeward-bound. Autumn had set in, and it was already getting dark as I gazed from the bus window at our companions, the formidable mountains, now menacing shadows, looming over the valleys, as the setting sun, a fireball of blazing orange, slid silently behind their blackness.

I was missing the Cotswolds, especially the farm and Our Mum. I even missed Nanny Oldfield, but most of all, I missed my friends, the dinosaurs in their Garden of Eden setting. I had the feeling that Dad had regretted returning to Cwmcarn, this way of life didn't suit his fastidious nature. Not once did I catch him with a blackened face at the end of a shift; he must have had a good washdown before clocking out. As vain as ever, he still dressed like a film star when he was away from the pit. The trouble was he had nowhere to go, except to continue spreading the 'Word', pouncing on any unsuspecting sinner and pointing him to Jesus, making me want to curl up and die. Anyway, he was wasting his time on the Valley folk, as there was nothing they didn't already know about the 'Word'.

On 13 November 1946, I turned eleven and had to attend school. The one assigned to me was a run-of-the-mill local school, a short walk from Cwmcarn.

A strange uneasiness filled me as I approached the school on my first morning. The gloomy school building reminded me of a photograph I'd seen in the past of a grim workhouse. I'd always loved school, but I had a bad feeling about this one. A sense of despair pervaded the atmosphere, while the behaviour of the children in the playground seemed unusually subdued, with no hint of exuberant high spirits.

A solid wooden door was eventually opened to us pupils, as we quietly formed a line, before making our way into the main hall for morning assembly, where we stood in rows, in silence, until the headmaster made his entrance. I felt an immediate aversion to the short, elderly man, with his mean, bitter face and humped back, which forced his head forward in a menacing way. Standing before us, he slowly took in each child without making a sound, peering from low-placed, searching eyes, before instructing us to join in singing a hymn. I stood silently, as there was no spare copy to hand of the Welsh hymn we'd been told to sing. The moment the hymn ended, he beckoned me forward, demanding to know why I hadn't been singing. I explained as best I could, but he didn't listen to a word I said. Taking a cane from his desk, he ordered me to hold out my hand, before bringing it down with all the strength he could muster. The searing pain inflicted by this man's unwarranted attack was almost too much to bear. Unable to stop my tears, I cried, not only from the pain and injustice of his actions, but I'd also caught a glimpse of the relish in his eyes as he brought down the cane.

Nothing exciting happened in this part of the world, but the same cannot be said for one particular Saturday, when for a change we took the bus into Risca, a lively small town, with an interesting choice of shops and cafés. Making our way into the town centre, we noticed the formation of small groups excitedly going over an incident that had taken place a few minutes earlier. It turned out the main street was in the process of having its tarmac replaced, causing quite a disruption, when a young man on his bicycle came up against a steamroller. Somehow the poor fellow and his bike were dragged slowly under the mighty weight of the machine. He was completely flattened, the driver of the steamroller totally unaware of anything untoward happening. We arrived on the scene, shortly after the gruesome event. Apparently, the young man's screams were horrific, causing a number of pedestrians to suffer panic attacks. I'm glad I didn't hear any screaming, it would have given me nightmares, but all the same, what a terrible thing to happen to that poor young man.

Little could we have known that the winter of 1946–47 was to be the harshest on record, rendering the whole of Britain paralysed for months. Mid-December saw the temperature drop to minus twelve. A week or so later, temperatures rose, the weather turning dull and damp before deteriorating again in the middle of January, when an easterly wind swept in from Scandinavia, bringing with it seven-metre snowdrifts. From mid-January to mid-March, the temperature never rose above minus two during the day.

The weather played havoc with people's lives, and with trade. Coal and electricity were particularly affected. Ships transporting coal remained frozen solid on the rivers, unable to move for weeks. Stockpiles of coal were at their lowest, with those remaining unable to be moved, being frozen solid. Vegetables froze in the earth, food rationing was reduced to its lowest level since wartime, and a worrying shortage of meat meant that rations were further cut. Whale meat and a revolting-smelling fish called 'snoek', loathed by everyone, were brought in by the government.

Coal and electricity had recently been nationalised by the Labour party. A boom in the sale of electric fires came about when the whole country rushed to buy one as coal became severely rationed. Power cuts were brought in. Between the hours of 9 am and 12 pm, and 2 pm and 4 pm, everyone was without power. I woke on the first morning of the big freeze snuggled up to 'Deaf Danny,' the snow piled high above my upstairs bedroom window. For several months, a temporary pavement remained on that level with no sign of a thaw.

Somebody kept the path to the lavatory cleared of snow. I never enquired as to who supplied this service, as the word lavatory wasn't included in the Davies' vocabulary.

The one mercy was that dreaded school was closed for six weeks, which gave me time to work my way through *John Halifax, Gentleman*, a Victorian novel I'd picked up for a penny or two in an old bookshop during my travels. I'd selected this particular book as I loved the mellifluous tone of the name Muriel, John's beloved wife. I must have shed many a tear as I became immersed in their varying degrees of joy and suffering. Somehow, I managed to mislay *John Halifax, Gentleman* on my travels, but as luck would have it, years later, I came across a copy, again in an old-fashioned bookshop. I bought it for a few pence, for sentimental reasons; sadly, it no longer held its magic for me.

Throughout this unforgiving winter, in spite of the daytime temperature remaining below zero, not once did we miss Sunday morning service. Forging forward, with assistance from the cheering hymn 'Onward, Christian Soldiers, marching as to war' ringing out, over frequently hazardous conditions, keeping our minds on the urgency of the exercise. Fortunately, the days were usually filled with brilliant sunshine in a cloudless blue sky. One Sunday morning after the onset of the first heavy snowfall, we were trudging round a familiar bend when, low and behold, we found ourselves transported to Fairyland. The Black Mountains, to the right, left and ahead, no longer frightening monsters, but snow-capped peaks of a million translucent crystals, sparkling like diamonds, each one winking back at the morning sun from its glorious setting. Mile upon mile of virgin snow stretched as far as I could see, before connecting with an azure sky. Throughout the harshest winter days, at every opportunity I retraced my steps to partake of this miracle. It was time well spent as I knew full well its beauty would soon vanish overnight.

Attendance at church would be high, unless there'd been an overnight blizzard. The small children, overjoyed by ceaseless holiday, never tired of building snowmen with assistance from the grown-ups, the bigger boys excitedly pelting each other with snowballs until an adult calmed them, reminding them it was the Lord's day. Brother John would be there, if he could get a lift. He had been known to arrive by horse and cart. He'd do whatever he could to get there, but his poor old chest would never permit him to walk so far. As with all Pentecostal Churches, the congregation were a generous lot, plying me and Dad with sandwiches and home-made cake, not realising our Sunday dinner was waiting for us back at our lodgings.

It was mid-March before winter released its iron grip. I woke one morning to the sound of rushing water overflowing the outside gutters, telling me the thaw had set in. Soon the snow would drain away, making it possible to see the other side of the road, and what's more, pedestrians would soon be able to walk at street level again. Downstairs, glancing through the kitchen window I regarded a gang of tiny birds, chirping cheekily in the privet bush outside the kitchen door, where kind Mrs Davies had made sure they stayed supplied with leftovers, chopped into bits and pieces. Cwmcarn had returned to life.

One lovely spring day, just as things were getting back to normal, Dad broke the news. We were going back to London. Just as I was starting to adapt to this strange place and acquire some kind of equilibrium, I was to be unsettled. I'd grown fond of the Davies too, as I had for Deaf Danny, and the palace of my dreams, the picture house.

Today Cwmcarn, together with many miles of what had been working mines in my day, have been transformed into a glorious Country Park. The small town of Cwmcarn appears to be unchanged from my time, but the dispiriting black coal slagheaps are today the foundation of beautiful Cwmcarn Forest, which stretches for miles through the Rhondda Valley. Its marked walks of varying distances have lovely names such as The Bluebell Walk. The forest is a favourite with families, walkers and mountain

Cwmcarn

bikers, and highly favoured by the world of professional biking. I like to think that my encounter with the magical snow scenes of 1947 foretold what was on the cards for the Rhondda Valley coal mines. Never will I forget the memory of those exhausted miners, as I waited for Dad at the gates of Cwmcarn Colliery, during the winter of 1946–47.

~7~
Lee, South East London

Our new home was two streets from Emmanuel Church in Lee, too near as far as I was concerned. Even worse, we were to live in a home for elderly Sisters of the church, who, finding themselves alone in their later years, were offered refuge. The home had been set up by Pastor Barnes' son, and his wife, who ran the place like clockwork. I remembered her well from earlier days as an unusually tall, most attractive lady, always wearing the latest fashion, with a penchant for exotic hats. Their son Steven, a boisterous three-year-old, was to be my lifesaver.

On the day we moved, we repeated the journey to Paddington Station, where once again we crossed London by double-decker red bus, dropping us at the familiar bus stop at Boone Street, a few yards from Emmanuel Church, where we crossed to the opposite side, remembering not to trip in the slippery tramlines. In a matter of minutes, we were outside our new abode, 41 Aislibie Road, London, SE12.

It was a tall terraced house, with a path leading to the front door. The path cut through an immaculate front garden, set out with borders of seasonal plants, centred by neatly mown grass. We were made welcome by Mrs Barnes Junior, who showed us our separate quarters.

Dad was given a charming room, overlooking a decent-size, neat enclosed back garden, set out with garden seats and a table. I was to sleep in a dormitory, with six elderly Sisters, where my bed had already been set up in a far corner, well screened from the others, in case I caught a glimpse of someone's corset. Miss Martin, a lovely old girl, was the only one of us to have her own room.

The leader of the pack was Miss Freemont, a French woman from Paris, with a naturally flushed complexion and full lips. Her strong, carrying voice echoed throughout the house - something that occasionally startled two hearing-impaired residents who couldn't detect her approach. At least I got plenty of warning, as her guttural voice could be heard throughout the house.

The home ran like clockwork. Each of us were given a seat in the dining room, from which we didn't dare deviate. The dining room would be set for tea before we took our seats. Each person's ration amounted to two slices of buttered bread, an individual portion of jam, one scone, and one slice of cake. Miss Freemont's position at the table was opposite me, her back to the window, causing me a considerable problem should the sun be shining, as the plate of delicious cakes were in direct line of her flying spittle. The only way to protect my portion was to select a well-hidden cake and watch it like a hawk until it was time to dive in. I didn't mention it to the others; most of them could hardly see, anyway, so why trouble them with petty incidents?

Tea was followed by prayers, offered to the Lord in rotation, according to one's position at the table. The prayers were not normal prayers, but what I called a free-for-all. Following regular blessings and thanks for the Lord's mercy towards we sinners, silence reigned until a passionate outpouring might well evolve, the person offering prayers becoming filled with the Holy Spirit, then letting rip, by speaking in tongues. I dreaded this happening. After all, it was most embarrassing.

It soon became my turn to pray aloud. Sitting in silence, a mounting sense of panic rising inside me, I uttered not a single word. Murmurings of, 'Give her strength, Lord,' and other encouraging sounds emanated through the quietness, until eventually, unable to take any more, I burst out with, 'I'm not doing it,' as I fled from the room. Unfortunately, the following afternoon, instead of moving on to the next in line, they returned to me, leading to a series of missed meals on my part. With time, realising they were flogging a dead horse, they gave up. However, without fail, whenever it should have been my turn, there would be a hint of a niggle from someone or other.

We'd been back in London for some time when I realised Dad had developed a keen interest in taking a bus to Marble Arch, in Hyde Park, on Saturday afternoons, to hear the preachers at Speakers' Corner deliver their personal stories of sin and repentance to the crowds gathered there, by issuing the dreaded warning, 'The end of the world is nigh.' To the majority of their listeners, it was a bit of amusement, something to pass the time heckling and jeering the speakers who seemed earnest in their beliefs, their personal route always being the true way to redemption. We wandered around, listening to their enthusiastic outpourings, 'The choice was yours, both Hell and Damnation are waiting to welcome you with open arms, or you may choose to live in the arms of Jesus for eternity.'

Being quite worn out after listening to so many ardent orations, I welcomed a nice cup of tea at a friendly stall, while musing over the reason Dad would choose to harken to this motley group of oddities, when he could listen to the Gospel every day in his own church. It came to me in a flash: he was honing his own preaching skills, picking up ideas, working out how best to get his own message across. After all, didn't Jesus counsel his disciples to travel far and wide, spreading the word, at home and abroad? All the signs were there. 'In the last days, there would be wars and rumours of wars.' Hadn't we recently come through the war to end all wars? The world would soon be decimated, and heaven help you, if you find you yourself unprepared.

Living so close to Emmanuel Church, I was spending more time there than I could reasonably spare. The whole of Sunday was taken up with services, or some such intrusion. Morning service began at 11 am, followed by a quick dash home for lunch, and all the routines that entailed. Back to the church for Sunday school at 3 pm, where my teacher was Miss Edna Wright, an unmarried woman in her late thirties. She had a slight build and a naturally rosy complexion, which was affected by a respiratory condition, emphysema, developed during London's winter seasons. She wore her hair styled neatly in a bun, and always dressed modestly, including a beret she seemed fond of wearing. She had a gentle demeanor and found it difficult to make direct eye contact.

Miss Edna Wright had a sister, Miss Winnifred Wright, of near enough the same age. She was also a spinster, and a Sunday school teacher of a younger age-group. Although she towered over her sister, she too was skinny but considerably prettier. The sisters worked as secretaries for small companies near their home in New Eltham, where they shared a house with their elderly parents, in an upmarket suburban area on the borders of London and Kent. Mr Wright, their father, a scrawny, bent figure, was one of the esteemed

Elders of the Church, a cowering, round-shouldered man. If you knew his wife you'd understand the reason he cowered. Not once did I hear him utter a single word from his hunched position of seniority, up in the gallery with the pastor.

His wife was a prominent figure in the church community, actively involved in many aspects of church life. She carried herself with a formal bearing, perhaps influenced by her military background. Her usual attire consisted of a well-tailored double-breasted brown tweed coat tightly buttoned to her chin, sturdy utility-like laced shoes, thick woollen stockings, and a distinctive trilby hat adorned with a jaunty feather perched in its band. Peering over the top of her pince-nez spectacles, perched precariously on the tip of her nose, she glared suspiciously at the poor soul being assessed before her, adding to the severity of her presence and making her appear more intimidating than she believed she was.

With the end of Sunday school, there was just time to raid the church's small kitchen for a slice of home-made cake and a cup of tea before making a dash to the Clock Tower in the centre of buzzing Lewisham for our weekly open-air meeting. The powers that be were anxious that I attend, believing my youth might help attract young people to the church.

Light-hearted, merry hymns were the order of these days of gratitude for the never-failing love of Our Heavenly Father, for sinners such as we. 'My cup's full and running over,' was always a good one to get things underway. Joyful sounds swelled through the air, as our voices floated up and away, over the recently opened Marks & Spencer, and other exciting fashionable shops, for both sexes, although massive craters and acres of flattened ground were still visible. Passers-by and bystanders joined in and sang the hymns with enthusiasm. Various members of the church offered

Pretty from the Outside

up their personal testimony, and unfortunately I got roped into this, blurting out at some point in the service, 'I was saved by the Lord on 2 March 1946. Praise the Lord', making me want to curl up and die. The meeting drew to a close on a cheery note, before we 'Children of the Lord' made our way back to Emmanuel Church, for the most important service of the week, the Sunday sermon. With any luck, I would be free from the church goings-on for the whole week, although nothing would stop Dad attending the Monday evening prayer meeting. Now, however, it was time to join the ladies for a good night's sleep.

Dad came up with a strange notion. I was to attend an exclusive private school, his reasoning being that if I attended a private school only to become a failure in life, I would have no one to blame but myself, as he'd done his best. It was arranged that I begin the following term at St Anne's School, a long bus journey from Lee, in a totally unfamiliar area.

So began a round of tailors and dressmakers. Never having experienced the fitting of expensive clothing, I found it more tiring than learning arithmetic. The school's colours were purple and a light shade of grey. A full-length grey coat for winter, with matching skirt, a purple blazer with the school's badge emblazoned on the top pocket, two grey jumpers, traditional knee-high grey socks, sturdy black shoes and a black brimmed hat, the hatband bearing the school's emblem.

Summer term called for two pure silk, pleated dresses in a soft shade of ivory, with expensive cream-coloured flat shoes, soft and dainty, like a fairy's shoes. The summery effect was finished off with a ladylike Panama hat, with of course the school's emblem on the hatband.

School was held in a large private house, enclosed by superb

Lee, South East London

grounds where lessons were taken, when possible, in the shade of the overhanging branches of huge ancient trees, still standing, having survived the onslaught of war.

Boarding a bus at Lee Green, at 8 am for an hour or so's leisurely drive to I never knew where exactly. I went by way of familiar bus stops. Inclined to daydream, I became lost in a happy reverie, aware that we passed through Lewisham, Catford, then through parts of London I'd never heard of. It wasn't long before I became entranced by the latest modern hoardings springing up of late in every town and city, strongly influenced by the United States of America. This development symbolised the optimism running throughout the country. Soaps and washing powders were now delicately perfumed, no longer smelling of carbolic soap, or rancid disinfectants, as at Longfords. Who wants to go about with lovely shining hair reeking of carbolic?

The town hall in the centre of Catford was a major changing point for many passengers, allowing me the time to gaze around. High in the air, displayed for all to see, was a monster hoarding promoting Dreft soap powder as being fragrant and feminine. Delightful shades of dainty lingerie swirled, free as air, a gossamer fantasy of pastels soaring high into a cloudless blue sky. Morning and evening, while the bus stood at that particular point, my mind drifted to Rita Hayworth in *Down to Earth* back at the picture palace in Cwmcarn.

The headmistress and owner of the school was Mrs May, an all-encompassing mother hen figure, of about sixty years of age, who idolised her girls as they did her. There were twenty or so pupils, all around my age, with Mrs May the sole teacher. The most important subject revolved around food, the service and preparation, together with the elegant art of eating and drinking in a ladylike manner, which I found a delightful exercise.

St Anne's was unlike any school I'd come across before. It was more like being on holiday; none of us were ever in trouble, and if a girl was poorly, she would be tucked up in bed with a hot water bottle and made a tremendous fuss of.

It proved lucky for me that Mrs May came into my life at this time. I was at an age when I was maturing rapidly, and it was Mrs May who gently guided me through this mysterious time of change. Returning to the old ladies was dispiriting to say the least. If the weather allowed, I'd be out at once with Steven in his pushchair, heading for the little park right behind our garden. I loved these times with a youngster, as it reminded me of glorious days on the farm with Baby John. We fed the ducks with chunks of leftover bread, and searched out new shoots pushing their way through the undergrowth beneath the bushes, watching their development over the coming months until they reached their day of glory. All too soon it was time to go back and deposit Little Steven to his grateful mummy.

The truth is, she was rather obsessed with work, never happy unless she was up to her elbows in flour and butter, or sorting out some muddle or other. I must say she did a marvellous job, always turning out for church looking as crisp as a model in *Vogue* magazine. Luckily for me, Mrs Barnes enjoyed women's magazines and was happy for me to borrow them. It was in one of these that I saw a pattern for a knitted bikini, all the rage in France for the new season. I reserved the wool from the local wool shop, in alternate shades of brown, turquoise and scarlet, paying for a couple of skeins whenever I managed to get enough money together. I worked at my own speed, tucked away in my little corner behind my screen, where no one entered without my permission. Dad would have had a fit if he'd found out what I was up to, but what the eye doesn't see, the heart doesn't grieve, and I enjoyed getting one up on him. I had no idea where I would wear my bikini, but I must say, after stitching the parts together and trying it on, it looked jolly nice. I'd find the right place to put it to use, being a firm believer that where there's a will there's a way.

The summer passed happily at school, with most of our time spent outdoors. Our lunch was prepared by an expert in the art of cuisine, relating to the palette and health of the human being, including the correct use of cutlery and which wine glass to use for certain wines, things not pertaining to my way of life at the time.

A delightful menu was selected for each day of the week, served, most days, from an outdoor buffet. I'd never tasted such food, luxurious meats, such as grilled chicken breasts, and salads served with French dressing, none of your rubbishy salad cream. Amazing fish dishes, always delicately eaten, thus avoiding any tiny bone, which may have escaped the chef's highest standards. Puddings were always special, such as strawberries and cream, with meringue, chocolate mousse, and always a delicious choice of imported Italian ice creams, the likes of which you would never find in a shop in England.

Quite often, if Mrs May had some urgent business to attend to, she would leave me in charge of the class. The only thing I could think to do was read from a book we happened to be studying. I always got through it, but I was no teacher, and couldn't help feeling the girls were being short-changed. Thank goodness, my services were rarely called on.

At the end of the school day, the majority of us were picked up in stylish cars, either by mothers, or chauffeured limousines. I didn't mind the bus, in fact I loved it. At least, being such a long way from Lee, I didn't have to worry about anyone finding out about the church and living in the home. God forbid, anyone from such a top school should hear Dad pointing souls in the direction of the Lord.

Despite enjoying every moment at St Anne's, I didn't learn a thing, apart from how to present myself like a lady in all situations.

In defence of Mrs May's teaching methods, in 1947 young ladies were expected to work in an office or shop, before marrying and becoming full-time housewives. As most of Mrs May's pupils were born into wealth, the social graces, and not much else, was all they needed to familiarise themselves with before tying the knot.

At the age of twenty-three, I had my appendix removed. The day after my operation, my surgeon visited my bedside. On reading my notes, he remarked, 'Twenty-three, and still not married? Men don't want to marry old women, you know.' That was the attitude in the 1960s. Young women were constantly being told: find a husband, or find yourself left on the shelf. If, by the age of twenty-eight, there was no man on the scene, one had failed miserably, leaving many women in their twenties deeply depressed, feeling they'd missed the boat. It was a bit like fishing, as not only did you have to catch the man, but you also had to land him, which was the hardest part.

Dad worked as a painter and decorator, sometimes working on a Saturday, leaving me free for the day. My favourite way of spending the day was a visit to Greenwich Park. On such days I rose early to allow ample time for loitering. Free as the air, I took the road to Blackheath, where I made my way into the central village, which had retained its old-world character from centuries past despite being part of the hustle and bustle of dusty London and a marked victim of the recent war. Exclusive shops, aimed at the well-to-do, lined attractive streets, their windows displaying the very latest in the world of high fashion.

I always forgot that Saturday was market day. Even at this early hour, cheap clothing, aimed at the young, were changing hands in the open square, sold by cheeky chappies and chatty women to working girls, eager to part with their hard-earned wages of the week. My eye was caught by costume jewellery, and various colourful curiosities, set out on trestle tables. Tempted as I was to linger, I resisted, reminding myself of my reason for setting out on this uphill hike that led me to my favourite starting point, overlooking Greenwich Park, where I rested, breathing in the clean air, while absorbing the majestic view spreading far into the distance. Directly below me, open fields stretched steeply down, before eventually opening onto wide grasslands with paths crossing hither and thither, where parents played games with their young ones, and gentlemen walked at a brisk pace, with their sprightly dogs.

The centrepiece of the whole scene was Greenwich Palace, with the River Thames flowing silently behind its stately structure. The creamy marbled stonework of the palace took on a pearly lustre, reflected from the soft light of this balmy day.

I stood, absorbing this spectacle from its highest point, a fierce wind tearing through my long, brown hair, as I reflected on the fantastic scene before me. London, North to South/East to West, proudly presenting this vast, unique canvas.

Wending my way down familiar paths, through wild woodlands, passing secret coverts where I'd taken shelter from harsh weather on earlier visits, until meeting expanses of green fields, leading ultimately to flawless lawns fronting the palace.

My final port of call was Greenwich Observatory, a sad image, standing abandoned since being destroyed by a German incendiary bomb in the war. Its glass dome shattered, its walls smashed to smithereens, exposed to all weathers, among overgrown and fallen trees, choking bushes and rampant undergrowth, each scrambling to overpower the once lovely lines of Sir Christopher Wren's design.

Time to get back, if I didn't want to miss tea. No more loitering. Hurriedly, taking the steep path back to my starting point, I gasped for breath, turning to take one last glimpse of my London, before heading back, full speed.

As usual, the first sound to assault my ears was the strident reverberation of Miss Freemont's tones thundering along the hall from the residents' lounge, where she held court over her followers. Luckily, her companions were happy to remain in her shadow. A rival would never be tolerated by such a leader, and God forbid it should arise, as it would certainly lead to pistols at dawn, which would be fun.

Miss Fremont made it plain she didn't think much of me. Many a time I'd hear her raucous complaining about some misdemeanour or other that must have been caused by that wicked girl.

I confess, I was guilty of startling her from time to time, just to liven things up a little, when life was particularly dull. I frequently overheard her regale her companions with tales of my wickedness. Apparently, my antics nearly caused her to have a stroke, or a heart attack. My first thought was always, 'What a pity she didn't.' In retrospect, I realise I should have shown more compassion, but it would have been asking a lot. If ever the Devil sent someone to torment me, it was surely in the form of Miss Freemont.

As this annoying old lady continued her attacks, I conceived a brilliant idea, designed to confuse her. During the Sunday morning service, at an appropriate moment, I would suddenly possess the gift of tongues. My heart beating wildly, when the right moment presented itself, I braced myself, taking to my feet, before letting rip with an eloquent outpouring, without the vaguest idea where it came from. This was followed a moment later by a Brother, with a heart-warming interpretation, bringing about the inevitable joyous reaction from the congregation. Returning home from the ill-deserved congratulations I received, the first voice I heard was Miss Fremont's telling anyone who would listen, 'We all know she's a wicked girl, but the Lord has chosen her, and we can't argue with that.' To this day I'll never know if my outpouring was real, or if I made it up in a moment of madness. I remember feeling most uncomfortable later, bitterly regretting my misdemeanour, hastily pushing it from my mind. Never again did I receive the gift of tongues, which is perhaps just as well.

Life continued as before, with noticeably more respect from the inmates of the home, which was gratifying. Life at school meandered along with not a worry in the world, until one evening Dad called me to his room and told me I was leaving St Anne's as he couldn't afford the fees. Next term I was to attend the local secondary school.

Maybe it was the size of Coopers Lane School in the London Borough of Lewisham that caused me such apprehension on my first day. A modern secondary school of mixed sexes, with thirty or more pupils in each class. Surprisingly, I took to it like a duck to water. I'd missed out on the 11+ exams, but the teaching I received here was first class. After the relaxed teachings of St Anne's, the new school came as quite a shock. There was to be no pampering here. I must put the social graces behind me for now and await a more suitable time in my life.

Pretty from the Outside

It wasn't long before I was making progress, loving most classes, especially subjects relating to literature and art. I learned to love the Bible, focusing on the beauty of the words, rather than sin and hellfire.

Two special teachers inspired me, each helping to restore my trampled confidence. Miss Miller taught literature and composition. A scrawny, fearless, grey-haired woman, looked on by lazy scallywags as a harridan, but revered by those of us who devoured her inspiring teachings. Then there was Mr Robinson, a tall, balding, humorous man who taught art, in all its forms. Inspired by the enthusiasm of both teachers, I soon found my feet, which is more than I can say for my relationship with the teacher of ballroom dancing, who was also the sports teacher.

An athletic young woman, with a short modern haircut, inclined to be laddish in her demeanour. With fewer boys than girls in the dance class, Miss Cooke decided that, being the tallest in the class, I should take the part of a man. No girls' shorts could be found, only one pair of ill-fitting men's cast-offs. Well aware how ridiculous I looked in my baggy shorts, I had no choice but to take my lady in my arms in front of the whole class. Panic-stricken, by now not feeling at all well, I froze to the spot. Unable to move, tears welled up as Miss Cooke forced me to go through the routine again and again. The more she drove me on, the more rigid I became. She was not to know that I was inclined to panic in such situations, having suffered years of Dad's bullying.

One day, when I was still a newcomer, Miss Cooke ordered an urgent meeting of the girls as a serious matter had been brought to her attention. Anticipating the worst, sure I'd done something dreadful, I joined my friends in the sports centre. It had come to her notice, she announced, we girls were rapidly maturing young ladies, with maturing bodies. It was imperative the larger among us should wear a brassiere with ample support. She went on about the dangers of running around the sports field, or taking any other strenuous exercise, for that matter, being too great a strain for our delicate breast muscles to cope with. Before long, we would ruin our young bodies, our breasts would sag and remain that way for the rest of our lives.

Thrown into panic at the thought of such a calamity, I knew I had to take immediate action.

I'd seen slides on a screen in geography class of women in hot countries prancing about at ceremonial occasions wearing nothing but tiny grass skirts, and some, even the young, suffered from this dreadful condition, I should imagine, from too much practice, poor souls. After school that day, I stayed on the bus, all the way to Lewisham. Racing into Chiesmans department store, taking the stairs two at a time, I rushed up to the ladies' underwear department. The brassiere recommended by Miss Cooke was in stock, in fact it was a bestseller, extremely stylish, in shiny pink satin, with elasticated support, which, the helpful assistant informed me, was extremely controlling in all situations. The price for such a necessary luxury was almost ten shillings.

After tea, I plucked up the courage to face Dad. I loathed asking for money, he always made such a song and dance about it, but I had no choice. Visibly shaking, heart pounding, I knocked on his door and rushed in blurting out that I had to have ten shillings. He demanded to know what I needed it for. Feelings of terror swept over me, but by some miracle I managed to utter the words, 'I'm afraid I can't tell you.' His reply was simply, 'I'm certainly not giving you ten shillings, if I don't know what it's for.' Wishing the floor would open up and swallow me, I forced out the words, 'If you must know, I need to buy a brassiere.' Dad, by now as confused as me, dug deep in his pocket, retrieving a ten-shilling note, handing it to me with the words, 'In future, ask for money for underwear.' Such situations cropped up frequently over the following years, always making us both uncomfortable, but if I played my cards right, it led to a nice little earner now and again.

I sallied forth the following Monday, head held high, snug and secure with a new uplifted profile. My clothes looked smarter, I appeared taller, slimmer, and surprisingly grown up.

I hadn't noticed how my appearance had altered over recent months. My footballer's knees had given way to long slender limbs that would give Betty Grable a run for her money. For the first time I had a waist, and a high, well-controlled bustline. In November, I would be thirteen, that's almost grown up. Two years later, I would go to work and get away from Dad.

Miss Cooke had hit the nail on the head when she noticed we were maturing young ladies. It was about time I acted my age, proud and serious, no more skipping along Coopers Lane like a child. Another advantage of my brassiere was the protection it gave me against Mr Pike, the science teacher, whose prime interest seemed to be brushing up against any girl's breasts, given half the chance.

School had become my lifeline to what I believed to be the real world, where I had the right to have an opinion. Making my way along Coopers Lane each morning, my aching loneliness fell away, as I looked forward to the pleasures awaiting me. Literature, composition, even my own efforts gave me pleasure, thanks to Miss Miller's ability to draw from me the substance of her offerings, and what a joy it was to have my eyes opened to the 'great art of the world,' as revealed by the delightful Mr Robinson, with his easy manner and wicked sense of humour.

Things failed to improve with Miss Cooke, however. I now shook visibly before her classes, my distress seeming to give her a perverse pleasure. Apart from my unhappy relationship with this lady, I couldn't have been happier, making friends with a special group, the closest being Iris, a sturdy outspoken girl, tough protector of the weak, taking on male or female offenders, who never stood a chance once Iris stepped in. Audrey was another dear friend, rather delicate, I remember her suffering agonising period pains, which, in the 1940s, one had to put up with. When she was back to herself, she was a sparkling wit, a fabulous-looking redhead, with a creamy complexion, adored by the whole group. After lunch, we gathered in our favourite corner of the playground, supposedly to discuss important girl matters, which invariably led to telling silly jokes and met with shrieks of laughter. The first time I heard a belly laugh rise in my throat, the unfamiliar sound made me almost jump out of my skin, it being such an age since I'd heard my own explosive laughter. I asked Dad if I could meet my friends out of school and during school holidays. Under no circumstances was I to have any contact outside of school with the offspring of sinners. There were plenty of people at the church who would make far more suitable friends.

Monday to Friday, I was a happy outgoing school girl, fitting in with my colleagues, a normal girl. Away from school, I was a misfit, the odd one out, repeatedly told I was under the influence of the Devil's agent, Satan, whose sole aim was to lead gullible souls, such as me, into the realms of despair.

One day, the headmistress Mrs Collins sent for me, and informed me she had had a visit from Dad. He was concerned I was going the way of my mother, who was a beauty, he said, but

Pretty from the Outside

a thoroughly bad lot. Mrs Collins told me she'd done her best to reassure him, saying I was a lovely girl, popular at school, one of the top in my class. 'Instead of worrying, you should be so proud of her, she's a credit to you.' That was a feather in my cap. Dad never mentioned his meeting with Mrs Collins.

Summoned to his room one evening, Dad gave me the news that I would be leaving the home.

It seems that I had become too much for Miss Freemont's delicate nervous system and was the cause of her recent digestive attacks. It's true I had surprised on her a couple of occasions, making her jump out of her skin, but clearly, she hadn't taken things in the spirit intended.

I was to board with an elderly widow, Mrs Butler, and her unmarried son, Henry. Henry was the youngest Elder of the Church, sharing a position of honour with his fellow Elders on Pastor Barnes' balcony, a person of some importance in the hierarchy of Emmanuel Church.

The Butlers lived in a semi-detached house, at the highest point of a horrendously steep cul-de-sac, the name of which slips my mind, but it was handy for school, being three bus stops closer to home, but a longer walk to the church.

Mrs Butler was a short rotund lady, well into her sixties, her style of dress typical of an elderly lady, made up of a sensible pleated, brown tweedy skirt, a pullover worn over her blouse, always finished off with a warm cardigan, under her coat, which was just as well as the house was freezing, and at her age you couldn't be too careful. A hardy great coat, worn with a knitted, woollen cap, completed her look, when she faced the outside world.

I had neutral feelings toward Mrs Butler and her son, Henry. He was reserved in nature and seemed uncomfortable in my company, which gradually developed into obvious disapproval. He was in his middle years, with thinning hair, and was very close with this mother.

The house was never out of order, with a place for everything and everything in its place. Even the matching cushions on the three-seater settee sprang back into shape the moment a human posterior was released from its embrace. Silence reigned at all times, unless by chance, an uplifting, suitable programme came over the wireless. 'Songs of Praise,' broadcast on a Sunday evening by the BBC, was not to be missed, though it called for a quick dash home, following Pastor Barnes' evening sermon. For a short period, I was invited to sit in on these sessions, but it wasn't long before they sussed me out as being a hopeless case.

The first time I opened the door of my little box room, I almost passed out. Shaken to the core, I somehow managed to stay on my feet. Directly hanging over the head of my bed, was a life-size portrait of William Holman Hunt's famous painting, 'The Light of the World'. Familiar with the painting, I recognised it as a sensitive portrait of the Lord Jesus, quite righty a sacred masterpiece when displayed in suitable surroundings, but the last thing I wanted was a life-size figure of Christ, his hypnotic gaze following my every move, with that mournful expression of sad disappointment burning into me day and night.

In the painting, Christ is seen standing in a derelict garden, wearing a crown of thorns, blood running freely down his face, as he stands mournfully among overgrown weeds. With one hand he knocks on a shabby wooden door, in the other he carries a brilliantly lit lantern, the softness of its beam radiating upwards, highlighting his haunted features. The painting, no doubt highly symbolic, was not one whose company I cared to share my life with.

Being happy at school made up, in many ways, for my gloomy home life. At the start of term, I'd been made responsible for the sewing room, including anything pertaining to needlework. I made sure I was the keeper of the key to the door, with nobody allowed to enter without my permission. I made sure the room was kept well dusted and tidy, my private sanctuary, a refuge from Miss Cooke, and a snug club house for our group in the event of a wet day. We certainly had some fine times in that hideaway.

Every weekday after school, I trudged up the long cul-de-sac to what I called 'The Haunted House,' inserting my key in the lock with dread. Mrs Butler was rarely there when I got home, being greatly in demand for her charitable works. The whole house was ice-cold and as silent as the grave, except for the sinister tick-tock of the grandfather clock standing in the hallway. Glancing around me, everything always in perfect order, cushions well plumped up, awaiting the excitement of the evening, when we might well take advantage of some life-enhancing broadcast over the wireless.

My group at school were, like me, keenly interested in fashion. From the end of the war, the English were much influenced by American film stars. We longed to be 'with it,' like the Hollywood stars, such as Lana Turner, the original, sweater girl, blonde and sexy, or radiant Ingrid Bergman, who played the part of a nun to perfection in *The Bells of St. Mary's*.

My room at the Butlers was littered with girls' bits and pieces. I can't imagine what 'The Light of the World' made of having to look at that mess every day, not to mention the constant ructions with Henry for hogging the bathroom in my efforts to style my hair like my latest film idol. There were no picture houses for miles around, so I couldn't catch up with what was showing locally, but one of the girls lent me her mother's weekly film magazine, *Picturegoer*, covering everything you could wish to know regarding the latest Hollywood goings-on. Each week I devoured the magazine from cover to cover but never found the courage to take it back to my room. Should Mrs Butler come across a glimpse of a lovely woman's naked shoulder or, God forbid, inklings of a lady's breast, such salacious subject matter might tip her over the edge, causing a fatal heart attack, and then I'd be arrested for manslaughter. Much better that *Picturegoer* remained safely in the confines of the sewing room.

My relationship with 'The Light of the World' deteriorated rapidly. Each moment I spent in His company affected me badly, it being impossible to rid myself of that mournful gaze piercing into me, with my every movement. At night, I slept out of weariness, but I never came to terms with those sandaled toes resting on my head, as they sank into my pillow each night.

The Butlers never mentioned the painting. Perhaps they were unable to sense what disturbed me so, but clearly, neither of them chose to sleep in its presence.

With the end of term, the long summer holidays loomed ahead, and I dreaded the long weeks to come. But, never say die. I soon learned the Butlers were going on holiday for a fortnight, somewhere on the south coast. Arrangements had been made for me to stay with Mrs Butler's married daughter, Mrs North and her family, at their home a few miles away.

On the day of the Butlers' departure, I took a bus to nearby Hither Green. It was ages since I'd been part of a family, but the moment I stepped through the front door, I felt at home. The house wasn't pristine, like Mrs Butler's, with everything in place, but right away, I relaxed into the laid-back feeling of a real home.

Mr North invited me to make myself comfortable, in one of the randomly untidy armchairs, the cushions all scrunched up, or thrown casually to the carpeted floor. Introductions were made to the four children of the house ranging from a toddler of about eighteen months, two girls near enough my age, and John, a boy of sixteen. I stood with Mrs North in the kitchen, helping her prepare a sandwich lunch, as we would eat a hot meal later in the day.

John, the sixteen-year-old boy, was charm itself, surprisingly at ease with girls, not like most of the boys at school who liked to be the smart alec in front of the girls, or tongue-tied with confusion. Around five o'clock in the evening, we all sat down to a proper cooked meal, followed by a squidgy, hot sponge pudding, with lashings of creamy custard. I remember talking way too much, a habit I'd grown into from spending too long in disapproving company. As the evening wore on, we all settled down in the sitting room. Aware of the warmth and closeness between the members of the family, so relaxed and natural, completely happy in each other's company, I too felt at ease and happy.

I thought of the March Family in Louisa May Alcott's book, *Little Women*. Drifting into a reverie, I imagined I was sitting in a theatre watching a scene in a play, where I'm the only person in the audience. As I watched my new friends cavorting before me, I was hit by the pain and loneliness of an being an outsider, of not belonging anywhere, and for the first time in my life I experienced the sharp pang of envy.

I gave my heart to Mrs North. A warm, average woman, with no airs and graces, not the least perturbed if the cushions got flattened, no rushing to plump them up the moment someone stood up. Most of all I enjoyed tackling the housework, being useful, chopping the vegetables for the evening supper, rushing round the shops with joyful energy, shopping for provisions and family necessities. I'd not forgotten my ration book; food was in short supply, and would remain so for years to come.

The North family belonged to Emmanuel Church, but were not pig-headed about it, tolerating others' beliefs. We all attended Sunday morning service, me with no sign of my usual heavy heart. Spotting Dad in his usual seat, I went over to say hello, which lowered my sunny frame of mind, but naturally, I had to be polite. When my two weeks was up and it was time to return to the Butlers, and the dreaded 'The Light of the World,' I crumpled. My heart breaking, I sobbed uncontrollably at having to leave this house where I'd been so happy, pleading with Mrs North, to let me stay. They agreed I could stay as a lodger, but Dad would hear none of it, saying they didn't really want me, they were merely being kind, so I hauled my broken heart back to The Haunted House and the Butlers.

My happy time with the North family soon slithered into a dream. For some time, my reaction to the happiness I'd recently known made me feel low, so much so, I felt it would be better if it had never come about. Thankfully, autumn term was just around the corner, and soon I'd be back with my comrades, and the marvellous Miss Miller and the laid-back Mr Robinson, who between them had given me a glimpse of a different world, waiting to be discovered.

In November 1948, as I turned thirteen, Dad decided I was to be baptised, following a decision made by himself, Pastor Barnes, and the bigwigs of the church, including creepy Henry Butler, who probably hoped it would cure me of my worldly ways.

The Pentecostal Church followed the teachings of the New

Testament, by plunging true believers into deep water by way of a formal ceremony to confirm their intention of spreading the Word of the Lord everywhere they went. Living with the threat of 'The Home' hanging over me, I had no choice but to go along with the plan. The evening of my baptism arrived. I walked into Emmanuel Church like a lamb to the slaughter, where Sister Rose was waiting, having been assigned to prepare me for my induction into the fold.

Leading me down curved stone steps to what had once been the cellar, now converted into small rooms, I was allocated a cubby hole in which to disrobe. Sister Rose assisted me into a full-length, cream-coloured gown, made of heavy, woven cloth. Ties attached to the inside of the garment were secured round each of my ankles to make sure the gown didn't float upwards, as I was immersed into the water.

We presented a mixed bag as we waited nervously for our big moment, some young, some older, all clad in identical gowns. Having passed the dress code to the attendant's satisfaction, we were led up the stone steps, where a row of chairs in front of the altar had been set aside for our use. A major portion of the floor covering had been rolled back, revealing what appeared to be a small, but extremely deep bathing pool, with a handrail, leading down steps into lightly steaming water. Taking our seats, we nervously regarded the packed congregation, already singing melodious hymns, suited to the happy nature of the occasion, when, without ceremony, Pastor Barnes, also robed in a cream gown, made his entrance, descending with businesslike aplomb into the chest-high water where he addressed us all, accentuating the huge admiration and respect he felt for the challenging step about to be taken by these Brothers and Sisters, willing, as of this day, to spread the Word, over land and sea.

The congregation expressed their heartfelt goodwill, and before I knew it, I found myself descending into the pool, robe billowing about my waist. Pastor Barnes drew my hands towards him, blessed me, making the sign of the cross on my forehead, before uttering a few words about keeping to the true path, when without warning I found myself tipped by the small of my back into the water. Gurgling blindly, deafened by the bubbling in my ears, Pastor Barnes helped me regain my balance, as I stumbled with my sodden gown towards the steps. Choking and spluttering, I clambered out of the pool, dripping Holy Water with every step. Sister Rose rushed forward, enfolding me in a huge towel as I coughed and dripped my way down the stone steps to the cellar. Fleeing the scene as fast as I could, the last thing I needed was a lot of enthusiastic admirers thinking I'd turned over a new leaf. Making my way back to The Haunted House, my prime concern was my ruined hairstyle for school the next morning.

~ 8 ~
Bromley

Before long, we were on the move again. I can only suppose, the poor old Butlers could take no more of my unacceptable habits, surely, designed to test the patience of Job. Breathing a sigh of relief at the thought of no longer having to live with 'The Light of the World' looking with marked disappointment at my every move, and the disapproval of my two companions, I couldn't wait to be out of the place.

This time, Dad had found lodgings for both of us, on the London side of the town of Bromley, which borders the county of Kent. Thankfully, I could still attend Coopers Lane School by taking a bus from the opposite direction, the same applying to meetings at Emmanuel Church.

Number 13 Highland Road was a huge, red brick, detached house, positioned in an oasis of calm, having narrowly escaped the bombs which had left heavily scarred wastelands in their wake. We'd been allotted one large room under the eaves, divided into two, the larger section our living room, with a double bed for Dad shoved in a corner. A small table and two dining chairs had been placed beneath a window, overlooking next door's brick red wall, which I could touch if I opened the window. A grubby mini-sized oven, with one gas ring and a grill, was stacked in a corner, along with other tired-looking cooking utensils, together with a selection of mismatched crockery and a wash basin with a small draining board. Between us, we had no cooking experience, except for a dozen current buns I'd whipped up in cookery class at school. If Dad was expecting cordon bleu standards, he was in for a rude awakening.

My little room was made up of pieces of plywood that formed a dividing wall of sorts separating me from the main room, and thankfully, providing me with total privacy. A fair-sized skylight flooded my personal space with bright sunlight and warmth. A small chest of drawers made an ideal dressing table, where, if I perched on the edge of my small bed in front of the mirror, it was possible to arrange my hair in the latest style, which, at that time was Veronica Lake's peekaboo look, utterly gorgeous, in her latest film, *The Blue Dahlia*, the not-to-be-missed film noir, currently doing the rounds, starring golden-haired Alan Ladd, and Veronica. All my friends adored her hair, but school rules meant short neat hair, or long hair in plaits, at all times.

Upon our arrival at Highland Road, the front door was opened by a woman in her early fifties, with greying hair, whose name I've forgotten, which is a shame, because she was a lovely being, always showing me great kindness. She had distinctive features that took some getting used to, including expressive eyes that held a steady gaze. She often wore a chiffon scarf around her neck, which occasionally shifted to reveal a swelling in her throat the size of a golf ball. I later learned that this was a medical condition known as a goitre. As our friendship deepened, I came to focus less on her physical characteristics and more on who she was as a person.

Bromley

The lady's much younger husband was well known as a bad-un, causing her much grief. Although a good-looking chap, he fancied himself as a bit of a dandy, forever chasing young women. He didn't care to work, preferring life in the fast lane, often ending up with a spell in prison.

Dad had decided I was to take on a newspaper round and with my earnings buy all my own clothes, his argument being if it had been good enough for him, it was good enough for me. I soon found a round with a newsagent out near Bromley Station. Although some distance from Highland Road, it had its plus side. It meant passing two picture houses on the High Street, where I could see which films were coming out and take a quick look at the current posters, guaranteed to set me up for the day ahead.

Setting off at an ungodly hour for my newspaper round, I headed for the picture houses, which were directly opposite each other on the High Street. Colourful posters were displayed outside locked gilded doors, which would be opened at 1.30 pm, giving lucky film-goers time to settle into their seats before the programme started at 2 pm.

I was always the last to arrive at the shop, my eager fellow delivery boys already mounting their model bikes, their newspaper bags slung over one shoulder. A number of the boys had two or more rounds to complete before school, needing to earn enough to pay off instalments on their slick bikes. Once I'd put my papers in their correct order for my route, not having been offered a bag, I had no choice but to hoist the hefty load against my chest then be off, on what turned out to be the hardest slog of my life.

Up and down, up and down, steep hills the like of which I hadn't come across since Gloucestershire. Blocks of flats with several entrances, each to be climbed one at a time, some with six flights of ascending stairs, before wobbling down again, knees trembling precariously, unused to such labour, then stepping out into fresh air, where, given time, I would regain my equilibrium.

In the 1940s, lifts were unheard of in blocks of flats, or office buildings. Only fashionable department stores had the luxury of a small lift, frequently operated by a disabled veteran of war, whose task it was to slide open the heavy iron gates at each floor, while listing the amazing range of foreign imports stocked, unavailable in this country since before the war. It didn't take me long to realise I'd been handed the dud round. A bicycle would have been useless on my route.

Down and down steep hills I went, leaving newspapers at shabby houses, newly built blocks of modern flats, and sometimes I'd have one lone delivery, sure to be the last house in an extremely long road.

What went down, had to go up. Up and up I climbed, until finding myself in an area of true countryside, where, thankfully I rested on a roadside bench on a small green, at the most agreeable spot named Shortlands. Here were grand houses, each set in its own grounds, framed from the world by tall sweeping trees. Immaculate lawns, designer ponds with ornamental fountains shooting water high into the air above darting flashes of gold, as the early sun showed its face between scudding clouds. Each of these delightful houses was reached by way of a wide gate, opening onto a long, curving drive, meandering past banks of nurtured growth before reaching the main entrance, where there might well be a highly polished limousine with its immaculate chauffeur standing by. I was delighted to learn that this genteel area lay at the lower end of Highland Road, a short walk beyond Number 13. It made me happy to know there was somewhere lovely near

Bromley

where I lived.

Back home after the scramble of early morning, there was just enough time for a quick bowl of cornflakes and to get dressed for school, before making a mad dash through several side streets to catch the bus.

If I was under the illusion delivering papers was hard work, it was matched by the runaround Dad put me through after school. He was always after special foods, from specialist shops, scattered in all directions. Only Hemmings bread, up by the station, would do. Marmalade had to be Marks & Spencer's own IXL brand, not to mention the many other items he desperately wanted. My consolation was to pop by the picture houses for a quick glimpse at the film posters of the week, as I headed for home.

Saturday morning was when I did the weekly food shop. Dad presented me with £1.00 for rations for two for a week, which was a constant bone of contention between us. Even in 1948, it was a ridiculously small amount to feed two hungry people.

Back from my paper round, I downed a quick breakfast, before I was off, first to Sainsbury's, a tedious operation, needing to queue at separate counters for different foods, waiting for each item to be weighed then wrapped, according to the number of ration books submitted.

Cheddar cheese in particular was a hassle, always sliced, in the customer's presence, by a long section of thin wire cutting cleanly through a wooden board, before being weighed, then wrapped in greaseproof paper. The weekly ration of cheese for two was about the size of a matchbox I could swallow with one bite. Happy to get the Sainsbury's stint behind me, I'd taken to dashing into Woolworths, next to Sainsbury's, where if I could spot the correct colour, I might be tempted to buy a cheap and cheerful pink lipstick.

My final call meant facing the bane of my life, a rotund, ginger-haired, thuggish fellow. The butcher. The weekly meat allowance for the two of us amounted to two lamb chops. I bet Ginger didn't survive on one measly chop a week, judging from the size of his belly. On my return to Highland Road, the first thing Dad did was check the size of the chops, always declaring them to be too small, meaning a return to the dreaded butcher, where I would habitually cower outside, fearing a repeat encounter with the enemy. Once I was inside, he'd make a snide remark about seeing me so soon. Each week I found the strength to blurt out, 'My Dad says these chops are too small.' Freckled face, turning purple with fury, Ginger tore aside the by now bedraggled newspaper wrapping, all the while uttering unrepeatable expletives, 'no doubt causing Dad's ears to burn,' selected two fresh chops and wrapped them in fresh newspaper, before grudgingly tossing them in my direction. Catching the package, I turned on my heels and was off as fast as I could. The replacement chops were always twice the size of the originals.

Later that day, I cooked them under our tiny grill, putting them aside for tomorrow's supper upon our return from church. I covered them with a plate to keep the flies off, not to mention the fattest mouse I'd ever seen, who, given half a chance, nibbled any fat that was left in the grill pan. We managed to get home from the Sunday evening service in time for 'Sunday Half Hour,' the BBC weekly programme of hymn singing, at 8.30 pm. With Dad happily immersed in hymn-singing, we tucked into the congealed fat of cold lamb chops.

One afternoon while wandering around the high-class shops, my eyes fell on a pair of shoes on display in the window of an exclusive ladies' shoe shop, priced at £2.00. With high heels, they were simple but ladylike, and played on my mind. Many trips later, I plucked up the courage to enter the shop. A smartly dressed female assistant found a pair in my size, in a shade of light tan, and invited me to try them on. Slipping my feet into them, they were not only comfortable, but even more stylish on than off. Every week I called in to the shop to pay for the shoes bit by bit with the money I earned from the newspaper round, until the day came when, packaged in the shop's personal wrapping paper, the shoes became mine. When Dad saw them, he said, 'That's all very well, but you still have to wear your long grey socks.' Needless to say, I wore my grey socks until I'd slammed the front door behind me. At that point, they were whipped off and stashed away in my pockets, permitting me to sally forth, barelegged.

Finding it increasingly difficult to feed us both on £1.00 a week, I came up with a bright idea to help eke out the allowance. I'd always been partial to pancakes, so I invested in extra milk, sultanas and a large bag of flour. I felt proud to have come up with a solution, thinking they'd be a great success, not only delicious, but helping to stretch the budget.

One evening, having presented my masterpiece perhaps once too often, Dad took one look at his plate and hurled it at the nearest wall, bellowing at the top of his voice, 'I'm sick to death of these puncture patches, get me something decent to eat.' Giving as good as I got, I screamed back, 'Then give me money to pay for it.' Unfortunately, with people like Dad, nothing changes.

We shared the top floor with a number of builders, mostly married men, who worked locally during the week, returning to their distant homes and families every weekend. They were always pleasant enough, passing the time of day with me if I met one of them on my way to or from the communal bathroom and lavatory, which were shared by the whole floor. I became aware of the landlady's dodgy husband hanging around with them. I became wary, as over time I noticed him easing his way along the landing towards our room. Well aware he was aiming to chat me up, I caught him mooching around our door one evening, so I tackled him. 'Stop hanging around here and clear off, or my Dad will sort you out the minute he gets back from his prayer meeting.' That scared him. He soon scarpered.

Dad was making my life miserable. Until Bromley, I had always been surrounded by other people, unwittingly offering me protection. Now I found myself alone, living with a crazed person. Morning to night, he tormented me with my many faults, my looks, my stupidity, every fault in the world was down to me.

Taking pleasure in being cruel, he enjoyed playing games. Sweets and chocolate were strictly rationed to 12 ounces a month, per ration book. I was a chocaholic, so no matter how hard up I was, my month's allowance was gobbled up by the end of the first week, whereas Dad saved his until the last day of the month, when he bought his full allowance, Mars bars, a slab of Cadbury's milk chocolate, Crunchie bars, always my favourites. Settling himself into a chair at the table, his eye-catching treasures arranged in perfect order, a drawn-out performance would commence. Positioning himself as close to me as possible, he would start the entertainment by deliberately relishing each item, looking directly into my face as he slowly devoured them one by one. After delighting in one or two delicacies, he'd suggest I ask for one. My reply was always the same, 'Please, Daddy, may I have some?' His answer never wavered, 'No. That will teach you to save yours.' With that, he'd slowly finish every last morsel, and every month I vowed never to ask again, but I'm ashamed to say that my love of chocolate always got the better of me.

Another means of taunting me was through my bad relationship with arithmetic. Anything remotely to do with numbers filled me with dread. My problem wasn't helped by Dad's insistence on helping me with, with what he termed, my sums.

As soon as our evening meal was over, he'd place himself next to me at the table, to sort out my problems. As hours went by, he became more and more aggressive, until my mind refused to think. I cowered, paralysed with terror, as he raged with such violence, it often came to blows. To this day I still panic at the word 'figures', although I'm pleased to report, it has never held me back from being an excellent shopper.

The torment continued from the moment he came through the door each evening.

My greatest failing, apparently, was that I was exactly like my mother, a temptress, driving innocent men to breaking point. His fury mounting to a crescendo, I was filthy, like my mother, no matter how much I argued I was clean. He took to strangling me with a towel, at the same time crazily screeching directly into my face. I tried to tell him I was clean, truly I was clean, but to no effect, although I fought him tooth and nail with a strength I didn't know I possessed. One evening during his rampaging he lost control, and catching my chin he knocked me out.

As I came to, I found him leaning over me sobbing like a baby, pleading for forgiveness. Feeling utter revulsion, I recoiled from the crocodile tears rolling down his cheeks.

It was about this time that I began to experience strange symptoms when I was on my paper round, particularly when I climbed the steep flights of stairs in blocks of flats. My body seemed to be taken over by my breathing which would become louder and increasingly threatening, my heart pounding with such force I feared I was dying. After one of these turns, I went on my way, soaked with the sweat of fear.

A similar thing happened when I nodded off at night. I would wake up with a start, my teeth seeming to grow bigger and bigger, until I was sure I was choking to death. My only relief was to touch my teeth, which to my surprise I found to be as they should be.

These nervous attacks stopped as soon as I got away from Dad.

Throughout the summer and early autumn, Dad enjoyed taking a country bus to somewhere of interest on Saturday afternoons. My favourite was Westerham, the home of our former prime minister, Winston Churchill, idolised by all for leading us through the war. In the 1940s, public transport was reliable, and with few cars on the road, traffic jams were as yet unheard of. Picturesque towns and villages abounded, reachable by a half hour bus ride from the centre of London, with cosy pubs, local shops, and welcoming tea shops, serving dainty sandwiches, hot crumpets, and home-made cakes, accompanied by a pot of strong Indian tea, as loved by the British.

These havens of tranquillity provided a respite for a population still recovering from the effects of war, and easeful days before the roads became clogged with traffic, and the town planners moved in.

Mr Churchill, the hero of our country, lived in his country estate, Chartwell, where he would live until he died in 1965. The love and respect felt for the great man could be felt in every nook and cranny of the town. Smiling shop assistants, proud to have Mr Churchill living in their locality, couldn't do enough to make visitors feel welcome. Every corner of the town paid homage to Our Saviour, in the form of posters, billboards, and street corners. A larger-than-life statue of a seated, relaxed Winston reveals his softer side, and takes pride of place on the town's green.

Another valiant warrior honoured by the town is General James Wolfe, hero of the Battle of Quebec, killed in battle in 1759, aged thirty-two. He too holds a prominent position on the green, where standing aloft on a towering plinth high against the sky in full military dress, he wields his sword heavenwards, as he charges into the fray.

After strolling around the shops for a while, it was time for Dad's favourite Eldorado choc ices, as usual two for him, one for me. He wolfed his down like a starving man, which he might well have been with my cooking skills.

Long walks were a vital part of these days. Dad would remain silent, finding it the perfect setting in which to communicate with his Lord. That was a blessing. As far as I was concerned he'd given up trying to convert me, doubtless realising it was a waste of time.

Westerham Hill is a steep upward climb of several miles, used by enthusiastic cyclists to improve their muscle strength and cycling skills. As we made our way up the hill, I would note the same ruddy face peddling for his life up this testing incline, before catching sight of the same face flying downwards, only to repeat the exercise over and over. Returning from our long hike, we took refuge in one of the town's comfortable tea shops, where I, worn to a frazzle, flopped into the nearest seat hoping that with any luck there might be a hot meal in the offing as well as the set tea.

Afternoon tea, a major pleasure of English life, keeping body and soul together until supper time, before turning in for the night. Supper might be Welsh Rabbit, or even nicer, hot toast

Pretty from the Outside

smeared with dripping left over from the Sunday roast. Taking the meat from the oven, Mother would pour the juices from the joint into a bowl, where slowly, they'd solidify into delicious dripping above jellied gravy, perfect for weekday suppers, when spread on thick slices of bread, toasted on a long toasting fork before an open fire. It was deliciously nourishing, a popular dish with rich and poor alike, best devoured as the last burning embers of a dying fire fizzle away.

Now came the part of the day I dreaded, the return coach journey to Bromley. Relaxed and sleepy after the excitement of the day and a tasty hot meal inside me, I'd be ready for a nap, but Dad had other ideas. Once the bus was on its way, led by the hand of the Lord, he would make his way to the front of the packed bus, where he dramatically faced the passengers, instructing them to repent their sins and seek salvation the only way possible, through the blood of Jesus. All those visits to Speakers' Corner had been to this end, to master the ability to prevent lost souls from marching headlong into destruction. I'd always known he was up to something. There was no stopping him now. Inflamed by the spirit, he poured forth his message of salvation, his audience making no attempt to hide their contempt. Slinking back into my seat, I vowed not to get involved, to pretend he wasn't with me, but as the jeering grew ever more threatening, I couldn't help myself pleading with him to sit down. His reply, always the same, his accusing finger pointing straight at my face, as he declared, 'Don't you stop me doing my duty by the Lord. If I'm struck down tomorrow, the Lord will ask, Brother Fred, why didn't you save those lost souls on that bus yesterday?'

Following the trip to Westerham, being close to Mr Churchill brought back memories of Longfords, all those 9 pm news bulletins throughout the war years. No matter how good or bad the news, Mr Churchill's thundering tones never failed to restore the fight in every flagging listener, power and conviction emanating from that magnificent voice, ending with 'We will never surrender'.

I missed the family at Longfords Mill, I missed everyone at Hankins Farm. I missed Mr Churchill taking care of us. Forlorn and feeling sorry for myself, I wept bitterly that night, but woke refreshed, my fighting spirit renewed.

With the onset of cold weather, the chill in the air on my early morning trek was noticeable. I wasn't good at balancing my clothes allowance; seven shillings and six pence a week didn't run to much in the world of fashion but my high-heeled shoes proved to be a good buy, adding class to any outfit I wore.

Apparently, others didn't share my view. Taking the wind out of my sails, Mrs Collins, the headmistress, sent for me one morning. It had been brought to her attention that I persisted in wearing summer dresses even though the weather was bordering on winter, closing with the words, 'Margaret, dear, you are a beautiful girl, you don't need to be so vain. It's time to wear your warm clothes. Now, off with you, be a sensible girl.' Feeling grim, after such chastisement, I told Dad about the meeting. This either touched a merciful side of him, or piqued his vanity, as the following Saturday afternoon we set off to the most exclusive ladies' clothing shops in the best part of town to buy sensible warm clothes. Eying shops I'd hardly dared glance at previously, it wasn't long before I found myself drawn to the loveliest shop window of them all.

The great French designer, Christian Dior, had recently launched his latest collection, causing upheaval in the world of fashion. Gone were the short skirts of the war years, the 'new look' had arrived, featuring mid-length voluminous swirling skirts, with the tightest bodices, nipped-in waists with one eye-catching button in the centre, emphasising a lady's tiny waist; quite the opposite of the utility clothes we were used to. Dashing towards the central display, my eyes alighted on my coat, no other coat would do. Once inside the shop, a friendly assistant picked out my coat and a selection from a rail of equally delightful Dior creations, with me insisting that no other coat would do.

That coat was designed with me in mind, of that I'm certain. In a light shade of eau-de-nil (the palest shade of green), with a flattering collar in water-marked taffeta, of the same shade of green. The sales lady enquired if Madame would require anything else. I chose a timeless, navy blue, pin-striped tailored suit, a choice I have never regretted, standing me in good stead for years to come, when I needed to look attractive, but smart. Chuffed to bits with my Christian Dior coat, the look I'd been searching for was complete, with the addition of my high-heeled shoes.

There was a rumour going round the school that Marks & Spencer had nylons at their Lewisham branch, a short walk from the Clock Tower. Before the day was over, I was on the bus heading to Lewisham Clock Tower, the site of our open-air meetings, this time with bigger fish to fry. Racing to Marks & Spencer, there displayed for all to see were nylon stockings, sheer and shining, in various subtle shades, for one shilling and nine pence a pair. I joined the queue of excited women and girls, where we exchanged tales of the wonders of these American beauties. When it was my turn, I was permitted to handle a sample. Easing my hand to the toe of this gossamer cobweb, my delight knew no bounds. Off with thick woollen stockings, off with spinster's lisle, forever. Womankind had been granted a miracle, designed to change their lives forever.

Nylons made a huge difference to my life, including my perception of myself. Naturally we couldn't make use of our new finds during school hours, having to put up with those ghastly knee-length, sensible socks.

One day, while out on my paper round, I was granted a divine revelation. Throughout the school holidays, Dad was in the habit of leaving a shilling on the table to buy myself a bite of lunch. Out of the blue, it occurred to me that the price of a seat for matinee performances at either picture house was at the reduced price of 9 pence leaving me with 3 pence – enough to buy three penny buns to see me through till evening. A short school break was coming up, a perfect time to experiment. Putting the plan in motion at the start of the break caused great anxiety, along with unpleasant pangs of guilt, but after getting a bun inside me to quell my nerves, I sauntered into this Palace of Dreams, bought a ticket like a regular film buff, and found a seat in the sumptuous foyer, where I gazed about me, thinking of all I'd been missing over the years. With time approaching for the performance to begin, I fumbled through the darkness to my designated seat. Peering about me in the darkening light, I made out the audience was mainly made up of old people, probably pensioners.

September Affair was my very first grown-up film, starring the beautiful Joan Fontaine, and the handsome Joseph Cotton, both huge Hollywood stars. The saddest song I'd ever heard, 'September Song' played repeatedly throughout the film, soon to become a worldwide hit. It still comes over the radio from time to time, bringing back memories of that never-to-be-forgotten day in my life.

The film features Joan as a world-famous pianist, and Joseph as an engineer, who find themselves quite by chance sitting next to each other on a flight from New York to Rome, when the plane develops engine trouble and is forced down near Naples. After taking a walk together for a couple of hours, they return to the airport, just in time to see their plane taking off without them. Later, they hear the plane has crashed, meaning they are believed to be dead. Realising they have fallen deeply in love with one another, they decide to start a new life together as lovers. Unfortunately, their love can never be. Joseph finds it impossible to forget his poor wife grieving back home, so although his true love is Joan, he has no choice but to return to his family. It was so heart-breaking I found my eyes welling up in front of the audience, particularly as that melancholy song played over and over again. I sobbed as the lights came up, revealing me blowing my nose, my eyes red and swollen all the way home, but I'd found comfort knowing I wasn't the only one going through a bad patch.

One afternoon, while shopping for Dad's extras, I popped into WH Smith, the well-known stationery shop and bookshop. I was well known to the shop assistants, though it was rare for me to buy anything of consequence, but no one batted an eye at my flipping through the film magazines, or glancing at expensive books. Wandering among the latest publications, my eyes were drawn towards a lovely photograph of Princess Elizabeth and her younger sister, Princess Margaret Rose, on the cover of a book of special interest, entitled *The Two Princesses: The Story of the King's Daughter's*. As a fervent admirer of the Royal Family, I longed to own it, but as that was out of the question, I pushed it from my mind. Having enjoyed the distraction, I left the shop by a door I'd not used before, to find myself at the entrance of a small park, right in the centre of town. Delighted to have made this discovery,

I sauntered around for a while, vowing to return when I had more time.

My heaven-sent park was to become my special place, second only to the picture houses. There was nothing fancy about this neat small park with comfortable benches dotted here and there, mostly occupied by old folks, or mums with babies in prams and enquiring toddlers set on chasing a squad of leaping grey squirrels. I found a favourite bench, under a tree, where I took to feeding a regular crowd of chirruping sparrows, flocks of tits of all varieties, not forgetting the friendly robin hiding away in the safety of the higher branches above, until he caught sight of my Christian Dior coat, and swooped to earth, knowing his luck was in.

With my fourteenth birthday looming, I dared to dream of the day in the not-too-distant future when I would be free to make my own way in the world.

You could legally leave school when you were fifteen years old. Coopers Lane School was well known for setting its school leavers on the right path, and I had complete faith in their ability to do the same for me. I didn't say a word about it to Dad. It would be just my luck for him to come up with something or other to do with the church, forcing me to run away and find my own way.

Aware of time racing by, I devoured the teachings of my two adored teachers, absorbing every smidgen of their individual visions. Towards the end of term, Miss Miller surprised us by taking the whole class to see a new play, 'The Browning Version,' a thought-provoking play by the British playwright Terence Rattigan, already a huge success in London's West End, and regarded by leading reviewers of the day as his best work yet. What made it even nicer for me was that it was being staged at the quaint Bromley Theatre in the High Street (today replaced by a spacious modern theatre, on the exact spot, renamed The Churchill Theatre), one minute from my special park.

On the big day, a charabanc picked us up from school and dropped us off at Bromley Station, from where we walked in tandem through familiar streets, past my newspaper shop, past Fat Ginger, the bullying butcher, still shouting his mouth off.

Feeling mellow after the trip to the theatre in the company of friends, I returned to our lodgings, where surprisingly, I found Dad in an unusually good frame of mind, a rarity. I was equally shocked when, at the end of our meal, he asked what I'd like for Christmas. As the last time he'd bought me anything other than necessities was back in the Longford days, I had good reason to be suspicious. *The Two Princesses: The Story of the King's Daughters*, the expensive book I had fallen for in WH Smith sprang to mind, but certain he would never approve of such frivolous subject matter so I promptly forgot about it. Imagine my surprise when I was presented with that very book on Christmas Day, beautifully wrapped in special Christmas paper. As Our Mum had been fond of saying, 'There's nowt so queer as folk.'

However, things were not all plain sailing. Over the last few weeks, I'd been knitting a pair of special socks for Dad, for Christmas. In a sensible shade of grey, I used the finest quality four-ply wool, knitted on four needles, which meant turning a corner for each heel, like top-quality socks but so tedious, many a time, I wished I'd never started the exercise. Somehow or other, something went amiss. One sock ended up a perfect fit, the other too tight over the ankle, the effort involved with trying to get it on causing Dad to break into a steamy sweat, turning his complexion a motley purplish hue, as he struggled to get the darn thing over his foot, all the while blaming me for cutting off his blood supply.

I apologised profusely, but I think it was really mean of him to broadcast my failure to the congregation on the following Sunday.

With the arrival of the school holidays, I faced the dull, dank mornings with a spring in my step, anticipating the pleasures awaiting me later in the day, when, tucked away in the darkness of the back row of the stalls, munching my way through three soft, spicy buns, immersed once more in a harrowing tale of misplaced love, to be resolved in the nick of time a moment before the lights came up in a cosy corner of, a *Den of Sin*.

That winter holiday saw me up to my eyes in wonderful films. Along with the hard weather came a period of breath-taking glamourous films, the idea being, I should imagine, to cheer everyone up.

The first truly glorious film I saw was *Pandora and the Flying Dutchman*, starring mind-blowingly gorgeous, Ava Gardner, who as soon as I glimpsed her up there on the screen, went to the top of my list of screen idols. Beautifully photographed, the film is set in a small Spanish sea port, where a Dutchman, played by James Mason, is doomed to an endless existence, sailing the world on his ghostly sailing yacht alone and tormented, until he can find a beautiful woman willing to give up her life to love of him. Ava, playing Pandora, a woman so exquisite men are willing to kill themselves in their desire of her, turns out to be the ultimate woman, giving up her luxurious life for love of the Dutchman. Ava, heart-rendingly lovely, though she doesn't look so great when she's washed up on the beach, tore me to shreds, as I left the cinema in tears. I couldn't help seeing the film several times. I don't think I'd give up my life for James Mason, but Gregory Peck, now that's more like it.

With it being Christmas, the film *Holiday Inn* was showing, starring that great crooner Bing Crosby singing the world-famous song 'White Christmas,' which lives on to this day, and also starring Fred 'twinkle toes' Astaire, the unsurpassable male dancer of that era. Scenes of jollity flew before my eyes, what wild, happy times were enjoyed during the Christmas season in other parts of the world, what beautiful scenes of happiness and love, much more to my liking than morning service at Emmanuel Church, Boone Street.

The moody film *Black Narcissus*, set in a monastery at the top of the Himalayas, left a permanent mark on me. Breathtaking scenery but, at the same time, hauntingly spooky. A group of English nuns are sent on a strange mission, led by Sister Clodagh, played by Deborah Kerr. Who could forget the ethereal beauty of that face, standing there in her nun's habit, her loveliness illuminated by her white veil, reflecting the purity of her virginal features. Things are spoiled by the diabolical behaviour of Sister Ruth, driven out of her mind by desire for the plantation manager, believing him to love Sister Clodagh. Clearly crazy, Sister Ruth determines to kill Sister Clodagh, who is saved in the nick of time, in a scene of terrifying drama, as she peals the cloister bells, with the sinister Himalayas looming in the distance. A brilliant, incandescent film, leaving me totally wrung out, I must say.

Having only recently joined the world of avid film buffs, perhaps I'd become complacent regarding my entrances and exits from the Devil's playground. One evening, Dad informed me I was to visit Mrs Wright, the matriarch of the church, at her home in New Eltham, the following Saturday afternoon, as she wished to talk to me. Off I went, arriving at the appointed time, whereupon I waited in the hall, before being summoned into the presence of the fearsome old lady. Ignoring me for some time, she continued with what I took to be important church business. Staring at this pompous presence, it was all I could do not to laugh at the ridiculous scene she presented, designed to terrify the unworthy, but to my eyes it was comical. After the conclusion of more urgent matters, she pushed her papers to one side, the better to grant me her full attention. 'Margaret, my dear,' she began, 'it has been brought to my notice, you were seen leaving a house of Satan.' 'Oh,' I replied. 'You mean, going to the pictures? That's nothing, everybody does it.' After trying to get through to me how my time would be better spent in Christian pursuits, I stood up to her, giving as good as she got, in my nicest, but firm, manner. Admitting defeat, she concluded, 'What a dreadful waste. You have such a winsome little face, to win souls for the Lord.'

Mrs Wright's two daughters, the Sunday school teachers, who occupied the top floor of this pleasant house, invited me to join them for a cup of tea, so after I'd tucked into several delicious home-made fairy cakes, I made my way back to Highland Road, completely satisfied I had made my point and held my ground.

The year of 1950 passed pleasantly enough. Dad continued to bully me and raise his fist to me, but I stayed strong, fighting him like a tigress at times. Good Friday was a dead day, with everything shut apart from churches, as thoughts were completely given over to remembering the true meaning of Easter.

Dad happened to be working on Good Friday, which meant I was a free spirit that day.

In anticipation of a lovely day, I armed myself with a huge bag of monkey nuts to stave off hunger, and made my way to my newly discovered little park, taking to my usual bench, in the company of my wildlife companions, including these days, tame squirrels, the little devils rifling through my bag of nuts with their usual over-familiarity. Nothing in particular made it such a perfect day. I have never worked out why on that particular day I felt at peace with the world. I think of that special day every Good Friday.

No mention was ever made of my meeting with Old Mrs Wright, or my visits to the picture houses, so I let sleeping dogs lie. All I needed to do was lie low for a few more months, and then I'd be on my way to who knows what? But it had to be better than this.

One of the joys of having a paper round was the chance to keep an eye on the comings and goings in the world of entertainment. Each morning, while on my wanderings, it was important to know what the big names in the film and theatre were getting up to. There were tales of opening nights, film premieres in London's West End, exciting events across the world, even as far away as Hollywood. One morning in May 1950, the front page of every newspaper featured the marriage of eighteen-year-old film star Elizabeth Taylor to the young heir to the Hilton Hotels, Conrad 'Nicky' Hilton. The photos of this young beauty glowing with happiness on her wedding day rival any scene from a movie. Breath-takingly beautiful, this raven-haired girl was to be recognised as one of the greatest beauties of all time.

Little could I imagine that morning, as I plodded my round, that five years later, I would dine with Elizabeth and Michael Wilding, her second husband at Claridge's Hotel in London, meeting not only one of the loveliest, but, more importantly, one of the kindest, most unforgettable human beings I've ever met.

One day, I read in the local paper that Princess Elizabeth was to visit Bromley, and one of the places she would be calling at were the Bromley Council Offices at a certain time in the afternoon. I worked out that I could just make it there after school if I got my skates on. I wasn't going to miss this, as the Princess was on my list of glamour girls. Sure enough, I made it in good time, finding myself positioned near the door by which she would eventually exit. Quite a crowd of mostly girls and women gathered, all of us thrilled to see the young lady who would one day be our Queen.

As luck would have it, the Princess came through the door, pausing so close to me, I could have reached out and touched her perfect, English complexion. Naturally, I would never dream of doing such a thing, but I was proud that she was our lovely Princess, and I could tell by her open face, she was a kind person, with no airs and graces, just ten years older than me.

I was over the moon at having seen her in the flesh. I tried to talk about it with Dad that evening, but he was in too much of a rush to get to his prayer meeting to be bothered about royalty.

Life continued in the same old way, me wrapped up in films and Dad absorbed in church business. It really was amazing how many films I managed to squeeze in, sneaking off at odd times when Dad was dwelling on 'Higher Matters'.

One Sunday, I was surprised when Miss Wright, my Sunday school teacher, asked if I would like to have afternoon tea with her the following Saturday at her home. Feeling rather cocky, I assumed that I must be her favourite pupil, as I was the only one in the class to be invited.

Mr Wheeler, the middle-aged Elder in the Church, had recently lost his wife, but he'd found a new lease of life by getting engaged to Miss Winnifred Wright, Edna Wright's sister. Off I went to tea with Edna, which was worth enduring if only for the home-made coffee cakes, and enormous slabs of Battenberg cake wrapped in thick marzipan she served up.

Saturday afternoon tea became a regular event until one day she enquired, 'Do you think your father would like to join us next week?' Our Saturday teas became a threesome, until one afternoon, I bounced into the living room, only to find Dad and Miss Wright locked in a steamy embrace, just like in the films. At that moment I understood it wasn't me Miss Wright liked; I was a fish being dangled on a hook to land Dad.

My life improved noticeably once Dad's romantic attachment was out in the open. I couldn't for the life of me understand how he could fancy such a scrawny bag of bones, especially after being married to my lovely mother. However, it didn't take me long to realise this love match was a godsend for me. Soon to leave school, I'd be free to lead my life as I chose. One evening, Dad brought up the subject of finance: 'I know things have been hard on you lately, we've had to cut back, as I have to pay out a large amount of money, but it will be worth-while in the end.' A car, that's what it must be. How exciting, what else could it be but a car? Summer drifted on, and the end of the school year came around once more. All we pupils congregated in Catford Town Hall for the annual ceremony. I was awarded first prize for scripture, and received yet another Bible to add to my collection. I spent the holidays being happier than I could remember. Dad's attention being noticeably drawn away from me, I revelled in film after film, weeping sad tears one day, howling with laughter the next. Every day I wandered round my little park, before resting on my favourite bench and joined by my wild friends, as hungry in high summer as in midwinter.

With the onset of autumn, Dad announced what he had been saving up for. It was to pay for a divorce. Throughout the years he had denied my mother this one thing, in spite of her having two children out of wedlock, which was a scandal in those days, forcing her and the man with the big boot to keep moving house, being frowned upon everywhere they went. Bitterly disappointed, after such a long wait for a car, I exploded. 'A divorce is for you, not for me.' He could see my point, he said. He would give instructions to the opposing party that I should be paid £20.00 at the end of the proceedings, which needless to say, never materialised. I perked up with, 'Why don't you marry Miss Wright?' He reacted to this with astonishment, oblivious to my seeing what was right under his nose.

The time had come to seriously consider my future. I was called to the headmistress's office to discuss the matter. Eventually, after considering various options, I chose to take up an offer from Erith Hospital, a cottage-style hospital on the borders of South London and Kent, which was planning a trial run for what were termed Pre-Student Nurses, due to girls leaving school at fifteen and finding other occupations, so being lost to nursing. The statutory age to take up nursing was eighteen, so many young women had already gone and started other careers. Sent away to think it over for a while, it didn't take me long, as I quite fancied the idea. I remembered the film *A Farewell to Arms*, based on Ernest Hemingway's, book, starring Gary Cooper as a wounded soldier, and actress Helen Hunt looking so pretty in her nurse's uniform, lovingly ministering to him in his hour of need. I could picture myself wearing a pristine uniform, tending to the sufferings of a handsome, wounded soldier. The decision was made. Nursing was to be the life for me.

Time flew until the day I was off to seek my fortune. I can't say I was sad to say goodbye to the newspaper round, with nothing left of my 7/6. a week to show for all that walking. It was a shame about the black stain on my Christian Dior coat, caused by the constant rubbing of black print pressed against my right breast, but I was pretty good at sorting out such peccadillos.

Things were hunky-dory for Dad. His marriage to Miss Wright was to go ahead in the new year. Sister Winnifred Wright was all set to move into Mr Wheeler's salubrious home as soon as they tied the knot, leaving the top half of 21 Thaxted Road free for Dad and Miss Wright to set up their love nest, from which Dad planned to start a decorating business, with Edna as secretary, expert in such matters as she was, having been an office worker all her working life.

I was devastated to be leaving Miss Miller and Mr Robinson, who between them had kept my feet on solid ground for several years, feeding my hungry mind with countless offerings. Their presence never leaves me. Each of them opened my mind to the things I hold most dear to this day. I've not forgotten my special school friends, the many borrowed film magazines hidden away in the sewing room, me being too scared to take them back to The Haunted House. My final port of call before the off was to my friendly little park, which had of late become such a comfort to me, where I dispersed my final bag of peanuts to the regular squirrels and tiny birdlife, dive-bombing the regular spot on first sight of my Christian Dior Coat. I aimed their booty far and wide, before tearfully leaving the park for the last time. I walked past my friendly cinemas, displaying this week's showings, their offerings no longer of relevance to me.

Pictures

*My mother circa 1935, the year
I was born.*

Pretty from the Outside

Me aged around 4 at the orphanage.

Pictures

Taken on a trip to a professional photographer in Cheltenham when I was 7 years old in 1942.

Me and my friends in the early 1940s. I'm on the left. At the top of the picture is my friend Mary. In front is Little John. Longford's Mill, Gloucestershire.

Pictures

Me and my friends. Little John sits on the left. I'm on the right. My friend Mary sits next to me.

The Hope Family. Back, from left to right: Grandad Oldfield Our Mum, Our Gran, Our Dad. Front: Our Barb and Our Ken.

Pretty from the Outside

The finals for Miss England, in The Lyceum Theatre Ballroom, 1955.

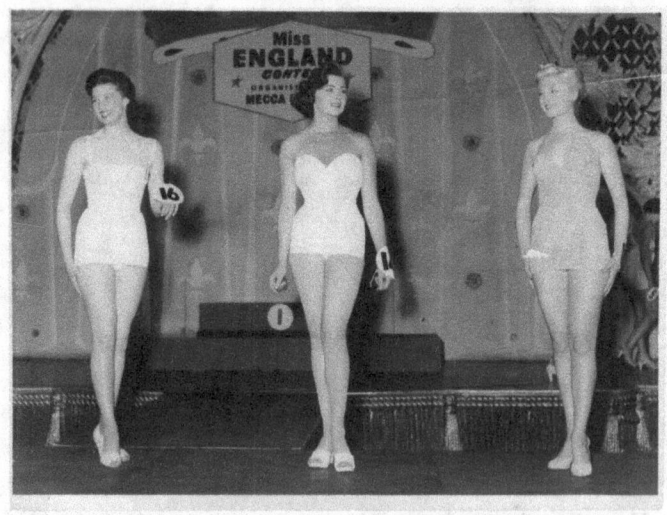

Both photos on this page printed with courtesy of Dance News

Pictures

The finalists, Miss England, 1955.
photo printed with permission of Dance News

Pretty from the Outside

Eating oysters with the other models on a boat trip in the Côte D'Azur.

printed with courtesy of Getty Images.

Pictures

The doorman from the Hotel de Paris in Monte Carlo protects me from the rain as I walk to a photo shoot.

printed with courtesy of Getty Images.

My father and I in Monte Carlo in the late 1950s after he had got used to the idea of my modelling.

Pictures

At the beach on the Essex coast. This photo was taken by my photographer friend, Gordon Hireson.

Pretty from the Outside

At an event in Harrods

Pictures

The Miss Universe Pageant in California, 1955.
Photo credit: Kelch - Rouzer. 20 Hart Pl, Long Beach 2, CALIF

Portrait taken around 1965.

~ 9 ~
Berkhamsted

It was a day in early January 1951 when I took my first step towards independence.

Dad's parting gift was a pair of heavy, black wellington boots, which were promptly deposited in the nearest waste bin. How could he burden a young woman dressed in a Christian Dior coat with such a grotesque offering, just as she sets off to seek her fortune? After all, I was to minister to the sick, not trundle through muddy fields. I suppose the poor fellow was so smitten with love for 'Ednakinz' he couldn't think straight. I know I shouldn't tell tales, but Dad was now Fredikinz. In cosy situations each becoming Kinzy. Hilarious.

With no idea of where I was heading, I followed a list of suggested bus routes passing through Woolwich, a name that vaguely rang a bell, but with the assistance of helpful bus conductors, I eventually found myself outside a cottage-style hospital, in an attractive semi-rural location. It was mid-afternoon as I heaved my suitcase through the main doors into the reception, before making my way towards a receptionist, who smilingly informed me I was the first of four expected Pre-Student Nurses. I was directed to a bedroom on the first floor, reserved solely for me, a nice enough room, tucked away at the end of a corridor. After unpacking my personal belongings, I made my way to be fitted with my uniform as instructed, which was quite a performance, but I was over the moon as I glanced in the mirror at my starched striped dress, worn under a stiff white apron, secured by a safety pin above each breast, all topped off by a dear little starched cap, which, I was pleased to see, suited both my hairstyle and my features. The completed look was finished off with black lace-up school shoes, and black stockings, which I'd acquired as soon as I'd knew the job was mine. Food and lodgings along with the upkeep of my uniform swallowed most of my wages, leaving me with the sum of £2.00 to get me through the next month. At least I looked the part, which gave my self-confidence a boost.

At 6 pm I made my way to the dining room, where I was given a permanent position at the far end of a long dining table as lowest in order of importance, next to my three pre-student colleagues, of which Greta was to become my good friend. It was somewhat disconcerting to discover the mortuary was next door to the dining room, but I reminded myself, the dead can't hurt you, as I slunk past the bushes camouflaging those solemn premises on wild winter evenings.

On my first morning, I took in the reflection of Nurse Rowe, pre-student nurse, before making my way to the nurses' dining room, where I consumed a substantial breakfast, partly to quell my churning nerves, before heading to the children's ward, with my three colleagues. This was my first encounter with Staff Nurse Rose, whose first words to me were, 'Nurse Rowe, return to your room at once and remove that lipstick.' Nurse Rose, a sober-minded German woman, and I were to have constant run-ins over lipstick throughout my time at Erith Hospital, me believing it cheered

Berkhamsted

things up, Nurse Rose, insisting it wasn't at all suitable for a nurse while on duty. We four pre-students were given strict instructions never to enter any other ward than the children's ward, so, out the window went my notion of ministering to a wounded Gary Cooper.

At first, I did very little ministering to anyone. The work consisted of bedpan rounds, emptying bedpans, before giving them a good scour in our workroom, 'the Sluice.' Cleaning beds and cot wheels was another regular chore, an absolute swine on the knees. However, things were not all doom and gloom; I found the greatest pleasure in dancing attendance on all the children, but it wouldn't be long before I was in trouble for getting them too excited. There were a number of long-stay patients, not requiring constant attention, resting in a fair-sized conservatory at the far end of the ward. The conservatory housed a happy bunch of mixed ages.

I especially remember Laurel, a delightful three-year-old blonde girl, who was born with deformed legs, realigned by surgery, now in plaster, a matter to be solved by time, and gentle Sheila, eight years of age, with a heart condition, fragile, and pale as a ghost, constantly panting for breath. These long-termers were my favourites. I was perked up no end when the conservatory inmates voted me not only their favourite nurse, but the prettiest nurse in the ward. Any child passing through, having had their tonsils, or adenoids, removed, or having undergone a minor operation, joined the permanent group overnight.

Of course, there was a serious side to the work. I would be called upon to change and bathe poor little mites, who were not expected to survive.

Life in the hospital was challenging, but I was happy. The

endless bedpan rounds and routine chores were a bore. By no stretch of the imagination was being a pre-student nurse glamourous, nothing like in the films, but once the hard slog of the morning was behind you, there was nothing better than spending time with the children in the conservatory.

If our work schedules allowed, Greta and I headed into the town centre from time to time, although we had to be careful with our money, being by no means rich. On our first trip I splashed out on a pink, silky blouse, with a decorative black velvet bow at the throat, but later I regretted my purchase, because I had to count my pennies.

Somehow or other, I found myself a boyfriend. For the life of me, I can't remember how we met. His name was Jimmy Porch, a respectful young man of nineteen, a soldier doing his national service, which was compulsory for young men at the time. Once a week, we went to the pictures, but with the war being so recent, the big American studios made rich pickings from glamourising film upon film, not with beautiful female stars, but with tales of American battles, filmed in technicolour, invariably won single-handedly by John Wayne, as in *Sands of Iwo Jima* and *Flying Leathernecks*. I told Jimmy I was sick of being bogged down by American heroics, I could take no more of John Wayne.

The kindest of men, in his eyes I could do no wrong. At the end of the evening, he'd kiss me goodnight at the nurses' door, assuring me that I had loads of, SA (sex appeal), making me feel good but in no way making me fancy him.

It wasn't long before he suggested we get engaged, as he was soon to leave for Egypt as part of his training, but I knew he wasn't the man for me. Besides, why would I want to saddle myself with a husband when my aim was to make my way in the world?

Berkhamsted

One turn-up for the books was when I received a letter from my mother saying she would love to meet me. Through all these years, Dad had kept control of me, insisting that if she wanted to see me, she would have to go back to him. Now, with his interests elsewhere, we were free to get together, so we set a date to meet up in August.

Making my way to the ward one day, I bumped into an attractive older staff nurse, who must have been about thirty. I'd often seen her among the hierarchy of the dining table. She said she'd been looking out for me, as she wished to invite me to London's West End the following week to see a new film based on the ballet *Coppélia*, a huge success, now showing at the Empire Cinema in Leicester Square. First, we would meet up with two charming gentlemen of her acquaintance, who wished us to dine with them after the performance. I waited excitedly for the evening to arrive. This was really living it up. Taking a train to Charing Cross Station, I made my way the short distance to the cinema in Leicester Square, where Staff Nurse, dressed to the hilt, in a flouncy dress, fancy high-heeled sandals, carrying a glittering evening purse, stood with two smartly dressed turbaned, Indian gentlemen, awaiting my arrival. The upmarket cinema was most impressive, although the film might as well have been in a foreign language, as far as I could follow the story line.

After the exhausting performance, we edged our way through teeming crowds to Piccadilly Circus, before entering the Regent Palace Hotel, where the Indian gentlemen had organised an Indian meal in one of the hotel's exclusive dining rooms. The dinner, being Indian, was a new experience for me. I vowed to take Jimmy to the rather shabby little Indian Palace, down a side street in Erith. At least it would be a break from John Wayne, or some other Yankee hero. At the end of a long evening, and not wanting to miss the last train, it was time to think of getting back to the hospital. As my escort exited the swing doors, I caught sight of Staff Nurse's splendid, sequinned rear disappearing into a taxi with the other gentleman, just as the door slammed behind him.

Left with the other man, I told him I had to head for the station. Agreeing to accompany me, we made our way through various mews and side streets, where, in 1951, ladies of the night abounded, holed away in the hidden nooks and crannies of London's West End Mews and various dark passages, selling their services. We must have passed a dozen or so couples partaking of the sins of the flesh, when I found myself rudely shoved into a vacant spot, where my escort tried it on with me. Never have I fought harder! I bit, kicked, shredded his turban with my nails, all the while screaming for help, but no help arrived. Eventually he conceded, but not before spitting with hatred, 'Get out of here,' as he landed a vicious punch to the side of my face causing me to stagger before crashing to the ground where he kicked me in my ribs.

With my night out reaching its inglorious finale, I shakily made my way to the station, where the last train took me to safety. Bumping into the friendly staff nurse at a later date, she enquired casually, 'Are you all right?' That was the end of that episode.

I was still a great admirer of the divine Rita Hayworth, Goddess of Love, who I'd discovered at the quaint picture house in Cwmcarn all those years ago. I'd long yearned for my hair to be cut in Rita's style. Somehow or other I'd saved enough from my meagre wage packet to fulfil this dream. On my day off, I took myself into town in search of a high-class hair salon. Unfortunately, there was nothing high-class about Erith in 1951, leaving me no choice but to settle for a rather mediocre salon, which had clearly seen better days. I described to Sue, the only stylist in the outdated salon, the look I was aiming for. Long, casual waves brushing my cheeks before cascading to my shoulders. Assuring me she knew exactly what I wanted, she popped to a backroom to make a nice cup of tea, as by this time I was clearly jittery. After laying out on a portable trolley the tools necessary for the operation, I was most disconcerted to see and hear a heavy, rusty apparatus, much in need of lubrication, descending from the ceiling overhead. This forbidding object had several electric wires dangling from it, each wire being connected to a section of my shoulder-length hair, before Sue ensured each tress was tightly secured. Now a prisoner of this mighty weapon, I suffered an acute panic attack, realising there was no escape. This was made profoundly worse when Sue switched on an electric current. Helpless in my chair, too late to change my mind, I heard the sound of crackling, accompanied by the stench of burning, which only relented when the power was switched off.

What had I let myself in for? Nothing could prepare me for the results. I was now the owner of a mass of frizz, the likes of which I'd last seen on my toy gollywog. Rushing back to my room, I hastily shampooed my hair, the worst thing I could have done. There was nothing else for it but to wait patiently for the effects of the perm to wear off. Jimmy was sweet about it. Nothing would put him off me. In his eyes I'd be perfect if I was completely bald.

August arrived, and with it Jimmy's trip to Egypt. For a while we wrote to each other, and at one point I posted a box of his favourite chocolates to him, for which he was most appreciative, but they never arrived.

One afternoon a tragedy occurred. I was alone in the

Pretty from the Outside

conservatory, amusing the children in my usual fashion, when terrified screams rang out. Blood splattered up the walls, over the children in their beds, and the floor become a slithering mess. Panic set in, as little Sheila, with the heart problems, succumbed to a horrifying haemorrhage. Her terrified eyes stared onto mine, but I was helpless, slithering to my knees in the bloody mess in my haste to get help. I raced to the top end of the ward in my blood-soaked uniform, and senior staff calmly cleared the conservatory, while Nurse Rose attended to the dying child. Anxious to get the junior nurses away from the scene, we pre-students found ourselves roughly bustled into the corridor. I can still see Sheila's pleading eyes as I write these words.

The day I was to meet my mother arrived, 18 August 1951, the last time being our unhappy meeting in Gloucester Park all those years ago. Arrangements were made, we would meet under the clock at 11 am at Charing Cross Station, fairly near the scene of my recent encounter with the Indian gentleman. Here's hoping today's rendezvous would turn out to be more successful, as it couldn't possibly be worse than that night.

Thank goodness my frizzy perm had settled down, and I was feeling confident in my businesslike, navy blue pinstripe suit. Thank goodness I'd had the gumption to choose it on that rare, remarkable day when Dad was forced to part with some cash when he paid for my faithful Christian Dior coat. With the sheerest nylons, and high-heeled shoes, I considered myself to be the perfect image of a successful businesslike, young woman, but I was neither confident nor businesslike, but sick with nerves, as I waited under the clock at precisely 11 am, eyeing a little old lady, her walking stick offering support to one side of her trembling frame, her free arm grasping the arm of another human being,

Berkhamsted

frantically praying she would not turn out to be my mother. After all, thirty-seven is getting on a bit. I was so caught up with watching elderly ladies, I didn't notice a beautiful, smartly dressed young woman looking into my face, enquiring, 'Are you Margaret?' Was it possible this smartly dressed, poised lady could be my mother? I'd quite forgotten how petite she was, as I towered over her, she oozing confidence, a picture of high fashion in her up-to-the-minute swing coat, her crisply cut hair worn in a smart DA (Duck's Ass) at the nape of her neck, standing beside me, a perfect picture of composure.

My mother suggested we pop into a ritzy-looking restaurant opposite the station.

Once inside, we selected a table close to an accomplished piano player, where my mother broke the ice by requesting the pianist play a certain Ivor Novello melody, 'We'll gather lilacs in the spring again,' so romantic, I could have wept. This led our friendly pianist to break into a string of wartime favourites, reminding us both of the years we'd been apart.

My mother encouraged me to eat something. I insisted I wasn't hungry, just a cup of coffee would do, although in truth, I was ravenous, but resisted the urge to tuck straight in. It would be so embarrassing if I left a crumb on my chin, and my mother noticed it.

'What would you like to do this afternoon?' she asked. 'Go to the pictures,' I instantly replied. I chose the film *Worm's Eye View*, starring the glamourous Diana Dors, the most popular English pin-up girl of the fifties, with her waist-length, platinum blond hair and curvaceous figure, known at the time as England's answer to Marilyn Monroe. The male lead was played by a long-forgotten comedian of the day, Ronald Shiner. Taking our seats in the stalls, my mother asked if I was hungry. Again I protested, feeling it was not done to eat in the stalls of a West End cinema. Trying to suppress the angry growls my stomach insisted on churning out quite spoiled the film for me.

Arrangements had been made for us to meet the man with the big boot, from Holcombe House days, at the Piccadilly branch of a Lyons Corner house, near to his place of work in New Bond Street, where he was an accountant for a top-notch ladies' fashion house. When we arrived, he was already sitting at a window table, a welcoming smile on his face. I learned that evening I now had a stepfather. Due to Dad's desire for a hasty divorce, my mother had at long last been made an honest woman. Thankfully, his easy manner, along with a glass of wine, helped us to relax, and best of all, I was finally able to tuck in to a decent meal. With hot food, including a splendid pudding inside me, I came out of my shell.

Replete and at ease, my stepfather asked what I would like to do next. Without hesitating, I replied, 'See a film,' and suggested *Captain Horatio Hornblower RN*, starring the handsome Gregory Peck as a swashbuckling captain, hero of the high seas, and his lovely passenger, Lady Barbara Wellesley, played by the blonde Virginia Mayo, a gracious lady of quality, who is crossing the ocean with a huge trunk containing a selection of breathtaking gowns, which seemed rather foolish to me, considering she's sailing on the open sea for weeks on end in the wildest conditions.

The film proved to be extremely tense, but after the excitement of the long day, we were exhausted and decided to call it a day. I was happy that night, even more so when, a few days later, a gorgeous lace blouse arrived by post. My mother was keen for me to live with them in Berkhamsted, Hertfordshire. Nurse Rose agreed with her, feeling a period of settled family life would be best

Berkhamsted

for me at the present time.

Within a month I had left my life as a pre-student nurse and moved to the old market town of Berkhamsted to start a new life with my new family.

My mother was now Mrs Florence Breen, leaving me the sole Rowe. We lived at 2 Chiltern Close, a high-quality, recently built four-bedroom house, with gardens to the front and rear, part of an attractive new development of council houses without garages, as the day of the family car was yet to arrive.

I was delighted to discover I had two aunts, my mother's younger sisters, living nearby. Aunty Peggy, who I was to learn was quite a girl, and Aunty Winifred, the complete opposite of both my mother and Aunty Peggy. A timid worrier, whose considerably younger husband, Uncle Frank, had an eye for the ladies, causing poor Aunty much anguish, and much running round the streets at night trying to locate which housewife he might be helping out. Each of the Aunties had several children and lived in similar houses, just around the corner from us, on the same Chiltern Estate. My only complaint about the modern homes of that day was the cold interior, it being impossible to get warm in winter. Central heating, unheard of at the time, was very much an expensive luxury, but it would have made such a difference to home comforts in the 1940s.

I grew fond of my two half-brothers, Patrick, the baby who had visited me at Holcombe House all those years ago, now a good-looking, blond-haired boy of twelve or so, and Martin, nine, a bit of a rapscallion, but good-natured and lovable. We got on really well together. I became especially fond of Patrick, a sensitive soul with marked artistic talents.

Right from the start, my mother and I hit it off, and before long, it felt like we'd never been apart, each one setting the other off with perpetual giggling, frequently finding ourselves in trouble when in public places. In spite of our mutual humour, not once did we mention the past, the sad times we'd been through. The only comment my mother ever made to me regarding Dad was that he was the hardest-working person she'd ever known.

With a twenty-minute walk, or a short bus ride into the centre of town, it didn't take me long to find I was living in a lively town. Berkhamsted, with its old-world charm, bore signs of affluence in every shop window, especially in the exclusive, couture shops, the cut of their stylish suits, and luxurious gowns, supplied by the cream of Mayfair Couturiers, designed to take a Lady of substance, to the most exclusive events. Our member of Parliament was Lady Davidson, a highly esteemed Conservative representative of the constituency.

I couldn't help but notice the number of pubs in the town. One side of the High Street boasted more pubs than shops, each of them once an old coaching inn, approached by a narrow archway, shadowing a long, cobbled drive, which in times gone by housed coaches and their horses overnight, so much so, I half expected to see a horse-drawn carriage clip-clop into the courtyard at any moment.

Luckily for me, there were two cinemas, The Court, comfortable and welcoming in the centre of town, and The Rex, further along the High Street, an outstanding example of an Art Deco building, with all the features of that era, an eye-catching interior with a magnificent chandelier in the foyer, and a first-rate restaurant on the ground floor. Many an afternoon tea, with superb Welsh Rabbit, have I enjoyed there. Two commanding curving flights of stairs leading up to the main auditorium were a marvel to behold. Unfortunately, during its latter years, The Rex fell into disrepair, becoming home to dozens of pigeons, a truly sorry sight, until rescued in the 1970s by a group of eminent British actors and businessmen, including Hugh Grant and Jane Asher. Reopened to huge success in 2008, the first film to be shown was Graham Greene's *The Third Man* in honour of the author, a Berkhamsted man. Today, set out with luxury chairs and tables, there's nothing more pleasing than relaxing over a glass of wine while snacking on nuts and titbits, enjoying one of the latest films.

In the early 1950s, the beautiful Chiltern Hills were as they are today, spreading their soft but spectacular beauty for miles around, with Berkhamsted at its centre. In spring, the beech trees take centre stage, the transparency of the pale green translucent leaves dancing to their own delicate tune, but come autumn, turning from deepest golden to vivid orange, then on to deeper crimson red, conjuring scenes of such perfection, it's hardly surprising that to this day, the whole world seems to turn up at weekends to make the most of nature's artistry.

Ashridge Estate, the centrepiece of the Chilterns, near Berkhamsted, is to this day managed by the National Trust, their offices nearby with a comfortable restaurant, and bookshop, next to The Bridgewater Monument, dedicated to the third Duke of Bridgewater, known as the Canal Duke, due to his expertise in designing canals, including the Grand Union Canal, which curves widely around these parts, popular today with holidaymakers relaxing on longboats throughout the summer months, with nothing to dwell on other than the many locks ahead. In the 1950s, the canal was kept busy by transporting essential goods from northern factories to the City of London. Today the boats provide comfortable homes for easy-going characters, preferring the simple life.

Providing you're fit enough to climb the 172 steep steps, it's quite an experience to climb to the top of the monument by using the internal narrow curving stone stairway, leading to a viewing balcony, from which, on a clear day, five counties can be viewed, including London's Canary Wharf.

My life settled into a comfortable routine. I was given a large bedroom overlooking the back garden. My stepfather allocated a small section of the garden to me, where each season I did my best to plant seasonal blooms, but it didn't take me long to realise that any small talent I might possess didn't lie in gardening. The question came up of what to call my stepfather. I couldn't call him Mr Breen, but I couldn't bring myself to call him Dad; having one was quite enough to be getting on with. Eventually, we settled on Pop, which was suitably informal without sounding sloppy.

I especially loved our regular ladies' get-togethers. Pop took an early train from Berkhamsted to Euston each working day, leaving the mornings free for the two Aunties to join us for a cup of strong English tea, a Rich Tea biscuit, and if finances were flush, things might stretch to a chocolate Bourbon or two, as we excitedly tuned into the BBC's daily instalment of 'Mrs Dale's Diary,' the everyday story of a provincial doctor's wife and her family. Although considered at the time a tale of ordinary families, today they would be seen as the upper classes, Mrs Dale calmly running the large house in an orderly manner, despite being up to her elbows in baking, and the worry of what to serve up for Jim's dinner that evening. Then there was her sister Sally, with her high-quality hat shop in the High Street, dashing here and there in her smart little car, not forgetting their old mother dashing around town like a spring chicken.

Berkhamsted

I barely heard from Dad during this period, and quite frankly that was fine by me. He was free to enjoy his newly found married bliss. He and his beloved were now husband and wife, safely ensconced in the upper floor of 21 Thaxted Road, where Dad had started his own business, with Edna as secretary to HF ROWE. Painter and Decorator. I was confident that Dad's business would thrive, with him being fastidious and a talented painter. I remember back in the Bromley days he was assigned to decorate the inside of a Catholic church, including painting a small statue of the Virgin Mary, which he worked on at our place. It was unbelievable. You'd have thought Michelangelo had painted it.

It was time to get a job. I'd enjoyed the break, but I needed to pay my way. Mum heard through the grapevine that the Old Mill House hotel were looking to hire a chambermaid. Back then, this hotel amounted to a worn old building, more in keeping with an old people's home, at the far end of town. Arriving there for my first morning, the tired old place gave me the heebie-jeebies. Tottering old folk wandered about the place, looking as worn as the Old Mill House itself. I was called upon to clean up some nasty messes, and empty more chamber pots than I'd come across at Erith Hospital. Feeling down in the dumps at the end of my first day, I knew it was not for me. Going over my depressing experience with Mum when I got home, she said, 'Don't worry, darling, I'll give the lady a call.' I marvel at how easily I got out of that, considering I'd been used to fighting my own battles. I am pleased to report that the Old Mill House is today a super-duper hotel.

My next job had a lot more going for it. I was to work on the till at a delightful café and cake shop. The Court Café, so named because it was one shop removed from the Court Cinema in the centre of the High Street. The café had a sunny air about it and was popular with a constant flow of customers, viewing the selection of tempting treats from the window, before coming in to place their order.

It was my job to switch from being a waitress at busy times to helping at the front, bagging up and taking money, when needed. This job was fun, with no time to get bored, and all the jam doughnuts I could manage.

I was working front of shop when the news came through; King George VI had died peacefully that morning, 6 February 1952, aged fifty-six. The whole country knew he'd been unwell, but it came as a tremendous shock all the same. I recalled those speeches he delivered every Christmas Day throughout the war years, when he battled against that dreadful stammer, never once letting his people down.

The newsreel at The Rex had shown him looking grey and gaunt a few days earlier as he waved goodbye to Princess Elizabeth and Prince Philip at London Airport, when they left for a tour of Kenya. The weather had been bitterly cold, a fierce wind blasting from the east. It was no place for a frail elderly gentleman, who'd have been much better off tucked up his bed with a comforting hot water bottle rather than standing on an exposed runway. Queen Elizabeth II would now reign over us, which would be quite different, but exciting.

Although I was happy at the Court Café, the world of cinema remained my priority. On Sunday evenings, The Rex showed top Hollywood films, some of which I'd missed out on in the Bromley days. Come snow or pelting rain, I wouldn't miss those special showings. Somerset Maugham's *The Razor's Edge* was great, with loads of big names, and the loveliest human being of all, the gorgeous Gene Tierney, her long dark hair very much like my own, only much neater. Somerset Maugham was fast becoming my favourite author, as I found myself riveted by his dark themes, such as *Of Human Bondage*, a story of mental manipulation by a devious woman exerting her mental power over an innocent young man, which really got me thinking. At least it had me dwelling on more serious matters than films about dancing, with all those chorus girls lined up in a row, kicking their legs in the air.

A cinema in Watford was showing the new foreign films with subtitles in English, enabling the audience to follow the story more easily. Patrick was interested in artistic films and asked if he could come along. He was clearly too young to view an adult film, which meant a disguise of some sort. The poor boy already wore strong spectacles, due to a bad reaction to a bout of measles in his younger days, leaving him extremely short-sighted. Wearing Pop's old mac, along with a trilby hat pulled well down over his naturally worried brows, he looked at least seventy. On the first of what were to become frequent trips to Watford, the two of us boarded a Green Line Bus, which dropped us off in the very centre of Watford by a modern parade with three, well-known top cinemas next door to each other. But for today, we had The Palace in mind, a speciality cinema down a side street that was showing an Italian film called *Bitter Rice*, a story of young people gathered together for the rice picking season in a section of the River Po, in Northern Italy, to earn money, as they were dreadfully poor. From morning to night, up to their thighs in muddy water, the girls wore mid-thigh-length stockings, held up by elastic bands, and the tiniest shorts ever. What a fine old time they had when they finished work, rollicking in the haylofts, getting up to what Dad would term 'sins of the flesh.' It was all a bit of an eye-opener, a lot of it brought on by the hot weather, I should think, but we certainly learned plenty from our frequent foreign film jaunts.

Mum and I were now more like a couple of pals than mother and daughter, enjoying having all the time in the world to get to know each other.

With time, she revealed other sides to her personality. The smart witty woman, always in control, was apt to fall apart when finding herself in the company of what she deemed the upper classes, seeming to crumple into a scared little girl. It made me want to give her a hug, because I understood how she was feeling, the difference in us being, she hadn't learned to bluff her way through it.

I learned she could be unreliable, which I found painful until I got used to it. One day, she produced from the attic a collection of knitting patterns, telling me to choose the one I liked, and she'd knit it for me. I looked forward to this special garment, until, as time went on, I realised it would never materialise or be mentioned again. As I got to know Pop, my stepfather, I had a feeling I had to be on my guard. I hadn't liked him at Holcombe House, and I didn't like him now. Permanently jolly, but ready to turn on a whim, I put it down to the suffering he'd received from thoughtless people who jeered at his handicap, his hip having been badly crippled from youth by TB. All the same, I was wary.

Mum was especially fond of The Crooked Billet, a local pub with a most genial host, two minutes from Chiltern Close, down at Billet End. One day Uncle Royston, Pop's older brother, rolled up. A bachelor sailor, 'more of an ancient mariner,' turned up out of the blue, which I learned could be once in five months, or five years. With a steady position on a Royal Navy ship, whenever he turned up unexpectedly, a fine time was had by all. Bearing fine gifts from exotic places for all the family, and pockets loaded with cash, The Crooked Billet was in the money, and before long, Uncle Royston and Mum had almost moved in there.

To give Pop his due, he refrained from the partying scene having to catch the early train to Euston for his high-powered job on Bond Street. But what a humdinger of a celebration come Saturday evenings. They tried to draw me into the fray, but I wasn't having any of it; standing around with nothing to do but drink yourself senseless wasn't my idea of fun. I preferred to stay at home listening to Radio Caroline broadcasting from the North Sea, very popular with young listeners at a time when the BBC declined to play music considered to be 'with it.' Uncle Royston's leave ran to a month or so before he was off on the high seas once again, leaving Mum to recover her health, and the remainder of us our senses.

It was around this time that my life changed. Again, Mum heard somewhere on the grapevine that The Swan Hotel, one of the best hotels in the town centre, were looking for a suitable young woman to live in, primarily as a waitress, and to help out generally during busy times. I met Mrs Thomson, a slender businesslike lady in her late thirties, immediately taking to her, as she did me, and we agreed a date by which I would move in and start work, returning to Chiltern Close at weekends. Being only sixteen, I was to have no dealings with the popular bar side of the business.

Sad as I was to leave the Court Café, The Swan Hotel was almost directly opposite, so I could always pop in to see my pals. I thought hotel life would be interesting and a step towards whatever I was eventually to do with my life.

Centuries old, this coaching inn was one of three, set next to each other in the High Street, The Swan being a particularly charming example of the historic past. Cosy with welcoming log fires in the colder seasons, low ceilings with brass fittings, subtle lampshades, everything about The Swan drew customers inside. My low-ceilinged, higgledy-piggledy bedroom welcomed me at night with a double bed, a deep feather eiderdown, so comforting, I found it hard to wrench myself from its embrace on winter mornings.

I took to my new job like a duck to water, rising early to take a pot of tea to Mr and Mrs Thomson in their bedroom. Around this time, Joan, the kitchen maid, would arrive, and we'd breakfast together at an outsized kitchen table. One of my first duties was to put the dining room in order, folding serviettes into neat points before standing one in each place setting for what was a popular three-course lunch. My first job on a Monday morning was to help Joan polish the many brasses from every nook and cranny in the pub. For this lengthy undertaking we settled into the comfortable snug, me popping out to serve morning coffee in the lounge, if required. Lunch service was hectic, at times frenetic, the home cooking always top-notch. Unfortunately, Cook fell ill soon after I started there and was replaced by none other than my mother, who was herself an excellent cook. Both our working days ended after the lunchtime rush, so after catching our breath from the madness of the last two hours, we relaxed in the kitchen over our own meal, before heading for home, pausing to dawdle round the shops, or maybe call at the Court Café to catch up with my old mates, before returning to Chiltern Close, where I stayed until it was time to make my way back to The Swan Hotel to sleep.

Mrs Thomson, was a business-like person, most agreeable as long as you took your work seriously, but she could be a real tartar with slackers. The person who annoyed her most was her own husband, a perpetual joker, always messing about first thing in the morning by chasing me round the kitchen, teasing me with a dead mouse fresh from the trap, or something equally horrid. One morning at breakfast, he was up to his usual antics, when his wife stormed in to find him wearing a tea cosy on his head, brandishing a mop, proclaiming, 'Father is King.' She soon gave him 'Father is King,' and sent him packing. I was concerned for her health, she looked so tired, forever getting herself so worked up.

Luckily, Mr Thomson, would soon be off in his sporty little car to his interesting job as a horse racing reporter for one of the national newspapers. Anyway, all we workers adored him.

The bar did a roaring trade, run by Mr Waring, the sick cook's husband, a quiet, hard-working man, happy to help we girls when a man's strength was needed. Many of our bar customers were local businessmen, popping in during the morning for a pint of something or other, or a quick whisky, whereas the ladies were more partial to a sweet or dry sherry, according to their palate. Of course, there was always high demand for a steaming cup of coffee, freshy made by Joan, and served by me. There were two particularly interesting bar regulars, with the names Hoagie and Johnnie, two men in their late twenties, both ex-pilots with the RAF. They spent hours in the bar, morning and evening, always courteous, but never mixing with other drinkers, while putting away pint after pint. Known as 'the boys,' they were always courteous to me, never drinking more than they could handle, but remaining a mystery to everyone.

The latest show to storm the London stage was *Bless the Bride* featuring a number of magical melodies, each of them becoming major hits on the radio, and whistling lads on the streets of 'Berko'. The favourite was 'Ma Belle Marguerite,' sung by the male lead

French actor, Georges Guétary. Soon, one of our regulars renamed me 'La belle Marguerite,' which was flattering and made me feel good, but soon I was known as 'La belle Marguerite,' all over town. Another regular was dear Mr Neil, the owner of Neil's Furniture, an exclusive furniture store located directly opposite The Swan. Arriving at 11 am on the dot for his morning sherry, his first words to me were, 'How's youth and beauty today?', making me bigheaded, although it was lovely everyone being so kind to me.

The year of 1952 was a happy year. Mum wasn't much of a walker, meaning I spent hours alone, exploring the beautiful Hockridge Woods around us. One day, I walked as far as the rolling slopes of Tring Park, where seeing the sign Rothschild Zoological Museum, I popped into the entrance for a quick look round. There were fascinating old photographs of the late Lord Walter Rothschild, whose habit it had been to be driven around the estate in an open carriage drawn by zebras back in the 1900s. The old Lord was evidently quite a character, and founder of the museum.

The small town of Tring, about five miles from Berkhamsted, had its own small cinema. One week I saw in the local paper a matinee performance of the film *Father of the Bride*, starring my adored Elizabeth Taylor, was to be shown on the following Wednesday afternoon. I talked Mum into accompanying me. The bus to Tring didn't run at a suitable time, so we borrowed the boys' bicycles, Martin's smaller bike suiting Mum's petite frame, while I took tall Patrick's. The only way a lady could hold her stockings up were by the use of garters or suspenders. Mum was always teasing me for wearing suspenders, insisting elastic garters were much easier to get along with, leading me to decide, today of all days, to experiment with garters. The ride to Tring proved to be hilly, quite knocking the wind out of our sails, unused as we were to cycling. Adding to my distress, I realised the garters were not behaving as they should. By the time we reached Tring, my stockings and garters had gathered in wrinkles round my calves, which would, quite rightly, be considered slovenly in the 1950s. On arriving in Tring, I had no choice but to resort to asking an amiable newsagent if I might have the use of his backroom to rearrange my attire. Both he and his assistant found the incident highly amusing, not so myself, being well aware it would be most unseemly for a lady to find herself caught out in such a situation.

The ride back to Berkhamsted was not only a graft but an embarrassment, leaving me without stockings and with painful blisters on my poor feet. I suggested Mum keep her new-fangled ideas to herself, but she seemed to find the whole thing highly amusing, which irked me no end.

Life went on, one day seeming to ease into the next, so much so, I woke one morning to one of my favourite sounds, the blackbird, the clarity of his tone reaching the last house in Chiltern Close. The cherry tree Pop had planted in the back garden was on the point of bursting into bloom, its delicate perfume filling the air with joy. As far as I was concerned, all was right with the world.

To my surprise, Dad called me that evening. It was so long since he and Edna had seen me, was there any chance I might pay them a visit soon? They could put me up for the night, if I wished. I quickly mentioned I had my job to consider, so I would come over for afternoon tea the following Saturday. To tell the truth, I wasn't keen on this meeting, but best to get it behind me. Whatever happens, I mustn't let on I worked in a den of sin. On the appointed day I caught a Green Line Coach from Billets End to Victoria Station, and from there a red bus took me to New

Eltham, dropping me off at the end of Thaxted Road. A brisk walk led me to Number 21, where I found myself stricken by an attack of collywobbles, plunging me into such gloom,

I wondered why I'd set out on this exercise. I tried my hardest to calm the sense of panic sweeping through my shaking body by telling myself not to be afraid, fear belonged to the past, my life was happy now. Recalling the hateful visits to Mrs Wright, Edna's mother, the dreaded Matriarch of Emmanuel, Pentecostal Church, I supposed I'd be expected to say hello to her. With any luck she'd be out.

It was Edna who opened the door to me, where surprisingly, my panic left me as quickly as it had arrived, leaving me tranquil, able to take on the very Devil himself. A lovely surprise was the adorable dog they'd acquired, a frisky golden retriever with the name Vagabond, shortened to Vaggy, the sweetest creature who did much to ease my tension. The two of them seemed very happy, business was going well, the subject of church not raised until later. Fortunately for me, Mrs Wright was away at a Pentecostal do of some sort. Sadly, her husband, the oldest Church Elder, Mr Wright, with the humpy back, had gone to a happier land, where he dwells at the feet of his saviour. It seemed Mrs Wright was in seventh heaven, running here and there, a new woman, having a fine old time in the service of the Lord.

After hearing the latest goings-on at Emmanuel Church, it was time for tea. As soon as Edna left the room to prepare our meal, Dad got in quickly with, 'How is she?', meaning my mother. I suppose he only took on Edna as second-best. He should have treated Mum better when he had the chance. Poor old Edna wouldn't hold a candle to my mum. She must have something going for her, but I couldn't see it. Tea was served, the usual high

Berkhamsted

tea of these days of hardship and food rationing. Starting with tinned salmon sandwiches, very nice indeed, followed by tinned fruit salad, with a tin of Carnation milk poured over it, tasting as good as cream, and the delicious little coffee fairy cakes she was so good at making, the same recipe she'd used to lure Dad, a regular Delilah she turned out to be. I waited for the House of the Lord to come up, but I'd become adept at changing the subject, influenced as I was by working in a 'House of the Devil'. He should have known it was all wasted on me, but he didn't give up. 'I think of my daughter in those dens of sin, watching those evil sinners dancing before her,' he'd say. I tried to calm his fears by pointing out that films were only actors playing their parts, earning a decent living to feed their families.

I must say I was glad when it was time to leave. The less I saw of them the happier I'd be. Glad to get back to good old 'Berko', I breathed a sigh of relief, although to be fair the visit had gone better than I'd expected, the nicest part had been meeting Vaggy.

I took constant delight in getting to know my close family living nearby, having been unaware of their existence before I came to Berkhamsted. In fact, it was exciting to find I belonged anywhere, and what was even nicer was being made to feel welcome. I made a point of spending time with both families as often as possible.

Aunty Peggy, the most gregarious of the three sisters, always good for a laugh, adored her husband, Uncle Cyril, a wine waiter in a smart local restaurant, and her three children, but that didn't stop her finding the time and energy to find love elsewhere.

Dear Aunty Winnifred, always in a state of worry, knowing as she did, her husband's roving eye. Uncle Frank was really into photography and was a member of a local camera club in town.

He asked if he might take some studio shots of me. Aunty was agreeable, so one evening I set out to their house, 27 Ashridge Rise, to find he'd set up a temporary studio in the front room, with special lights and umbrellas, like a real photographer. Aunty said she'd keep out of the way and made herself comfortable in the kitchen, listening to the wireless.

Uncle Frank made a point of positioning the lights in the most flattering angles to ensure I looked my best, both of us giving it our full attention for what seemed like an age, until Uncle suggested we take a short break.

I was quite tired by now, glad to sink into the relaxing sofa, when, after a long day's work, I must have dozed off, only to be brought to my senses by a hand gently stroking one of my beasts, then finding myself overpowered, and a husky voice whispering in my ear, 'I must have you.' 'Have me? You must be out of your mind, you're my Uncle.' He didn't find that an obstacle to us caring for each other, was his reply. Shocked, more than I can express, I retrieved my accessories and made for the kitchen, where trusting Aunty Winifred, was listening to the latest news. Appalled that my own uncle would behave in such an outrageous manner, I made for home.

Uncle Frank worked for a famous aeroplane company, de Havilland, or some such name, based in Hatfield, not far from Berkhamsted. Frequently sent to Florida for work, his job being plane maintenance, it wasn't long after my arrival before he absconded, choosing to live in Florida with an American lady by the name of Joselyn, with whom Aunty Winnifred formed an unlikely, lifelong friendship, at first through letters, then by phone as the telephone service improved with the passing years. This unlikely friendship continued well past Uncle Frank's demise,

Berkhamsted

until both Aunty Win and her friend Joselyn died, well into their nineties.

Drifting along, I'd never been happier, apart from never-ending conflict with Pop, who could be quite waspish at times. Aware of my popularity in the town, he felt that I should be spending more time at home helping out, instead of galivanting around, as he put it. A black-and-white television had been installed in the front room, which claimed a decent amount of our attention. A cumbersome object, with a small screen, inclined to getting frequent snow storms – interference was the technical term – but when it was working, the television could be most entertaining. The news seemed more interesting when read by a lady, usually Sylvia Peters, looking very pretty in her best dress, sitting in a smart studio at Alexandra Palace, in London. I suppose most men bought a television for the football, but family entertainment, was to prove a towering success, and before long TV was regarded as a household necessity. The following year, in June 1953, London would see the Queen's Coronation, a good enough reason to invest in a television set. Coronation Day was to be an amazing affair, the whole day being televised, even the moment the crown is placed on the Queen's head. Crowds would line the streets, like when the war ended, and later in the day the wedding group would gather on the palace balcony in all their regalia and finery, to wave to the loyal crowds.

One unseasonable Sunday in June, hot and steamy from never-ending rain, I was making my way to The Swan, after Mum's unmissable Sunday roast with crisp golden roast potatoes spring cabbage, she even made cabbage a crunchy pleasure, followed by apple pie with custard, seemingly simple, but, so good.

As I neared the High Street, the clouds separated, the blinding brilliance of sudden sunshine on the sodden tarmac causing clouds of steam on this humid afternoon. As I entered The Swan, who should I bump into but my boss, Mr Thomson, taking me by surprise with, 'La bella Margarite, it's stopped raining. Let's go for a walk.'

So, off we went, quite a distance as it happens, all the way to Hockridge Woods, where multitudes of beach trees massed together, meaning the earlier rain had barely left its mark on the rich mulch we trod. Mr Thomson said I should call him Tony, but it felt quite wrong to do so, what with him being my boss. I must say it was good to have a serious talk, although, as always, by the time we got back to The Swan he had me in stiches.

Our walks continued from time to time. I'd be picked up from a regular spot in Hockridge Woods, and we'd zoom off in Tony's sports car to one of the many quaint inns to be found in this part of the country, where we had become regulars, Tony with his whisky, and me sticking to Britvic's delicious tomato juice. Our regular meetings continued all summer, and it wasn't long before I had fallen in love with this charming, older man who apparently idolised me.

My seventeenth birthday fell on 13 November. At Tony's suggestion, I'd arranged to have the day off. It was fun hurtling to the Ashridge Monument, where we parked the car, before dashing up the 172 steps to the top, where we took up position on the breezy balcony, taking in the spectacular sight of seven counties, all clearly visible on this special morning. Bronzed beech leaves swirled about us like confetti, as Tony opened a bottle of French champagne, filling two special glasses he'd borrowed from The Swan, as we drank to our relationship.

One of the first things Tony dealt with was my wardrobe,

Berkhamsted

insisting I must have some decent warm clothes. He whisked me away to the nearby town of Amersham, where we visited a quality ladies' establishment with stylish, but sensible clothes. I was soon the thrilled owner of a pair of soft but strong winter boots, guaranteed to be waterproof. A sensible but stylish winter coat, buttoning up to my chin, as well as a smart but feminine pure wool dress, as Tony remarked, will take you anywhere. All in all, I was thrilled to bits with my wares.

We decided it would be better if I stopped working at The Swan, making our meetings easier to arrange. As luck would have it, this coincided with the return of the previous cook, who'd been off sick, freeing both me and Mum.

To my surprise, I found it hard to adjust to a life without work. On the days I saw Tony, he picked me up in his speedy little car from our regular meeting point in the woods, before heading off to one of our familiar ports of call, where we knew there'd be a welcoming fire, as by this time, winter was heavily upon us. Tony didn't work every day. Being a racing correspondent, he only worked on race days. Most racecourses were within the Home Counties, making any trip from Berkhamsted a pleasure, passing through old-world towns and countryside, today more likely to be modern homes and shopping precincts, with only the bare skeletons of a previously beautiful setting to catch the eye here and there.

Arriving at our destination, I'd decide whether to see a film or attend the races, much depending on the weather. On a brisk sunny day there was nothing I enjoyed more than parading my luxurious winter coat and waterproof boots. My poor old Christian Dior model coat had long been dispatched to the rubbish bin, having served me well over the years. When the weather was bad,

I preferred cosying up in a nice warm picture house, watching one of the latest releases. No matter which choice I made, the afternoon always ended with a pot of tea and toasted tea cakes, in a nearby tea shop, before making our way back to 'Berko'.

Throughout the winter months life went on in the same relaxed way, perhaps too relaxed. I tried my hardest to dispel the restless irritation hanging over me of late. I was bored with the easy life I was living. The sense of purpose I'd always thrived on lay dormant, and I missed it, my sense of hope rising as the days grew longer.

As it happened, my situation resolved itself without any help from me. It turned out that Aunty Peggy, a devilish woman at times, had heard tittle-tattle, that I was running around with Tony, and couldn't wait to rush round to give Pop the news, who then dashed as fast as his poor old legs would carry him to The Swan to pass on the scandalous tale to Mrs Thomson.

Things didn't go down at all well on the evening when Tony rolled up at Chiltern Close, clutching a nicely iced bottle of champagne, to drink a toast to 'La belle Margarite', together with a fancy box of chocolates for Mum. Like a red flag to a bull, Pop almost exploded with what he termed, 'the dammed temerity of the man,' as Tony insisted, in no uncertain terms, he would never be parted from 'La belle Margarite.' Things almost came to fisticuffs on the pavement, but poor old Pop was too handicapped to put up much of a fight. Of course, Mum found the drama highly amusing, not so Pop, who was the kind of person to hold a grudge.

Highly indignant at the way things had ended with Tony, Pop was convinced I was still meeting him, and so concerned was he, he decided to get me away for a while, well out of the way of that dammed man's clutches.

It so happened, some years earlier, Mum had taken a seasonal job as a waitress in the seaside town of Torquay, in Devon, finding the position through an agency in Frith Street, in the Soho area of London. Pop contacted the same agent, where, there and then, he arranged similar positions for the two of us to work as waitresses for the summer season at The Paignton Ritz Hotel on the seafront in Paignton, Devon.

When the day came for our departure, we excitedly made our way to Paddington Station, and after a long train journey found ourselves breathing in the clean, salty air of Paignton. Carrying our suitcases, we headed for the seafront, where we couldn't miss The Paignton Ritz, due to the deafening sound of jazz music blaring from its open windows and along the seafront, from what appeared to be a sleazy nightclub, rather than an hotel. Mum started to panic, so after making our way to our allocated room, where the walls trembled from the thunderous sounds of the latest jungle rhythms, I reassured her we would stay overnight, then make a run for it first thing in the morning. Being the start of the summer season, there must be dozens of jobs.

Awake at first light, we hurriedly dressed before slinking down the stairs with our suitcases and sliding silently through the front door, onto the promenade, to the sound of an angry male voice shouting from behind, 'Where are you two girls off to?' 'Keep running, Mum,' I said, as I grabbed her suitcase and stormed ahead. We soon shook off our pursuer, before resting awhile on a low wall, where we retrieved our composure somewhat, before seeking an early morning café on the seafront, where we tucked into a full English breakfast special. We stayed put, relieved to be out of that hell-hole, waiting for the rest of the world to wake up,

Mum, enjoying a second pot of tea. while puffing away on her first cigarette of the day. At a suitable hour, I left her in charge of the suitcases, before, as Humphrey Bogart would have put it, 'casing the joint,' by strolling along the front taking in the many hotels of various standards. After some time, my eye was caught by a particularly attractive hotel, and instinct told me this was the one for us. Set well back from the sea front, behind a walled pebbled frontage, with a number of palm trees, a monkey tree, and other exotic plants, with parking for a few cars, and a notice indicating a car park to the rear of the hotel, the hotel was unusually named The Tembani Hotel.

Knowing that breakfast would be tailing off by now, I made my way in to the foyer to find an elderly man assisting with the clearing-up. This turned out to be the hotel owner, Mr Christmas, an exact embodiment of the original, plump, ruddy-cheeked, easy-going, original Father Christmas. After listening to my explanation of the situation Mum and I found ourselves in, he welcomed me with open arms. 'Delighted to have you both on board,' was how he put it. He mentioned a little cottage he owned about a mile away, and would we mind sleeping over there? Feeling excited at the outcome of my expedition, I made my way back to the café where I'd left Mum. Without giving her time to light up another cigarette, I rushed her off to The Tembani, to introduce her to our boss. Before departing for our cottage, a housekeeper selected identical black uniforms and a package of freshly laundered, white aprons, which were to be kept in a changing room at the hotel, where they would be recycled on a regular basis.

The Tembani couldn't have been a nicer place to work. A family hotel, welcoming old and young, set in a perfect setting, a few yards from the beach, with its traditional deck chairs to rent

Berkhamsted

by the day, donkey rides, every variety of ice cream, and of course, candy floss, that sweet delight I'd fallen for all those years ago at Barry Island, where Dad first turned against me.

Our working hours were made up of serving breakfast, lunch and dinner, with afternoons free, and one day off a week. There were four other waitresses, mainly locals, and a smart tall woman who was an expert on wines, in charge of all the drinks served at table. Each waitress was allotted a group of tables, a station, and was responsible for the same guests for the whole of their stay, usually a fortnight. Most of The Tembani customers returned every year, happy with the service they received there, always making sure their 'girl' was seen 'all right' on the day of their departure, which turned out to be an excellent opportunity to put money in my Post Office Savings account towards my new life.

We were happy in our little cottage, with everything supplied, but the walk to work was more like two miles rather than the one Mr Christmas had mentioned. Finding it too far to return home for our afternoon break, we took the opportunity to get to know Paignton, a welcoming town where we wandered around the busy High Street, with its amusement arcade, and its modern cinema with daily showings of the latest releases. Handy, not only for us, but for holiday makers finding themselves caught out by the odd, rainy day. One of our pleasures was to wander down to the harbour where we lounged about, soaking our poor old feet, while licking delicious ice creams, or watching the fishermen unload their earlier catches, before packing their bright-eyed cargo into slatted boxes, ready for instant distribution.

Each morning, on our way to work to start breakfasts, we passed a cinema. I noticed the main feature for the current week was Rita Hayworth's new film

Pretty from the Outside

Salome. I'd been a staunch fan of Rita all the way back to the Cwmcarn days. She hadn't made a film for some years, having thrown away her magical career in Hollywood to marry the illustrious Prince Aly Khan, for love. The Prince, known worldwide as a playboy, renowned in the gossip columns for his fast living and philandering ways, always racing around in sports cars pursuing beautiful women, leaving poor Rita alone and brokenhearted. Unable to take the pain, she divorced Aly, and returned to Hollywood with her young daughters, to the life she knew so well. *Salome* was the film she hoped would restart her dwindling career.

A few days later saw the two of us sitting in the stalls, waiting for Rita to make her long-awaited appearance. That old actor, Charles Laughton, by now well past his best and overacting madly, took on the part of King Herod. Stewart Granger, a celebrated British actor, played the love interest, and another British actor, Alan Badel, took the role of tragic John the Baptist, most movingly, I felt. I waited anxiously to see how Rita had weathered the years. Age had not withered her, as she hurled herself dramatically across the palace floor, writhing at King Herod's feet, driving the poor fellow mad with desire, weaving her sensuous spell throughout the rousing 'Dance of the Seven Veils,' discarding seductively one rainbow tinted veil after another, until, on reaching the final veil, she abandons herself at the feet of King Herod, by this time crazed with desire, at very moment the bloodied head of John the Baptist is carried in on a silver salver.

There was no doubt about it, Rita had everything going for her. It was as if time had stood still while she'd been away although at times I glimpsed a sadness in her eyes, which hadn't been there in the Cwmcarn days.

That summer was a special time for Mum and me, giving us

the perfect opportunity to really get to know each other after all the years we'd been kept apart. It was great to find we were so at home in each other's company, giggling at the same ridiculous nonsense, asked on occasion to quieten down during a moving scene at the pictures, when like guilty children, we slunk down into our seats, trying our hardest to regain an element of self-control. Not once did we mention Dad, although we were well aware of what each had suffered at his hands. Never again would he be allowed to intrude on our relationship.

Mr Christmas made sure none of the staff missed the television coverage of Coronation Day on 3 June 1953, the day our new young Queen Elizabeth was to be crowned in Westminster Abbey. We took turns to slip away to watch sections of this momentous day, as Mr Christmas had placed a large television screen in the staff rest room, where we could indulge in a delightful drop of bubbly.

Our summer continued in the same manner, with not a care in the world, a voyage I'd never wanted to embark on, but which was to prove such a happy experience for us both.

Although glad to be back in Berkhamsted, I couldn't rid myself of a niggling itch, reminding me the time had arrived when I had to try to make my way in the world. My relationship with Pop was not good, he refused to let up about Tony, convinced I was still seeing him. Another thing he couldn't tolerate was my hogging the bathroom, in my never-ceasing efforts to style my hair like Rita Hayworth's. 'Rita Hayworth, nothing but bloody Rita Hayworth,' echoed round the house. Now was the time to call a truce, he and I would never see eye to eye, I would head for London.

Before long, I was on a Greenline Bus heading for the city.

Pretty from the Outside

The only part of London I knew well was Marble Arch, where I'd spent so many Saturday afternoons at Speaker's Corner, listening to endless Bible punchers pitching their own version of the same old story. The first thing I thought of as the bus dropped me off at the familiar corner was food. It was some time since breakfast. Mingling among the teeming pedestrians, I soon found a J Lyons Corner House, next to The Cumberland Hotel. Feeling much better with a hot meal inside me, it was time for business. As I was about to leave, I caught sight of a discarded copy of the *Evening Standard* on the next table. I might as well take a quick glance at the jobs section.

As luck would have it, The Cumberland Hotel were looking for suitable young women to work as waitresses at their prestigious hotel at Marble Arch in Oxford Street.

With no time to waste, I made myself presentable in the ladies' rest room, before heading for the staff entrance of the hotel, which proved easier said than done as it took an age, being unexpectedly hidden away in nearby Bryanston Street. As fortune decreed, I eventually reached the door I'd been seeking, where a uniformed member of staff directed me through a maze of spooky underground tunnels, until, quite by luck, I found myself outside the correct room where I sat nervously alone in a designated waiting area, until I was called into an office by a pleasant man in his forties, who, after making me welcome, suggested I tell him about myself. I filled him in on my recent positions, including my latest stint in Paignton. I was suitable, he said, and he would love to employ me, but the only problem was I had to be at least eighteen. I practically begged him to reconsider as working here was all I wished for, after all, my birthday was only a few weeks away. He didn't want to lose me for such a short time, so I was

Berkhamsted

signed up. I was to work five days a week, starting the following Monday at 6.30 am, working through breakfast, luncheon, then dinner, until my last diners departed, at approximately 10.30 pm. My afternoons were free, which would be handy, for the Pavilion Cinema I'd spotted directly opposite the hotel specialised in the foreign films I was so taken with. I would be paid £2.00 per week, with any tips received my own, and two free days a week. Before I left, I was to collect my uniform. The only things I needed to provide were a sensible pair of brown lace-up shoes, and stockings. After fitting my uniform, my next task was to find somewhere to live.

~ 10 ~
London

On recommendation from helpful Londoners on the Edgware Road, I was advised to try Kilburn in my search for a bedsit. I hopped on a bus, alighting a few minutes later at Kilburn High Street. After scouring adverts in newsagents' windows, I found what I was looking for, so headed towards the nearest red phone box.

In the 1950s, red telephone boxes were abundant, on many street corners, but even so, there'd frequently be a queue of irate hopefuls, tut-tutting as some timewasting idiot insisted on hogging the line. On summer evenings family members all over England were to be seen scurrying along to the box on the corner, clutching a scrap of paper, ready for a quick chat with Cousin Mabel.

The landlady of the bedsit invited me to view the room. After walking for what felt like miles, Alexander Road was surely the longest road I'd ever walked, running from Kilburn all the way to Swiss Cottage, a more desirable area than Kilburn, and as it turned out, only a ten-minute bus ride from my work. At last I reached the house I was seeking, a tall Edwardian house, with steep steps leading up to the front door. An efficient middle-aged woman led me to a box room on the second floor, so tiny its wardrobe had to stand on the landing. The whole place was scrupulously clean, with a good-sized kitchen where tenants could cook a meal and have the use of a large refrigerator, handy to keep a pint of milk for that cup of coffee before leaving for work on cold winter mornings. I paid my first week's rent of £1.00 and a deposit of £4.00, before being given a key to the front door, and arranging to be back on Sunday with my belongings, ready for work on Monday. Returning to Berkhamsted, I pondered over the long day, and judged it to have been a great success.

It was with trepidation that I ventured forth on Monday morning at the unearthly hour of 6 am. My journey, a straightforward, twenty-minute bus ride taking me down Baker Street, then turning into Oxford Street where I was dropped off opposite the hotel, and a quick dash saw me outside the staff entrance. Pushing open the door, I was met by a man in uniform who showed me how to clock in on entering and leaving the building, then presented me with six teaspoons, along with strict instructions not to part with one of them. Six must be handed in on leaving the building. If so much as one was missing at the end of the day, it seemed, I'd be sent to the scaffold. This was a worrying start, I would have thought a huge company such as J Lyons wouldn't need to worry about a single teaspoon. This problem was to be the bane of my life, as it was for all the waiting staff, throughout my time at The Cumberland. It was so easy to forget to grab your spoons, when frantically busy, and you were depositing a heavy tray on to a fast-moving belt, carrying any debris round the bend and out of sight in a flash, meanwhile, returning to your station, customers would be yelling out for teaspoons, while you, completely helpless with not a soul to help you out, being in the same boat themselves.

On that first day, the staff areas being vast and underground,

London

it was luck that led me to the women's changing room, and my allotted locker, where I changed into my brown uniform, including two matching rosettes, one to be worn on either side of my hair. I knew I was in trouble as soon as I put on my brown lace-up shoes, when I found the right one to be too tight. Not having enough money to replace them, I could do nothing but break them in, but the truth is, they broke me in. To this day I rue the day I bought them, as my burning bunion never lets me forget.

At 6.30 am on the dot, I present myself at the head waiter's desk in the splendid restaurant, where, even at this hour, a pianist's gentle tinkling soothed the ears of early-risers. Mr Braed, the head waiter, was charm itself, tall and elegant, with brown hair, he was never seen dressed in anything other than a white tie and tails, always courteous, he took an interest in his workers, treating them with respect at all times. Escorting me to my station of four tables, he introduced me to the girl working the next station, requesting she show me the ropes. The girl was Irene, and before long we were good friends. Life could be hectic at The Cumberland. Breakfasts were a doddle, but lunch and dinner service had me running around like a headless chicken, what with all the worry over teaspoons, having to watch their every move like a hawk. The moment a customer so much as raised a buttock on departure, I was in there, grabbing my precious contraband, which was dropped into my secret pocket, ready for a quick rinse when I could grab a moment. This vitally important pocket not only housed The Cumberland silverware, but any precious tips that came my way.

Things weren't all doom and gloom though. Frothy coffee, the latest Italian craze, was popping up overnight, in all the new styled, glamorous cafés throughout the West End of London.

The height of modernity, with tall stools lining the bar,

customers might choose to perch casually, or relax at ultra-modern, continental tables and chairs. Irene and I soon got into the habit of slinking out for our mid-morning break where, quite by chance, we came across one such café, right on the corner of the Edgware Road. Anyone who was anyone had caught on to this new heady lifestyle, so sleek, so desirable, like in the American movies. Not only was the coffee delicious, but customers could also have their fill of rock and roll, or pop music, which could be played on the jukebox for a penny or so. Revitalised, we returned to our stations in a cheery mood, ready to face the mayhem of the lunch session. Following on, we might recover over a meal in the staff canteen, or spend the afternoon as we liked, as long as were back for the dinner service by 6.30 pm.

Dinner was an altogether different experience. Evening transformed the restaurant into a realm of finesse and glamour. The restaurant dimly lit, an orchestra playing romantic numbers from Ivor Novello, the composer of the some of the most moving songs of the war years, as well as great American musicals, such as Rodgers and Hammerstein's *Carousel*, all absolute bliss, quite taking my mind off my work as I waltzed about my station, with tray aloft. The Cumberland's leading light of the moment was the lovely Lizbeth Webb, a huge star from the stage show *Bless the Bride*, with a purity to her voice like tinkling bells. From time to time a different mood took over, a favourite was 'Top of the Pops' singer Alma Cogan, forever in the top ten, loved for the chuckle in her voice, who was to die tragically young.

When the last of my guests took their leave, I was free to return to my bedsit. Getting past the man on the door was a bit of a procedure, his hands running lightly over my whole body, my pockets and bags searched for contraband. Teaspoons counted and handed in, they could keep their teaspoons as far as I was concerned.

My eighteenth birthday arrived, and with it the right to work legally as an adult. I travelled to Berkhamsted at least once a week, staying overnight in my own room if it tied in with my free days. Of course there was always the telephone. With growing familiarity with The Cumberland and its idiosyncrasies, I became more relaxed, casting my net further along Oxford Street. Of prime importance was a visit to the Pavilion Cinema, with its ever-changing choice of foreign films, completely different from home-grown offerings. It's hard to imagine what those hot-blooded Latins got up to. I should think it was the hot weather that did it. I grew up quite a bit and was intrigued by, what Dad would call, things that shouldn't concern me. My admiration for female actresses knew no bounds. In my opinion, Italian women ruled the world for their stunning beauty. The names Gina Lollobrigida and Sophia Loren would soon become world-famous over the following decade, and beyond. I remember seeing each of them in small parts, before Hollywood glammed them up. One afternoon, my beady eyes spotted a clip of Sophia playing the part of a handmaiden, long before she became a star. In this particular scene she kept her face and hair veiled, but she'd forgotten to put on her brassiere. A fine figure of a woman she was too.

It wasn't long before I discovered the famous department store, Selfridges. I began by looking in the windows, which was more like a theatre production, their displays having won many awards, especially during the Christmas period. World-class designers showed their latest creations, including my hero, Christian Dior. One afternoon I found the nerve to enter the domain of the wealthy on the second floor, but after admiring

Pretty from the Outside

several collections, when I dared to ask the price of a snazzy French suit, I could hardly believe my ears. Thinking I might be arrested for daring to ask, I took off as fast as I could, to search out my meagre price range. Still, it gave me something to aim for. With time, I grew to know the layout of the store. There wasn't much I could afford, but finding a classy hair salon on the top floor, I thought I'd treat myself by getting my hair done by a senior stylist. The young assistants addressed me as madam, as did the mature gentleman who cut my hair beautifully, which bucked me up no end, even though it cost an arm and a leg.

For several mornings in a row, an elderly lady took breakfast at my station. One morning she handed me an entry form for a beauty contest she'd cut out from a newspaper, and said, 'You should enter this, my dear. I admire your beauty.' I thanked her profusely, flattered that she'd paid me such a compliment, and thought no more of it.

Spring came around. Winter had been a hard slog, what with dark mornings and dense periods of smog, causing upheaval for traffic and walkers. I worked on Christmas Day and New Year's Eve, entailing long shifts and long walks, as buses didn't run on Bank holidays.

A new waitress, Betsy, had joined the restaurant team, and her station was close to mine.

It hadn't taken me long to suss out that we girls worked on less desirable stations than the faster, stronger men who were given the pick of the customers, those who looked like they'd be good tippers, whereas we girls seemed to end up with little old ladies, leaving sixpence under a plate, after hogging the table for hours on end with their endless chatter.

Betsy turned out to be quite a girl, wise in the ways of the world, but great fun. It wasn't long before she joined our mid-morning frothy coffee club. Being the sole occupant of a double-size bedsit in Pimlico with a spare bed, she suggested we share it, which seemed an excellent idea, saving money for both of us.

I took a bus to Claverton Street in Pimlico, close to the Thames Embankment and directly opposite the Battersea Power Station. I hoped to meet with the landlady's approval.

Mrs Mead, a cheerful cockney woman in her mid-fifties, and I got on as soon as we set eyes on each other. The owner of two huge adjoining houses, both rented out as furnished rooms, she lived in the basement of one of the houses.

Naughty Betsy had omitted to mention that her boyfriend joined her at night, sleeping, if it can be called sleeping, in her bed where, well into the night, they made sweet but noisy, music. Making me feel unsettled and unable to sleep, I had a quiet word with Mrs Mead, who offered me a superior room in her other house, with two divans on the ground floor, directly above her own flat, where I soon settled in. Poor old Betsy didn't take the news very well, blaming me for being unreasonable, crying all over the place, making me feel an absolute brute. We soon resolved our differences, and with no grudges between us, we remained good friends.

The longer I worked at The Cumberland, the more I was sure I wanted to become a model. Admiring customers frequently remarked I was wasting my time as a waitress, that I should find work where my looks would be appreciated.

I'd saved a fair amount in my Post Office account, enough to see me all right for a while, so I decided to bite the bullet and apply for a modelling course I'd seen advertised in the back pages of chic fashion magazines. When it came to leaving The Cumberland, I spoke to Mr Braed, telling him of my aspirations. He was shocked, saying, 'But you're one of my best girls! If you find it doesn't work out, come back, anytime.'

Working for J Lyons proved to be a happy time for me. Although it was hard work, I was treated fairly and with respect. One episode stands out. For many years J Lyons & Co. owned the catering rights for the Olympia Exhibition Centre in Kensington. In between exhibitions, they ran courses for their staff from time to time, on the finer points of dining. I was sent on the course during the snows of winter, enjoying every minute of learning the most fascinating things about the world of catering. During that week, I absorbed so much, it's proved invaluable to this day. My eyes were opened to the service of fine wines, where they originated, the correct wine with the correct course, where to place the correct glass, from which side to serve each guest, how to work from a silver service, how to keep on the move with several plates balanced on each arm. What an incredible week that was, almost making me want to go into catering. I've never lost those skills, using them to this day to impress friends who are amazed at my dexterity.

After researching the ads in the back pages of *Vogue* magazine, I was drawn towards the Helen Angel Model Agency, with its own training school, which, for a substantial sum of money, ran a six-week course for prospective models, the aim being to put successful applicants on their books provided they proved themselves to be up to the exacting standards demanded. The agency was situated two doors from Christian Dior's London showroom in exclusive Conduit Street; any Christian Dior connection spoke volumes to me. In such esteemed company, I must be onto a winner.

Without thinking to make an appointment, I went to the

address, where I cautiously made my way down narrow curving iron steps, to the basement entrance, and marched straight in. Helen Angel herself welcomed me. I had done the right thing, she assured me, an appointment wasn't always necessary. It so happened, I was the type of young lady they were looking for. A most successful mannequin herself in her younger days, adored by the greatest designers in the highest echelons of Paris, I must say she still looked pretty good for her age, with a chic hairstyle, only attainable by a person with years of experience and impeccable taste. She led me to a reception area, where breathtaking photographs of gorgeous girls in dreamy outfits adorned every wall, before my attention was drawn to a recent shot of film star Robert Mitchum posing on the beach at Cannes at the latest Cannes Film Festival. Standing behind a comely young lady, his hands are wrapped around the lady's ample but naked breasts. The photograph had caused quite a storm when it went to print, horrifying regular readers. Helen proudly informed me that the lady in question was on the agency's books. Not quite certain if this was a good or bad recommendation, I handed over £30.00 of my hard-earned money. I was eager to get my career underway.

Dying to tell Betsy my exciting news, as soon as I got home I raced next door to put her in the picture, only to find her news far more interesting than mine. She too had left The Cumberland Hotel and taken up modelling. However, the work Betsy was going to do was nothing like the work I aspired to. In fact, I was quite horrified when she filled me in with the details.

She was working for a photographic studio situated on Tottenham Court Road, and was one of several models whose job it was to sit in a small room waiting for any male passer-by wishing to photograph a glamourous model to walk in, no appointment needed. Some clients didn't own a camera, in which case they might hire one, but a number of these men had no interest in taking photos, only interested in watching a pretty girl prance about in a seductive outfit of his choice. The selected young lady would don the chosen garment, before leading the client to a room at the back of the building, set up with studio lights and various accessories to enhance the effect of these so-called artistic works.

The outfits to choose from were provocative – a cheeky housemaid wearing the shortest skirt, black stockings and high-heeled shoes, saucily peeking over her shoulder in an inviting manner was a favourite. A selection of seductive brassieres for the fuller-bodied models were always in demand, but most popular of all was a pretty girl dressed in a school uniform, pretending to be a naughty schoolgirl, dressed in the tiniest skirt, posing in titillating poses. Betsy was always asked to dress up like a schoolgirl, her insolent demeanour and mass of blonde curls reaping her rich rewards. The list of unusual requests was amazing, all designed to stir the male psyche. There was one regular client in particular, the sweetest, timid little man, whose ultimate pleasure was to sit quietly while pelting cream buns at her points of seduction for an hour, with no interest in photography whatsoever. To Betsy's way of thinking, cream buns were an absolute hoot.

It was with nervous excitement I arrived for my first day at the Helen Angel School of Modelling at Dineley Studios. Dineley Studios was a block of studios, situated at the top of Marylebone High Street, mainly housing rehearsal rooms for forthcoming theatre productions in the West End. Situated at a junction with Euston Road, which in the 1950s was a tranquil, tree-lined spot, but today, with endless traffic, it was a junction of madness.

Ten hopeful, would-be models registered, each one anxious

to learn the fine art of making the least appealing item of clothing look a million dollars.

The girls turned out to be a friendly bunch, but how some of them thought they could be models was a mystery to me, as only two of us were anywhere near the required height of five feet, eight inches. At the time, the average height of an English woman was five feet, three inches, the usual shoe size no larger than sizes three to five. When I bought shoes I found myself embarrassed to ask for size seven, considered exceptionally large, and invariably out of stock. On the fashion front, the name Eastex, catering for the five feet twos, were without doubt, the best seller in every classy store. Fashion shows were an important part of the changing seasons, especially in spring and autumn, when ladies wouldn't think of buying their new season's outfit before viewing the exciting incoming trends on attractive models.

All fashion shows featured one five foot, two model, but not many girls who could earn a living as a model, the exception being a girl of outstanding beauty, who might well reach the top as a cover girl, or by gaining a long-term contract with one of the top names in the field of cosmetics and beauty.

Getting to the nitty-gritty of why she had invested in so many shorter girls, Helen assured us it was possible to grow taller, by stretching. Our days began with exercises to that effect, the most important being to flatten one's back against a wall, before pressing the back of each hand as high as possible up the wall, then push, with every sinew in your body. The idea being to reach for a marked point on the wall, pushing, until unable to push any further, then push again.

Helen was fond of reminding us that the most successful models owned the catwalk. Without the ability to make the catwalk her own, she would never reach the heights. I particularly liked this idea. It must have been the show-off in me, to saunter along the catwalk, the world at my feet, while deep inside, I was terrified of tumbling off the end.

A poised lady must have the self-assurance to stride out while working a long, slim umbrella, very much à la mode in the 1950s. One, two, three steps, plop, one, two, three steps, plop, one, two, three, plop, all the way to the end of the catwalk, where, with confidence, one swung the umbrella under one's right armpit, before striking out confidently back to the start, ready to scramble into the next outfit. All hopefuls were allotted points for their prowess in working a long umbrella.

Helen's knowledge of the refinement of the modelling world knew no bounds, although, not once in my career as a model was I called on to 'work an umbrella.'

All prospective models were advised to keep a notebook throughout the course. After following this advice assiduously throughout the weeks, I never so much as glanced at it again.

The time came for Go-sees, where potential models were viewed by various wholesale companies, and photographers, always on the lookout for exciting new faces. Filled with dread, I made my way to the showroom of a run-of-the-mill, ladies' suits manufacturer, tucked away in a back street behind Oxford Circus. The moment I entered the premises I was overtaken by an overpowering odour, permeating from rail upon rail of utility grey suits, immediately causing me to sneeze and my nose to run uncontrollably, which I learned was an insect-proof spray, used to protect the important collection of suits from invading moths. Whatever it was, my eyes streamed, and my nose refused to stop sniffling, ruining my immaculate make-up. The boss, who'd been expecting me, suggested I try on a suit jacket, but try as I may to force my arm through the narrow sleeve, it proved impossible. I checked the size and found I'd been handed a size eight, whereas I was size twelve. Feeling foolish, I stood before the company boss while he regarded me, moving his head sadly from side to side, murmuring under his breath, 'Why did you do it? Why did you do it?'

I was a bit down after that but perked up when I arrived at my next Go-see in Great Portland Street, a fashion house specialising in the prettiest summer dresses, all with tight, pulled-in waists and voluminous mid-length skirts, dainty and very much the look of the day. Nervously entering the showroom, I was greeted by a young man, probably the boss's son, who selected a dress for me to try on, guiding me to the dressing room. As I was removing an item of my clothing, I became aware of the door slowly opening. Quick as a flash, I shouted, 'I'm not dressed yet,' At that, the young man replied, 'You won't do.' Hastily donning my own clothes, I stealthily returned to the showroom, and with no sign of the young man, I made a swift exit, glad to be out of that pickle.

My next Go-see looked more promising. A designer of glamorous lingerie, supplying only the most elite of London stores, such as Harrods and Fortnum & Mason, was in need of a glamourous model to demonstrate his exclusive range of lounge- and nightwear to valued customers for the whole of the following week. Helen felt I was ideal for this type of work, and recommended me to the chairman of the company.

The showroom for 'Ladies' Luxury Lingerie' was on the top floor of an address in Regent Street, high above the shops on the ground floor, with its constant parade of shoppers.

With my recent failures at the forefront of my mind, it was

with apprehension that I slid open the heavy gates of the tiny lift and went up to the top floor, where vast glass windows looked out on what appeared to be the whole of London. I was greeted by the owner of the business, Mr Goldberg, a wizened, extremely old man, retaining, however, a healthy head of thick dark brown hair, who welcomed me with open arms. Although I'd caught sight of a typewriter on desk in the distance, there was no sign of anybody else on the premises.

Mr Goldberg suggested we make ourselves comfortable by way of getting to know each other, before I modelled a selection of his star pieces. I must say, those garments were something to behold. Never had I imagined night clothes could be so luxurious, layer upon layer of floating featherlight glamour, with low seductive necklines. I had no choice but to remove my brassiere, in order to show them to their full advantage. I imagined myself as Rita Hayworth, floating down to earth, all the way from heaven, in that magical film *Down to Earth*. Mr Goldberg remarked that he'd never seen anyone show his collection so magnificently, insisting I take my favourite outfit home with me. Later that day, I heard from Helen. Mr Goldberg had spoken well of me, booking me for the whole of the following week for the vast amount of £25.00, subject to my paying her 10 per cent commission.

The following Monday, I headed for Regent Street, excited beyond belief at the thought of fulfilling my first booking as a paid model. Confidently slamming shut the heavy gates of the lift, I found Mr Goldberg at the door of the showroom, waiting to welcome me with open arms. He insisted on making us a pot of coffee, to relax me after my journey, was how he put it, before positioning ourselves on a comfortable double-seated sofa before a coffee table, fashion magazines and order books to hand. We sat chatting about this and that, with no sign of any staff arriving, and no telephone calls. Mr Goldberg insisted there was no hurry, but later on he'd like me to run through the complete range.

He understood that I was new to the modelling game, but did I realise that in the tough world I had chosen I would need protection? I'd never survive in such a jungle without protection. I assured him I'd be fine on my own, as my boyfriend was extremely possessive. Even though I had no boyfriend, it seemed wise to get that in. I'd need an expensive wardrobe for Go-sees, he insisted. I could hardly believe my ears. Was he putting himself up for the job? After breezing through the fashion show, being allowed to exhibit such delights had been a privilege in itself, I had never looked more attractive. Pity it was all wasted, with no customers to share the experience.

Mr Goldberg suggested I take my lunch break and to take all the time I needed, as he wanted me to buy a top-of-the-range outfit for Go-sees. With that he thrust a bundle of banknotes into my hand, and I was on my way to Dickins & Jones, a top-notch fashion store, a mere stone's throw from the lingerie showroom. By now, hungry as a horse, I took myself off to the self-service restaurant specialising in health foods, fancy salads, and that sort of thing. Strength renewed, I reflected on my good fortune and the morning's events. Had I imagined Mr Goldberg had suggested he be my protector? He was pretty ancient to be protecting anyone. I must have got the wrong end of the stick. Deep down he was probably terribly lonely, giving pleasure to people less fortunate than himself, providing him with a much-needed sense of fulfilment. Anyway, it was an unexpected pleasure to be searching for a Go-see outfit. How kind he was to consider my future. After browsing every floor, I chose a slender-fitting suit, designed to show off one's figure, as worn by a confident, self-assured woman of the world.

Mr Goldberg was thrilled with my purchase, bless him, saying, 'It won't be long before you're on your way to the top.' Taking my leave at the end of my first day, he packed me off with not only my new outfit, but weighed down by several carrier bags of heavenly negligees and loungewear.

My second day was much the same as the day before, with no sign of staff or customers, and the telephone hadn't rung, apart from a call from Helen, enquiring as to how I was getting on. Mr Goldberg sang my praises, which I found encouraging. Come midday I took my lunch break as instructed, along with a fair wad of notes, my aim being to accessorise yesterday's outfit, which meant a high-quality handbag, costing the earth, and the latest high-heeled shoes to show off my legs.

Back at the showroom, the boss was pleased with my acquisitions, approving heartily of my good taste, before surprising me with, 'Oh, by the way, I've made an appointment for you with my hairdresser on Saturday morning, at 10.30.' How marvellous to have my hair styled by a top-notch hairstylist, and how sweet of him to think of me.

The week continued in the same mode, just the two of us. Not once did I leave at the end of the day without that day's booty, and never had I been so spoiled.

It was mid-morning on Friday, when Mr Goldberg informed me we were to visit Paris the following weekend. Shocked and horrified, I responded with, 'I am certainly not going to Paris, or anywhere else for that matter. I told you I have a boyfriend.' At this, the poor chap got himself into a right old state, clutching my breasts, refusing to release me, leaving me with no choice but to give one almighty push whereupon he flew through the air like a feather in a breeze, landing on his poor back, just as his hair flew across the room, exposing a bony, bald head.

Not realising my strength, I rushed to his aid, gently guiding him to his usual reclining position on the sofa, making sure he was unhurt, before retrieving his hair, which I tried my best to place on his gleaming scalp, but for some reason, it refused to stay put, insisting on sliding from one side to the other, clearly in need of an adhesive of some sort. His pride terribly wounded, he hurled insults at me. 'You've taken me for a ride, no one's ever made a fool of me before.' Feeling it might be time to take my leave, I grabbed that day's goodies, and without waiting for the gated lift, fled down six flights of stairs, away from trouble.

It was later in the day I remembered my hair appointment for the next morning. I was a bit scared, but relished the thought of my hair being expertly cut. The salon, in Robert Adam Street, consisted of smart Edwardian Houses, many still private homes, all with black-and-white paved frontages, and small conifer trees, immaculate in their individual urns, just two minutes from the back entrance to Selfridges. Steadying my nerves, I made my way in, half expecting to be thrown out but relaxed a little on finding they were expecting me. The friendly receptionist escorted me to a single cubicle where I was introduced to my stylist, Richard, an older man of deferential bearing, who shampooed, then expertly worked wonders on my wilful mane. Delighted with the result, I enthused wildly until I heard that familiar voice invading my space. Mr Goldberg was in the next cubicle getting his wig attended to. I should think so too. Aware that it was high time I made an exit, I stumbled to the reception with a pounding heart, fully expecting a squadron of police to be standing by, waiting to arrest me.

Thankfully there was only the receptionist who'd welcomed me on my arrival. 'There is no bill, we're pleased to have been of service,' was the way she put it.

My next Go-see was to the fashion house Herschel, manufacturers of the highest-quality ladies' outdoor clothing, situated in the prime position of Bruton Street, in Mayfair, next door to her Majesty the Queen's couturier, Norman Hartnell, which tells you something. It was the preference of the head salesmen, Mr Edmunds, to work with his own personal model rather than use the in-house models, conveying her, together with his latest samples, to the customer, rather than have the buyer traipse all the way to Bruton Street.

I arrived at the simple but classy showroom, where Mr Edmunds greeted me warmly. After displaying several of his best-selling models, he said the job was mine.

It was at the House of Herschel that I learned I was the fortunate owner of ready-to-wear shoulders, designed to make the cheapest of coats and suits look expensive, acting much as a coat hanger, whereas girls with sloping shoulders were more suited to delicate evening gowns. Not once during my time as a model was I turned down by coat and suit manufacturers.

To my surprise, I'd landed the job. I was to start the following Monday at the amazing wage of £25.00 per week. In seventh heaven, I hurried home to share my good news with Mrs Mead.

The House of Herschel was without doubt the most exclusive company I'd been employed by. The following Monday morning found me trembling and dry-mouthed as I crossed the threshold of this celebrated fashion house, where the light from a huge chandelier cast its glow over the whole showroom even at this early hour, as though it were Buckingham Palace.

London

I shared a large dressing room with the house models who instantly made me feel at home, my shyness vanishing over coffee and biscuits, before it was time to apply our make-up in readiness for the day ahead. After an hour or so of small talk, Mr Edmunds popped his head round the door, requesting I be ready to leave in ten minutes. Carrying two designer coats over his arm, he ushered me to his car, parked directly outside the showroom (parking on Bruton Street was not a problem in the 1950s), then we were off to the Ladies' Designer Room on the first floor of Harrods where we were expected. I glanced at the display of the newest trends as we whizzed past, longing to take a closer look, but we were here to make money, not spend it.

In all such establishments, the top buyer of each department reigns supreme, her very presence oozing authority. Harrods was no exception. A straight-speaking, rather portly lady with greying permed hair, wished to get on with the matter at hand. I sensed she was not one to tolerate time wasters.

This formidable woman placed an order with Mr Edmunds before remarking on how well his new model displayed the garments. With success under our belts, we made our way to Harrods restaurant for a cup of coffee and a Danish pastry. Back at the showroom we did little for the rest of the day other than fitting new garments that had been sent up from the factory in the East End.

The following day ran on the same lines, except it was Barkers of Kensington on Kensington High Street that we made for, with a different selection of samples from the day before, Barkers of Kensington being less upmarket than Harrods. However, the Barkers restaurant was first class at the time, not only for excellent dining, but for the stunning views over the city from its famed position on the top floor. The remainder of the week followed a similar pattern, with visits to several other stores, where I noticed Mr Edmunds was frequently complimented on how well his model wore Herschel's quality designs.

On Friday morning Mr Edmunds brought up the subject of a spectacular show Harrods were presenting the following day in their exclusive Fashion Theatre at 11 am. He felt it would a good idea for me to see the cream of today's models strutting their individual styles. He would pick me up at an arranged time the following morning.

Wildly excited about the forthcoming experience, I waited for him that morning, and what a magical morning it turned out to be. I sat next to my boss during the show, as he pointed out the individual qualities of each flawless model strutting her stuff, every single one of them owning the catwalk in their own incomparable style, with not an umbrella in sight. Mesmerised by the perfection before me, it took a while to clear my mind, before I found myself entering a kosher restaurant in Poland Street in the heart of the rag-trade world, where I nervously joined my boss in devouring three courses of rich, kosher food, quite new to me, but delicious all the same. As we left the restaurant, Mr Edmunds suggested we go back to his flat for a drink. Alarm bells sounded, and quick as a flash I got in with, 'I've arranged to meet my boyfriend.'

Feeling pretty good about life, I arrived for work on Monday morning, only to have the wind knocked out of my sails when the secretary asked me to come to her office and informed me I was being dismissed, for lack of experience. I was to work the week out, finishing on Friday.

Stunned beyond belief, I realised why I'd been fired. What a dirty trick to play on anyone. Although I knew the reason why I'd been sacked, doubts began to creep into my mind. Maybe Dad was right, I was useless, nobody wanted me. Feeling small and insignificant, I longed to run away, but I had no choice but to sit the week out, with nothing to do but watch Mr Edmunds come and go, his merchandise slung over his arm.

Throughout my miserable last week, Mr Edmunds completely ignored me, never so much as glancing my way. Thankfully, the same couldn't be said for the rest of the staff, the house models in particular were sympathetic. My favourite among these ladies encouraged me to keep going, and move on. Never was I so relieved to see the back of a place as I was that Friday afternoon.

I took my dismissal from the House of Herschel much to heart, my inner doubts resurfacing. Who did I think I was? Was everyone thinking how ridiculous I was?

I found myself avoiding Go-sees, wilting away as I hibernated in various Lyons tea shops, drinking endless cups of coffee, terrified to pick myself up.

Altogether things had fallen rather flat, other girls felt I should look for another agent. It seemed my present agent was not highly thought of in the business. Eventually, I made up my mind to repair my shattered ego by working a summer season as a waitress at a seaside resort once more. Darling Mrs Mead urged me to follow my instinct, saying she would use my room for short lets until my return at the end of September, and not to worry about my belongings, she'd hang on to them in her own flat. Betsy's photographic studio were delighted to take my lingerie collection off my hands at an excellent price. I held on to my favourite negligee, because you never know, do you?

I'd managed to save a fair amount in my Post Office account, so with the money I made from selling my lingerie things were well under control. Once again I would aim for the seaside in glorious Devon, work the summer season, saving every penny, before having another go at modelling. Having made that decision, I revisited the friendly catering agency in Frith Street.

~ 11 ~

Saunton Sands

I was heading west, but this year I'd base myself on the north coast of Devon, at the remote but delightful Saunton Sands. As far as I could make out, there was nothing there but the Saunton Sands Hotel, an extensive, elegant, white-painted, art deco building set on the highest point of a sheer cliffside.

Rounding the final bend of the bus journey from Barnstable Station, I caught a glimpse of what appeared to be endless golden beach, enclosed by multitudes of grey-green grasses wafting in the breeze, beside mile after mile of soft sandy dunes, beside a calm blue sea, sparkling under the summer sun, without a soul in sight. A sense of peace filled my being. In this lovely setting, I would happily wait on tables.

The staff residence stood directly opposite the hotel, a smaller replica of itself, painted a dazzling white, each resident staff member having their own room, along with a comfortable sitting room where we could get together over a cup of tea, or anything else we fancied. It was altogether most welcoming.

The main restaurant ran the entire length of the hotel, each table overlooking a panoramic view of breathtaking surroundings, the sea lying beyond. Early mornings presented no hardship to me. I found the sights, sounds and salty air intoxicating, even on a dismal morning, when ill-tempered sea and sky presented a mystical glory of their own, especially when viewed from the safety of a panoramic dining room.

My fellow waiters and waitresses were made up of locals, and agency workers, such as myself. The waiter whose station was next to mine was an agency man, although I can't imagine how he landed the job as from the start, as he suffered from an affliction, most unsuited to our line of work. Murphy, an Irishman, well into his fifties, was unfortunate in that he trembled throughout his body, caused, I was soon to discover, by a deep-seated affection for whisky. The sound of trembling crockery and jingling cutlery echoed loud and clear, noticeably during early breakfasts, when few residents were fully awake. Many a guest, awaiting his bacon and eggs, would anxiously hold his breath until the moment of touchdown, ever thankful for a safe landing. For reasons unknown, nobody ever complained.

Can you guess who ended up serving two stations throughout that summer?

Murphy and I became the best of pals. I could never say we were close friends, as there was an elusiveness about him, best ignored. His home was in exclusive Hampstead Village in London, where he lived with his wife, personal secretary to the film star Elizabeth Taylor, who had divorced her first husband and was now married to the much older, English film star Michael Wilding, also residing somewhere in Hampstead.

Murphy's regular job was as a waiter at the Rembrandt Hotel, on the Brompton Road, close to Harrods, where he held his position all year, until the arrival of summer, when due to it being a quiet season in London, he was let go, returning for the autumn.

Saunton Sands

At Saunton, he kept regular hours, disappearing, as soon as each service ended to do his own thing, except for the odd afternoon when he accompanied me on the local bus into the little town of Braunton, to buy what he termed necessities.

I enjoyed my trips into town with or without Murphy, where I would enjoy a good rummage around the quaint little shops, ending my visit with a creamy Devon ice cream. Hardly venturing further afield, even with a free day each week, I contented myself by staying put. The kitchen made me a packed lunch, but in spite of my intentions to brave new horizons I hardly took advantage, finding myself content to munch my sandwiches on the beach below.

Alone on the beach, my poor old bunion, relic of Cumberland Hotel days, took comfort in the transparent lapping waves, a hundred tiny tiddlers nipping at my cooling toes in the vain hope of discovering something edible. On such afternoons, my heart sang, thoughts of London and modelling a world away. Yet I was aware that had I not had those dreams and aspirations, I wouldn't be cherishing these afternoons as I did.

It wasn't long before I took to exploring the whole length of the beach, starting with the sand dunes, amid miles of waving grasses, wild and free as the sea itself. On occasion, I met dog walkers making the most of such surroundings, their pets shackled by a tight lead, for fear of losing them down a thousand and one rabbit warrens among the dunes, dogs being prone to revert to their natural instincts when tempted, oblivious to their training by mere humans.

Later, as I returned alongside the sea edge, I might catch sight of the same creatures racing freely through unsullied sand, leaping in and out of the undulating waves, delighting in their new-found freedom.

With no let-up in Murphy's shaking, and me doing the hard work when things got busy, I devised a routine whereby he didn't handle any freshly prepared dishes, his task being to clear away between courses, when only elderly ladies of a nervous disposition might be disturbed by his trembling hands. Once we had this arrangement on track, things went swimmingly.

I managed to persuade him to join me on the beach now and again, to let the pores of his poor, clammy face respond to the healing sunshine, but he didn't relish these episodes, itching to get back to his room. You can lead a horse to the water but you can't make it drink.

Things continued in a relaxed manner until towards the end of the season, when it so happened, two American gentlemen arrived, and were placed at our stations for meals. Both were courteous to the staff and open in manner, as Americans are inclined to be. Somehow or other, Bart and Ben, with me and Murphy, formed a comradeship, the Americans, with their natural ease, managing to win Murphy over. Bart was the quieter of the two, tall, beautifully dressed, his understated poise appearing to be a happy accident, whereas Ben was shorter, a bit of a scruffy roly-poly, fair-haired extrovert, always on the go.

Like me, our friends loved the beach, especially having the place to themselves. Some mornings I'd spot them meandering along the water's edge deep in conversation, their socks and sandals strung by laces from their necks, as I, glancing from the window, diligently put a final polish to the wine glasses and cutlery in preparation for the lunch service, when, on the dot of midday, the door would crash open, exposing a charging army, famished as usual by the Devon air, in spite of putting away a hefty breakfast a few hours earlier. Murphy, always on time, did his best to assist with the rush, his clattering momentarily silenced by the commotion made by guests, who, not wishing to miss a thing, clamoured round the most popular buffet table, with its specials of the day.

Bart and Ben usually arrived when the lunchtime rush had eased somewhat. I noticed Ben was helping himself to smaller portions of late, probably encouraged by Bart who, keenly aware of his own image, was less greedy than his podgy friend.

Now and again the four of us would travel further afield, for a change of scene. On one such outing, we ended up in a pretty place called Lynmouth, on the north edge of Exmoor, bordering onto the sea, I was especially interested in this part of the county as Dad, now the owner of a caravan, sent me postcards of places where he, Edna, and dog Vaggy, spent their favourite weekends. I knew he was especially fond of this part of Devon, as I frequently received cards from Lynmouth. I was pleased to learn he was enjoying his new life, but surprised they would dare to tear themselves from their beloved Emmanuel Church quite so often.

It was during one such outing, while gorging on delicious Devon Cream Teas, it hit me in a flash, I was falling in love with Bart. Hardly able to believe my heart, it was simply that he was perfect in every way, just the kind of man I longed for.

I confided in Murphy. He seemed to think nothing good would come of it and recommended I put such thoughts out of my mind, it was just a whim which would blow over once I was back home. What did Murphy know of a woman's passions? Time rushed by, soon it would be time to leave, and there was me becoming more and more obsessed with my perfect man. I found it almost impossible to get to sleep. If love was supposed to make you happy, it was a failure as far as I was concerned. Transformed from a cheerful outgoing person, I'd become a bundle of nerves, my mind focused on one thing, my beloved.

As our departure dates drew closer, Bart asked for my phone number, as we'd already decided to meet up for lunch in London. Surely, this was a sign my feelings were reciprocated. I phoned Mrs Mead to sort things out for my return. Unfortunately, she had let out my room until the day after my return. I said not to worry, I'd find a way round it somehow or other, anyway, I was dying to see her, to fill her in with all my news. It so happened that Murphy's wife would be away for a few days, so I could sleep on his sofa. Problem solved.

~ 12 ~
London

A short taxi ride saw Murphy and I outside his garden flat, an unexpected pleasure. What must have once been a family mansion was now divided into a number of apartments, with Mr and Mrs Murphy owning the whole of the ground floor, including a terrace, and a fair section of the beautifully maintained garden, the interior, clearly in the taste of a woman whose home was her pride and joy. Standing at various points of the delightful sitting room I couldn't help noticing a number of silver-framed photographs of Elizabeth Taylor in the company of an older woman, clearly a close friend, who I rightly took to be Murphy's wife. Musing over what kind of woman would be married to Murphy, I didn't have to wait long to find out.

Enjoying the luxury of a lie-in, I found myself rudely brought back to reality by a stream of foul-mouthed abuse coming from the mouth of a sturdy, mature woman, barging into the room where until a few minutes ago, I was lost in the land of nod. Slowly coming to my senses, the woman asked no questions but repeatedly screamed at me to get out of her house. Murphy eventually surfaced, but, scared out of his wits, could offer no explanation as to my presence. The furious woman really had it in for me, never letting me get a word in, but Murphy, by now terrified, was of no help. I reasoned the sooner I left, the better chance I had of staying alive, so putting my mind to that purpose, I calmly, gathered myself and my belongings together, meanwhile the frenzied female turned her attention to her husband, while I made a dash for it. Somewhat shaken I reasoned it was small wonder Murphy couldn't stop shaking. I, too, might be drawn to a wee dram or two, if I was married to such a harridan. With no idea where I was going, I followed my nose to the nearest bus stop and jumped on the next bus that came along. Luck was on my side when I found myself dropped off at the end of Claverton Street.

Fortunately, I had a telephone extension in my room, meaning, personal calls could be put through. Sure enough, Bart called within a day or so to arrange our get-together. On the appointed day I made the short trip to an address in Hertford Street, just off Park Lane, a classy gentleman's club, where I was expected, then escorted to an upper-floor apartment by a courteous, well-suited young man. Excited to see each other, we three exchanged enthusiastic hugs, thrilled to be in each other's company following those weeks of comradeship in glorious Devon. Murphy wasn't included in this get-together, which came as no surprise. He was quite likely doing penance for imagined misdemeanours.

My friends were staying in what appeared to be an exclusive, private apartment, with a comfortable lounge, a dining room, and a bedroom, which I didn't enter. Easing myself into an armchair, the eerie silence of the club made it feel more like a Sunday than mid-week in the heart of a churning city. Bart set about making us real American coffee, while Ben and I relived our exploits, so recent, but now, seeming a lifetime ago, including my tale of Murphy's wife, which the boys found highly amusing as did I, looking back from a safe distance. As Bart, always the perfect gentleman, refilled our coffee cups, he reached over Ben's shoulder in such a familiar way, I knew without doubt, it was Ben he loved, not me. Shaken to my core, I made every effort to hide my feelings. After making the necessary adjustments to my thinking, we made our way to a first-class restaurant, where, much to my surprise, with a heady glass of wine inside me, I felt as free as a bird. The remainder of the day was spent enjoying each other's company, vowing as we parted to always stay good friends.

On my return to the city, I missed Saunton Sands more than I believed possible. Now it was down to the real nitty-gritty, but with my savings, I could relax a little and hopefully see more of Mum. Mrs Mead reminded me that having a double room, I was entitled to have a friend to stay at any time.

My next job was a permanent position in a family-run business, Glenmore Sports, that manufactured mid-priced ladies' dresses at a dreary factory in Whitfield Street. This narrow side street ran parallel to Tottenham Court Road and was only yards from Heal's, the furniture store for the mega rich, loved by newlyweds for its ultra-modern, mainly Scandinavian, designs costing an arm and a leg. Prices then were well out of reach of the average buyer as is still the case in the year 2025.

A nine-to-five job, the only thing in its favour being the Number 24 bus which picked me up from the bottom of my road and dropped me off right outside Heal's, where a minute later I was inside the factory. I went to meet the family, an elderly couple who ran the factory side of things, and their two sons who, I learned, spent most of their time on the road, bringing in the business.

I modelled a few dresses, which looked as good as they could, thanks to my ready-to-wear shoulders. Pleased with the way I showed off their designs, they signed me up on the spot, arranging for me to start the following Monday at 9 am. The showroom was to be my office, situated at the factory entrance, an isolated position where I hardly saw or spoke to a soul, the exception being business calls on the phone, as I was to act as a secretary, dealing with all telephone calls.

Another means of keeping me busy was by button making. Most of their clothing included matching buttons, made of the same fabric as the dress, considered a touch of class in the 1950s. It was my job to form these buttons by cutting out small circles of the original dress fabric, before placing two of the said pieces over a small brass ball, then fixing the item by way of a heavy, powerful vice which squeezed the two together, the vice remaining a permanent fixture on my desk.

Winter was fast approaching, and to say I was unhappy was an understatement. From time to time I found myself called upon to try on a new sample, but it was a rare occurrence; usually I sat at my lonely desk making buttons, for which there seemed to be a never-ending demand, or I was kept busy on the telephone. Always relieved when my lunch hour arrived, I might cross over to Heal's to gaze at the tempting displays of modern furniture in their window displays. I admit to succumbing on the odd occasion to one of their scrumptious hot chocolate drinks, served in the special drinks bar, where, taking my place on a stool, I supped from a long slender glass, while enjoying a dainty chocolate wafer served alongside.

I couldn't afford to spoil myself at Heal's too often, but luckily, I'd found a café right next to the factory where I could buy a cheese roll and a hot drink, before parking myself on a bench in the teeniest patch of parkland between Tottenham Court Road and Whitfield Street, while feeding hordes of London sparrows and pigeons with what little was left over of my cheese roll.

At the end of the working day, I'd join the scramble for the Number 24 bus, longing for the friendly comfort of my room. I knew I was being taken advantage of at work, and knew I could do better. I reasoned I'd be happier back at The Cumberland Hotel rather than working my butt off for very little reward, so I handed in my notice.

Another birthday rolled around on 13 November 1954, making me nineteen years of age.

Things began to perk up for me about this time. Strolling the streets one day, I came face to face with a colourful street hoarding. Mecca Dancing, famous leaders in the popular world of ballroom dancing, with dance halls in every major city in the country, were to present the 1955 Miss England, Beauty Contest, at their prestigious Lyceum Ballroom in London the following June. The memory of the elderly lady breakfasting at The Cumberland Hotel suggesting I should enter a beauty contest came to mind, encouraging me to go for it.

Area heats were to be held at their leading dance halls nationwide, starting shortly in London, before working their way up and down the country. With nothing to lose, I knew I had to have a go so with fortitude, I set about planning my campaign.

The first thing I did was buy myself a top-notch swimming costume, the simpler, the better. I was aware the exclusive Parisian store, Galeries Lafayette, had a branch in London's Regent Street. Their swimsuit range was highly thought of in the fashion world for its range of French swimwear. What could be more suitable? It wasn't long before I hopped on a bus to Regent Street. It must have been my lucky day, as there was just one, crystal white, one-piece swimsuit in my size, the price horrendous, but with my confidence riding high, I made the purchase.

It occurred to me, a suntan would be just the thing to show off the simplicity of my white swimsuit. With the finals in early June, I would be unlikely to have gained a suntan naturally, but I felt the matter to be of prime importance. Back in my Cumberland Hotel days, I'd sometimes looked in the window of a ladies' beauty salon in Wigmore Street, behind the back of Selfridges, and it was there I went, seeking advice.

I knew as soon as I walked in, it would be an expensive business, but after going over my plans with the professionals, they too became excited by the idea. The manageress suggested I undertake a course of sun tanning treatments, but that was way out of my league. After much discussion, we concluded that the best thing would be for me to rent a tanning lamp at a special rate, for a long-term rental. I sat before that lamp for forty minutes every day, ten minutes on each section of my body, front and back, wearing goggles to protect my eyes, making the procedure extremely difficult as I could hardly see a thing, but I never missed a session, no matter how exhausted I might be at the end of a working day.

Keeping an eye on my funds, I popped in to see Betsy, to see if she had any ideas as to how I might earn money. As always, I found her in the devil-may-care mood, still happily working at the walk-in studio, raking in cash while steadily acquiring a string of private clients. Explaining my situation, she suggested I call on a reputable agent in Springfield Road, in Paddington, who represented the cream of artistic commercial photographers, whose speciality was the female nude. Trying to cheer me up, she asked if I fancied a weekend in Brighton. One of her regular clients, an elderly man, now retired from the legal profession, regularly booked her for a whole weekend, staying in his magnificent mansion, dining at the most exclusive restaurants, generally spoiling her rotten, all together an absolute sweetie. All he required was she cut a dash by posing on a ladder in his extensive library, donned in the briefest of titillating outfits, with the tiniest skirts and high-heeled shoes, her impish grin playing a vital role, as she scoured the shelves for a particular book, while he directed proceedings, taking dozens of images from the comfort of his director's chair. He especially liked her to take a friend along, that way they might well explore play-acting, making full use of the ladder, adding versatility and humour to the proceedings. Quite certain her client would adore me, what did I have to lose? After all, he was incredibly generous. Yet once again, I told my friend, that wasn't the line of work I had in mind, but I would contact the agent in Paddington.

Winter was well known as a quiet time in the life of a freelance fashion model, everything slowing down in the run-up to Christmas, then dead as a dodo throughout January, so I took myself off to Paddington, as Betsy had suggested. There I met a businesslike woman in her mid-fifties, a nice enough person, whose name I've long forgotten, who signed me to her agency. Dealing only in high-quality work, she handed me a long list of the rigid rules applying to glamour work, the principal one being, photographers were not permitted to touch a model, under any circumstance. She felt certain that as a model of quality, I would be in great demand, working only for the best.

Would I consider a regular position as the regular model for a leading camera club in the Stockwell area? Arrangements were made there and then for me to attend the camera club the following Thursday evening for a trial run, leading to a weekly position if we hit it off. I set off on the following Thursday evening, nerves jangling, for my first session as a life-model.

Stockwell was an easy spot to reach from Pimlico, my fears being eased by a lengthy stroll along the Thames Embankment in the early autumn evening, my carefully tended hairdo, soon ravaged by the wildest winds, dashing to the pavement the last leaves of London's plane trees. At Vauxhall, I took a bus to Stockwell, and within minutes I was at The Oval Underground Station. Taking my life in my hands, I raced across a convoluted junction, where I almost fell into The Brixton Road Photographic Studio, situated beneath a sweetshop. My nerves mysteriously vanished the moment I entered the premises, whereupon I found myself heartily welcomed by a charming middle-aged man, the club secretary, who after making me a cup of tea in a mini kitchen, showed me to a small, well-heated room, where I set about repairing my battered locks, before removing each item of clothing – the last thing anybody wanted was the imprint of underwear on such precious skin – then speedily taking refuge in my own dressing gown and slippers.

Shortly, my new gentleman friend tapped on the door, inviting me to take up my position in the studio, where a small stool, draped in black velvet, stood in the centre of a simple set-up, where I was invited to take up my pose before a group of men of various ages. Removing my slippers and allowing my dressing gown to fall, I took up a simple but graceful pose, which after adjusting to my satisfaction, caused a buzz of approval, heartening me somewhat. The group's leader offered various ideas as to the positioning of banks of studio lights before welcoming the opinions of eager students.

I purposely observed the reaction of a group of men to having a live woman posing naked before them, but with their minds on more important matters, there was not a flicker of interest, other than the placement of light on my body. Under the subtle gaze of these avid would-be expert photographers, a model was an object, she might as well be a block of wood, the only thing concerning them was how the light might fall on the subject. I found taking up a pose the most natural thing in the world, instinctively falling into natural positions. The enthusiasm of the photographers rubbed off on me, and I learned to love my Thursday job, earning enough to cover a week's rent.

The Helen Angel Modelling Agency kept their models supplied with an up-to-date list of clients, such as fashion houses and photographers constantly on the lookout for new faces. I thought I'd spend some time doing the rounds. One afternoon, while covering the Soho area, I called on Gordon Hireson, a photographer based in Gerrard Street, Soho, never dreaming that Gordon and his wife, Miriam, were to become my lifelong friends. In the early afternoon of that grey December day I pressed the bell of Number 41, bringing to the door a smiling fellow, who welcomed me inside. From that moment we were pals. There was nothing pretentious about Gordon, what you saw was what you got, which meant I felt at ease.

A tall, fit man in his late forties, he specialised in glamour work. Throughout the 1950s, there was demand for swimwear-clad, attractive young ladies, wearing white, high-heeled shoes to grace the covers of light-hearted newspapers and magazines, influenced, as always by Hollywood, where pin-up girls and starlets wouldn't dream of posing in anything other than beachwear, and high-heeled shoes. With time, the trend would move on to the kittenish look of France's Brigitte Bardot, in her miniscule bikinis, but for now, the demand was for a beautiful woman in a well-cut swimsuit.

Making myself at home in Gordon's office, I ploughed my way through piles of magazines and newspapers featuring his images, recognising high-quality work when I saw it. After chatting for some time, Gordon proposed we have a coffee at a popular spot further along Gerrard Street. Gordon was to keep me working on a regular basis, and it wasn't long before I became used to seeing my own face smiling down on me from newsagents' shelves. Before long, we were meeting every day, when work permitted, except for weekends, when he returned to Miriam, and their home, a family-sized, static caravan, at Burnham on Crouch, in Essex.

Having a true comrade with mutual interests, with no funny business on the side, provided with me with routine, and the support of someone who believed in me. Spending time around the coffee bar for hours, it became clear our friendly coffee shop was a meeting place for resting entertainers, actors, singers, all types of showbusiness hopefuls. It was only when cast as James Bond that I recognised Sean Connery as one of a regular group monopolising the same corner day after day with the as yet unknown world-class singer, Shirley Bassey.

From time-to-time Miriam, Gordon's wife, would spend a day in London, the three of us meeting up at the studio, before treating ourselves to a gourmet lunch. Miriam was a gentle soul, completely bewitched by her husband's models, emulating them with not a hint of resentment. Her main interest was making her own natural beauty preparations, mostly based on honey, quite tasty when planting a quick kiss on her rosy cheek on meeting.

Throughout that winter I was to spend many happy weekends in their convivial company, snuggled into a feathered eiderdown in their cosy caravan, between lengthy walks alongside the River Crouch, where resting small boats huddled tightly together, waterproof coverings protecting them from the many ill-tempered onslaughts the blistering Siberian Winds might have in store.

With the arrival of the new year, it was time to think of the first heat of Miss England, 1955, scheduled to be held in late January at the Tottenham Mecca Dance Hall in North London, an area unfamiliar to me. On the evening of the contest, I felt relaxed, having undergone my usual session with the sun lamp, in spite of there being no sign of the slightest tan as yet. The Northern Line tube whisked me through the winter darkness, to emerge some time later into the bright lights of outer London. The dance hall was already heady with young people, keen, it being a Friday evening, to enjoy the fruits of their week's labour. Directed to the back entrance, I joined a band of other would-be Miss Englands. The twenty or so other contestants were a friendly bunch, most of them familiar to the World of Beauty contests, knowing each other from previous years, chatting and exchanging plans for the upcoming season, when they'd be doing the beauty rounds. On the whole they weren't too threatening to my chances, but there were a few dark horses like myself, new to the game. The old-timers spent an age getting ready, involving coiling lengths of artificial hair into a coronet and placing it on the crown of the head, the idea being, to convey sophistication. Those with long hair might thread it through with flowers or ribbons, thus suggesting a beach belle. Quite a number did an excellent job of smearing their bodies with some kind of tanning lotion, whereas we newbies presented ourselves as nature intended, with very little artifice. As the time neared for us to exhibit our various assets, each girl was handed a number to be attached to her wrist, and then it was on with the parade. Before the off, the judges were announced. There would usually be a well-known comedian, sure to be a character off the television, together with the local mayor, or a counsellor of some importance, a film actor or actress of distinction, and a representative of Mecca Dancing.

When it was my turn, I sauntered up and down the catwalk with none of the flaunting thrown in by the regulars, walking tall, with a happy natural smile. By the end of the evening I was thrilled to be placed second, the winner, a petite, well-endowed, blonde. It didn't take me long to realise, comedians always went for busty little blondes.

It was roundabout this time I received a booking from my new agent to work alongside two of her illustrious figure models, for *Health and Efficiency*, an artistic magazine featuring a section of society preferring to live without clothing, believing it to be natural and health-giving. I'd frequently glanced at copies of the magazine in WH Smith over the years, the cover invariably featuring several well-built attractive young women in a natural outdoor location, far from prying eyes, their faces directed towards the sun. I was to meet up with two models at an appointed spot at Victoria Station, at an unspeakably early hour, before taking a train to Dorking in Surrey, where we would be met by the photographer and his crew.

On the appointed day, the radio advised that snow was on the way, reaching South East counties by late morning. Approaching Victoria Station with a biting wind already making its presence felt, I feared we were in for a tough day. After meeting up with my partners in crime, we grabbed a steaming drink, before boarding the train, transporting us like lambs to the slaughter to meet our fate. Before pulling into Dorking Station, I'd already noticed the odd fluttering snowflake, confirming our fears. We were met by

London

a young male photographer and his two assistants, a male and a female, each broaching their concerns about the weather, as we piled into a people carrier taking us to a familiar parking spot, somewhere outside of town. Luckily, we parked at an official stopover, with all the amenities, including a service station with café attached, open all hours for the use of lorry drivers, hill climbers, and such. The photographer advised us to grab a hot drink and use the toilet, while we had the chance, before taking to vaguely visible hills in the far distance. With the weather closing in, it was thought best to get the job under our belts as soon as possible. As we ascended, the sun taunted us now and then, giving us false hope, but to no avail, as nearing the point we were heading for, I caught sight of the first prancing snowflakes.

After parking at an isolated spot, which on a lovely day would have been delightful, but today declining to display its charms, the three workers, raced off to select hopefully, a sheltered position, as by now, not only had a cruel wind whipped up, but snow clouds were becoming increasingly ominous by the minute.

Apart from facing the elements there was nothing required of we three models, but to relax in the warmth of a running engine, prior to facing the real thing, somewhat later. I'd recently taught myself when facing a daunting prospect to empty my mind completely, removing my mind from my fears. Using this self-taught technique at the appropriate moment enabled me to perform calmly, which in years to come became a form of meditation.

On the occasion at hand, when called forth, we girls put a brave face on things, making a mad dash for the set-up in the distance, where our three stalwarts waited, teeth chattering, noses streaming, frozen to the core. Flipping into action, I played my part without a care in the world, embracing the elements, joyfully facing the heat of the sun in the spirit of the exercise, as did my workmates, professional to the end.

Knowing he'd got some great shots, the photographer rushed to pack his equipment away, while we naked girls tore back to our friendly van, where, with the vehicle's engine still running, our lifeblood slowly seeped through our bodies, until, with time, my burning feet were part of me. We all knew the session had gone well, but with the snow settling in, it was thought best we make a prompt descent. In no time at all, our carriage was hurtling crazily round by now hazardous bends. With luck on our side we made it to the car park, our first call being the café, where the warmth, together with a well-earned bowl of piping hot soup, gently eased us back into the real world.

The next day, I recounted our exploits to Gordon. He was of the opinion it was a hell of a nerve getting girls to work under such conditions, after all, we might have caught pneumonia. I reminded him that we girls were naturally well upholstered, and anyway we were being well paid for a quick dash through the snow. I must say, the day had been tremendous fun.

Recently, Gordon had searched out another coffee house to ring the changes, although nothing could keep us away from our regular haunt for long, with its showbusiness ambiance. Rather than turning left on leaving the studio, we turned right and wandered through a maze of interesting lanes leading onto busy Charing Cross Road. Each of these cut-throughs were fascinating, each with its own charm. This section of Charing Cross Road specialised in the sales of rare antique books, with quite a few smaller shops selling paperbacks tucked away in our cut-throughs, the cheapest being in the basement.

London

Before long, I was rummaging through the poetry section of one such cubbyhole, vowing to return when I had more time to browse. The busy shortcuts were home to a selection of bric-a-brac stalls, as well as the usual essentials, such as a chemist and newsagent. Best of all, our latest coffee house wore a friendly face with its stream of regulars rushing to or from nearby Leicester Square Underground Station, at the start or end of their working day. Our new find soon became our second home from home, a special port of call.

Always held on a Friday, the day arrived for the second heat of Miss England, which on this occasion was to be held at Mecca Dance Hall on Streatham High Street, in South East London, another area unfamiliar to me. Less nervous this time, I settled into the lengthy bus ride, indulging in my habit of daydreaming, or feasting my eyes on the latest ladies' fashions, a favourite occupation of mine now the shop windows were permitted to light up in the evenings.

The bus drove through the High Street where it was impossible to miss the evening's venue, due to the flashing neon lights, blaring music, and the din of the enthusiastic queues, all wishing they'd just get on with the show. By now I was getting the hang of things. Making my way to the stage entrance, I slipped into the routine like an old-timer, acknowledging the regulars on my arrival. Already working on their well-lacquered immovable hair, piled high on their heads, their one-piece swimsuits fashioned like tightly fitting corsets, always worn with white winkle-picker shoes, with such spindly heels, it was surprising they didn't break their necks. There were homely young girls as yet lacking polish, learning the ropes, the usual round-up of bosomy blondes, and interestingly, as last time, several dark horses, any one a possible winner.

The judges were of the same ilk as last time, only today a comedy double act, fresh from their recent television successes, already somewhat overacting while providing customers with a hefty slice of their routine. Soon we ladies were off on our usual routine, the enthusiastic audience routing for their favourites, the regulars running slickly through their routines, not a sign of a nervous twitch among them, a few newbies wobbling unsteadily on the unfamiliar height of their heels, and as before, a selection of real beauties, any of whom might be the winner. That evening I was awarded third place.

The following day I put Gordon in the picture, regarding the results of the contest. All he ever said was, 'Don't worry your head about it, you'll be all right.' After putting the world to rights over our usual refreshments, he returned to his studio to photograph a young lady for one of his regular clients, leaving me with time to scour a few of the specialist bookshops. For reasons unknown, I made my descent to the poetry section, tucked away in the basement of a dingy building. Time flew, as I flicked through works I'd adored back at school. About to take my leave, I almost missed an old edition of *Palgrave's Golden Treasury*, tucked away on a low shelf. Miss Miller reckoned you couldn't go far wrong if you choose Palgrave, a good all-rounder for inquisitive minds. At a reasonable price I bought it, and straightway became emotional about the teachings I loved, which I'd neglected of late what with all the running around and leading such a helter-skelter life.

Clutching my memories to me I moved on to the cubbyhole bookshop I'd vowed to return to. Finding myself alone, I settled myself in, before exploring the shelves of well-worn early paperbacks. There were biographies galore in that tiny den, but what should my eyes light on, but an early edition of William Wordsworth's

London

poem 'The Prelude.' I'd read snippets of this enchanting tale back at school, but here was the complete book, battered though it was. Trembling with emotion, I related my story to the shop owner who seemed to understand my excitement, and for just a half-crown that grubby little book became my champion. In times of loneliness or in need of courage, my roughed-up companion was sure to be tucked away somewhere about my person.

Time marched on, and it was soon time for the third heat of Miss England, this one to be held at Mecca's show place, the Lyceum, on the Strand, a famed old theatre, and Variety Palace. My mother, fascinated by the whole thing, was to stay with me for a week. Having seen little of her lately, I was surprised by how excited I felt, as I picked her up from the Green Line Coach at Victoria Station. After settling her in, I introduced her to my landlady, who invited us down for a good old cup of strong tea. The two of them were like peas in a pod, and it wasn't long before the house was alive with raucous laughter. It did me good to see Mum so happy, I don't believe there was much laughing back at Chiltern Close. The next day I took her to meet Gordon, moving on to our coffee house with its mixed bag of theatricals. There was no doubt about it, my mum was a true Londoner, being her real self when mixing with her own kind. With my time devoted to her, we caught up with a few of the latest films, too often reverting to being childish, one starting the other off, giggling guiltily, tears rolling down our cheeks, attracting whispered complaints from other patrons. It never went as far as being thrown out, but we came close thing on several occasions.

Friday was the big day. Apart from my usual ritual, I thought I'd have a go at fixing false fingernails, as worn by several of the regular contestants. I'm ashamed to say, I was guilty of the childish habit of nail-biting, most inappropriate for an aspiring Miss England. What a hassle those nails turned out to be. Why had I started it? By the time we left home, my hands were a disgrace, and by the time we reached the Lyceum, three nails had mysteriously vanished, leaving the fixing glue a sticky mess, picking up any grubby mite floating in the night air.

Being Mecca's Prime Dance Hall, the evening was more of an occasion. Already heaving with fun-loving crowds, we pushed our way to the stage door, escaping into the allotted dressing room near the back door. The evening ran on much the same lines as before, although in vast and more prestigious surroundings. Once more the judges were made up of the usual line-up, on this occasion including the actor Tom Conway, popular star of *The Saint*, solver of crimes, a well-loved character in the cinemas throughout the 1950s. Tom was blessed with a caustic wit, bringing humour to the role, much in the sardonic style of George Sanders, his real-life brother, a major Hollywood name.

There were more entrants in the contest this time, perhaps due to being held in the West End, but essentially it was a replay of the usual routine, with me being placed second, having remembered to keep my three disgusting sticky fingers tucked well into the palms of my hands.

The actor was accompanied by his agent, a heavy-breathing, rotund gentleman, who'd taken a shine to me, heading swiftly in my direction as soon as the presentation was over. Reunited with Mum, the agent whose name I have long forgotten, introduced us to Tom, suggesting there might well be a part for me in the new *The Saint* film, being filmed at Shepperton Studios. By the end of the evening I had an appointment to attend the gentleman's offices in elegant Hanover Square, the following week.

London

It was a joy to find Mum and I got on so well. Always happy in each other's company, she relaxed in my company, as did I in hers. A born Londoner, she should never have left the city. Her idea of heaven was to while away the time in the bustling surroundings of busy coffee houses, enjoying a cigarette or two in the company of mad-cap Londoners like herself. I had noticed she didn't turn to alcohol as she did back home. One small sherry in the early evening sufficed, though she was partial to a lager, around midday.

With Mum back in Berkhamsted, the day arrived for my appointment with Tom Conway's agent. Arriving at his smart office, on the top floor of an impressive address overlooking Hanover Square, with Vogue House directly opposite, home to the ladies' fashion magazine of the same name. Welcoming me with open arms, I was surprised to find him alone in these impressive surroundings, where we sat chatting for some time, before he suggested we avail ourselves of a first-class lunch, before getting down to business. Finding the two of us chest to chest in the tiny, gated lift was a little too close for comfort, with me breathing a sigh of relief on reaching the ground level without incident. A short walk led to the swing doors of the renowned Claridge's Hotel, where we were welcomed by a smartly uniformed doorman. After making a trip to the palatial ladies' rest area, where a young lady handed me a warm towel after washing my hands, I returned to my escort waiting in the foyer, who'd already ordered an aperitive in the bar, leading me to partake of a glass or two of champagne, which on reflection was an unwise move knowing how inclined I am to become wildly talkative, whenever I imbibe without discretion.

We were to dine in the grill room, to which the head waiter escorted us in due course.

Pretty from the Outside

Our food was served from a trolley, each item covered by a silver salver, by willing waiters with all the time in the world, unlike the mad house that was Cumberland Hotel. Eventually my host called for the bill, and this is when I started to panic. Suppose he expected me to pay my half, or even worse he might call for payment of a different kind.

Emerging from the sanctuary of the hotel, the shock of the hectic world struck me. At that moment I could think of nothing I'd like more than to find myself cocooned within the comfort of its womb-like security, for ever.

Back at Hanover Square, we eased ourselves into the over-friendly lift, me fearful as to what lay ahead. Back in the comfort of the office, still with no sign of another human being, I nervously pursued a line of small talk, waiting for the expected pounce, which eventually happened, but was such a feeble attempt that all I had to do was persuade the gentleman I wasn't that kind of girl, offering to pay for my lunch, praying inside he wouldn't accept my offer. Following a lengthy talk about this and that, I realised he was a kind, but lonely man, long past his days as a Lothario.

Before I left he insisted the film role was still on, his office would soon be in touch. Fully expecting that to be the last I'd hear about it, much to my surprise I was contacted within a few days with full details. I was to report to Shepperton Studios on a certain day, to play the part of an air hostess in the forthcoming *The Saint* movie, for a fine sum of money.

On the morning of my acting debut, I woke up feeling sick with nerves. Completely new to the film world, especially with a speaking part, I couldn't believe my luck. Although to be honest, I wasn't the least bit interested in acting, all I cared about was looking glamourous, like the Hollywood stars.

London

It so happened I had a most enjoyable day, starting in the make-up room, where I found myself placed in front of enormous mirrors surrounded by light bulbs, their brilliance highlighting the many flaws in my naked complexion. Things were much improved once the make-up expert and the hairdresser had worked their magic, leaving my skin seemingly flawless, my shoulder-length hair dressed in the elegant style of a 1950s Pan American Airline hostess. Pan-Am girls were renowned for being easy on the eye. Sitting next to me, waiting for her hair to be dressed, was the leading lady, an up-and-coming actress, Jill Ireland, who made me feel welcome. Jill was to make quite a name for herself in this country, almost a full-blown British star, before departing for Hollywood, where she married the American actor Charles Bronson, living there happily, until she died of cancer in 1990. I was terribly upset, especially when I recalled her natural kindness, and the way she put me at ease me that day.

The young male lead was Richard Thorp, who during his later years would make his name as the landlord of the Woolpack, in the long-running ITV soap opera, *Emmerdale*. Tom Conway was as always his laissez-faire self, with perfect manners towards both the hierarchy of the studio and those of lower order.

My big moment came after we returned from lunch. The scene was set in the interior of a Pan American aeroplane, where the Saint is flying to the United States on a major assignment. The hostess passes through the centre aisle offering various titbits, pausing when she reaches his seat to ask, 'Are you comfortable, Sir? Is there anything you'd like?' With that, the camera moves slowly down my body, the focus lingering on my legs. The naughty Saint runs his eyes over my shapely calves with his trademark quizzical raising of one eyebrow.

Pretty from the Outside

My day of glory was soon over. While visiting Mum a short time later, I noticed the film was showing at Berkhamsted's Court Cinema, so we took ourselves to view my shining moment, which, much to my surprise, wasn't bad at all. Tom Conway's agent went on to send me a handsome cheque, along with a film clipping of my first speaking part, today tucked away in a box in the attic.

My last chance to gain a place in the final of Miss England rolled around, this time being held at a Meccas Dance Hall on the outskirts of London, where I came second, meaning I had no place in the final.

A bit down in the dumps, I tried to get back to normal, although for reasons I didn't understand, and tedious as it was, I continued my daily routine with the sunray lamp.

Meeting up with Gordon was comforting. As my greatest fan, nothing would convince him I wouldn't be Miss England, 1955. With no sign of that happening, I'd accepted a six-week modelling commission with a foremost designer based in Hanover Square, starting in early June. Meanwhile, once evening set in, back at my room it was to Wordsworth I turned, starting with the first section of 'The Prelude,' Childhood and Schooling, memorising special passages, the ones that spoke directly to my heart, particularly the scene where the young Wordsworth takes a boat out on a lake just as darkness is falling. A threatening black cliff looms suddenly overhead, filling him with such a sense of ominous doom, he races home in terror.

I loved too, the magical skating scene, filling me with joy, causing my whole body to tremble, plunging me back to my years at Longfords Mill, when I was the owner of a thousand woodland nooks and crannies. With the beauty of Wordsworth's words in my life, I could tackle anything.

London

Strolling around the streets of Soho with Gordon one day, we caught sight of a poster announcing that Mecca Dancing were running a photographic section of the forthcoming Miss England Contest, inviting young ladies to enter by posting a recent photograph of themselves wearing a one-piece swimsuit to an address in London. With any luck there might be a chance for me after all.

Gordon was thrilled to bits, agreeing to take the photograph in the studio, where a few days later I arrived with my immaculate white French costume, matching winkle-pickers with the latest spindly, four-inch stiletto heels, my shoulder-length brown hair glossy and gleaming with health. Being a simple shot, the operation was soon behind us, Gordon, wanting to bring me luck, insisted on completing the necessary paperwork, then posting it with our chosen shot to Mecca's Head Office. Breathing a sigh of relief, with everything now in the lap of the Gods, we were free to return to our regular pursuits.

With Whitsun Bank Holiday only a fortnight away, Gordon suggested I spend the weekend with him and Miriam at their caravan, where, if the weather allowed, we could spend our time taking shots on the beach, and around the more interesting sailing boats. Having no reply from Mecca Dancing, and the contest less than a week away, I took it that I was out of luck and put my mind to enjoying the Whitsun weekend with my friends.

On the Friday of our departure, I met up with Gordon as usual, this time laden with all I needed for a weekend's work, the weatherman having promised sunny weather over the whole of the Bank Holiday weekend.

Blessed with the sunshine we'd been promised, we worked from morning to evening, taking short breaks to eat or laze around

Pretty from the Outside

in perfect conditions, the sun bringing forth from my head to my toes, front and back, a golden tan, with no sign of burning.

At last I was reaping the benefit of all those hours in front of the lamp, Overnight, I'd turned into a sun-kissed maiden.

I've never forgotten that weekend, made even more perfect when I arrived home on Monday evening to find lying on my door-mat a telegram informing me that I was the winner of the photographic heat of Miss England 1955. Would I present myself at the Lyceum Theatre Ballroom, stage door entrance, at 2 pm the following Wednesday afternoon, to take part in the final?

On Tuesday morning I reported for my six-week booking in Cavendish Square, confessing to having to take the next day off. When Mr Shine, the boss, heard the reason, he became as excited as me, as were his employees, to think such a notable happening could be taking place in their corner of the world.

The next day I spent the morning preparing myself for what I deemed the most important day in my life. After all the winner goes to New York then to Hollywood, of all places. No false nails, I'd learned my lesson and had been making a supreme effort to stop my childish nibbling. Already my nails looked half decent. Who would believe a sophisticated young lady would bite her fingernails down to the quick?

Arriving at the Lyceum, it was a relief to find I wasn't nervous. With things happening so speedily, the reality hadn't yet sunk in, so I took the whole thing in my stride. In the changing room, the thirty or so entrants were making their usual preparations, immaculate hair styles and artificial tans. A number of the regulars pounced on me, demanding to know how I'd managed to get such a fantastic sun tan. Feeling guilty for some unknown reason, I put it down to the sunny weather over the past weekend which up to a point was true, but I wasn't about to let them in on my secret.

I was asked to hand over my evening dress in order to run an iron over it. There had been no mention in the telegram of an evening dress, causing me to panic, until someone came up with the idea of borrowing the dress of the singer who sang with the dance band in the evenings. Luckily that solved the problem; the dress was a perfect fit, and nicer than anything I owned.

Each contestant was issued with a wristband with her number attached, mine was number fourteen, to be worn on the right wrist throughout the proceedings. With that it was on with the show. Off we sauntered in order of number, until an unnerving sight hit me. Beyond us, almost hidden in the murky darkness, a dozen or so frozen faces sat behind a lengthy table, eyeing each girl from top to toe as she showed herself to her advantage, the powerful stage lights focused solely on we hopeful Miss Englands.

The time came for us to parade individually, and this I approached like a lamb to the slaughter. After completing my round, one of the judges requested I repeat the exercise, as my shoes didn't do me justice. Knowing my legs would look their best with as much height as possible, I completed the second round on tiptoe, bringing the house down, lightening the mood. After a period of discussion among the judges, the list of hopefuls was reduced. Luckily, I was still in with a chance, and after much discussion among the judges, the list was cut to four girls, three being the first three, the other girl, unplaced. Having made the cut, we four faced individual interviews with a nice young man off the television, whose name I've long forgotten. The time arrived to reveal the winner. I stood silently as the forth and third places were announced, aware I was either the winner or unplaced. An announcement came over the loudspeaker, the most unanimous decision they'd ever had, the winner was Number Fourteen.

I remember checking the number on my wrist, and sure enough, I was Number Fourteen, Miss England 1955.

From that moment, with newspaper reporters and newsreel cameras closing in on me, who should appear from the back of the crowd but Gordon, yelling above the din, 'I told you, didn't I?' Then it was up to the roof of the Lyceum, where I continued smiling for eager photographers, until it was time for serious matters.

Hearing that London's leading model agent, Eddy Franklyn, had been one of the judges, my reaction was one of relief. If I'd known beforehand, I would have been even more scared, and what's more, he was anxious to sign me to his agency. Eve Arden, another judge, was to become a good friend. As the senior representative for Max Factor Cosmetics in England and head of their Showcase Beauty Salon in New Bond Street, she taught me the finer art of applying make-up, loading me with all the costly creams and potions a girl might need for a year, presented in a cream-coloured, leather vanity case, which was to accompany me on my many travels.

In the 1950s, a parent's permission was needed to obtain a passport up to the age of twenty-one. Brian Martin, high up in the Mecca team, had been assigned to take care of me, insisting we speak to my father right away. My heart sank. I was certain Dad would never give his permission for a daughter of his to parade around in a swimsuit in public. We called him right away, finding him confused and complaining the phone had never stopped ringing, with endless calls from newspaper reporters, what was going on? That evening Brian and I drove to 21 Thaxted Road, bringing me down to earth with a crash, remembering so many unhappy episodes connected to that address. I'd taken my presentation floral bouquet for Edna, hoping the gesture might help things along. Thank goodness for Vagabond, now a magnificent full-sized golden retriever, who, although months had passed since I last saw him, hadn't forgotten me. Edna said from the moment they told him Margaret was coming, he'd not left his position at the window where he'd kept an eye out, leaping to his feet as soon as I emerged from the car. Brian went through the day's events with Dad, explaining why I needed a passport. At this, Dad's religious beliefs took over. He wasn't sure he approved of a strange man flying across the world in an aeroplane with his daughter, he must ask the Lord's permission. I speedily got in with, 'We're in a dreadful hurry, Dad,' but he was adamant. Without the permission of the Almighty, he wasn't signing anything. Longing to die from shame, I knew what we were in for. Making a reverent sign of the cross, Dad invited us to kneel on the floor, while he had a word with his Lord, with me panicking, sensing we were in for one of his theatrical outbursts. Pleading with the Lord for divine protection of his daughter, things rose to a crescendo, verging on heartrending tears, making me squirm. I'll say one thing for him, though. Dad could give the great Shakespearian actor, Laurence Olivier a run for his money. Finally satisfied with his performance, Dad signed the necessary papers, leaving the two of us completely ravaged, longing for our homes.

Brian was keen for me to familiarise myself with the bus route to Mecca's headquarters in the London borough of Southwark, and from there he would accompany me to get my passport sorted out. On the bus the following morning, I was forced to battle my way to the front in order to get a seat. Passing by rows of passengers I couldn't help but notice the number of open newspapers, all featuring photographs of me. Unable to stop myself, I blurted out, 'That's me, that's me in that photo.' The whole bus stared as if I'd lost my mind, but nothing stopped me telling all and sundry that was me in their newspaper.

After signing a few papers at Mecca's headquarters, Brian drove me to the passport office, which in those days was in Petty France, nothing to do with the country of France, as far as I could make out. My papers had been finalised in advance, so all that was needed was my signature and I would be free to travel the world.

Then began a period of racing all over town. A visit to The Eddy Franklyn Model Agency was my first port of call. Eddy, a jovial, silver-haired man soon put me at ease. After signing me up, he told me of various things he had lined up for me. The following Saturday evening I was to appear on the television show *In Town Tonight*, broadcast weekly, live from the BBC television studios at Lime Grove Studios in West London, featuring people of interest who happened to be in London that weekend. On the evening in question, a chauffeur-driven car transported me to the illustrious television studios, from where I was escorted to a reception where my two fellow guests were already relaxing over a tipple of some sort. Being an avid film buff, I recognised them as film stars Derek Farr and his wife, Muriel Pavlow, from the many British films they'd starred in, usually as a team. At first I felt overwhelmed to be appearing on the same show as these highly respected actors, when all I'd done was be pretty. With the downing of a glass of sparkling champagne I soon discarded such negative thinking, and as for my companions, they turned out to be normal people, with no airs and graces, and by the time we went on air, we were like old friends.

The Miss Universe Contest was several weeks away, launching

in New York, before the major opening took place in Long Beach, California.

Meanwhile, Eddy had booked me for a top-notch job. *Picture Post* magazine were organising a cruise centred on five models. We girls were to be flown to the South of France, before boarding a sailing yacht in Monte Carlo Harbour, where we were to spend twelve days cruising round the Mediterranean, spending time at celebrated ports of call, presenting fashion shows of swimwear at each resort, while being on call at all times, by the great Bert Hardy, *Picture Post*'s senior photographer, renowned for being one of the first photographers to enter Belsen concentration camp in the final days of the war.

I had my work cut out, rushing around town, having fittings with several designers, each a part of a team working on my wardrobe for my forthcoming American experience, when I would be representing my country. My main relief was meeting up with Gordon at every opportunity.

During this busy period, I was constantly in touch with Mum, our happy summer as waitresses in Devon seemed like a lifetime ago, but in reality was so recent. My landlady, Mrs Mead, proved a staunch ally, as always. I don't know how I'd have managed without her friendship. One problem she sorted out was that of nuisance phone calls. Some fellow had managed to get hold of my phone number, persisting in calling endlessly with the suggestion, 'Margaret, may I talk to you about your bust?' I, being rather naive, slammed the phone down whenever I heard his voice. He called one day when I was out so Mrs Mead took the call. On being told I wasn't at home, he suggested as I was not available, might she be willing to talk about her bust. Quick as a flash, she replied, 'If you saw it, you wouldn't want to talk about it.' With that, my admirer was gone, never troubling either of we ladies again.

It was about this time, some bright spark advertised nude photographs of the current Miss England for sale. It could only be someone from the camera club, and it could only be the most innocuous images. Mecca, however, were concerned, fearing I might have to resign my position. Who should come to my rescue? None other than the greatest star in Hollywood at the time, Marilyn Monroe. It so happened that in her youth Marilyn had posed naked for a series of glamourous shots, aimed at the calendar market. At the time, it was unheard of for a star of Marilyn's magnitude to pose naked. Marilyn was to break the mould. When asked why she'd resorted to doing such a thing, her reply was that she needed to pay her rent. Asked if she'd had nothing on at all, she replied, 'Yes, the radio.' The bigwigs at Mecca concluded, 'If it's all right for Marilyn, it's all right for our Miss England,' thereby putting an end to the kerfuffle, much to my relief.

In order to enter the USA, it was mandatory to have a smallpox jab, so I made an appointment with my local doctor. It was a matter of a mere scratch on the arm, over in a flash, but as I left the surgery, I crashed to the pavement and knew no more. The first thing I was conscious of was waking up in a strange bed, with no idea how I'd got there. Before long, a kindly woman came to check on me and told me I had fainted on the pavement, where a passing pair of sturdy workmen had carried me to the flat above the surgery, leaving me in the caring hands of my saviour. After a hot cup of tea and a biscuit, I began to feel the lifeblood returning to my limbs, and after resting awhile, the doctor came to check on me. It seems I'd had a good reaction to the jab, which was preferable to coming down with the real thing.

Summer raced by, and soon it was time for the *Picture Post* cruise. The days before leaving were caught up with a hundred last-minute chores, including returning the sunray lamp to the beauty salon on Wigmore Street, for which I'd paid several times more than the price of a new one, but without resentment, as I reasoned it had served me well.

Finding myself near Cavendish Square, I called on Mr Shine, the gentleman I'd let down by winning my title. Delighted to see me, he'd found a model to replace me, although he insisted no one could take my place. I couldn't help but notice, he forgot to mention the priceless publicity gained for The Shine Fashion House by having himself featured in every newspaper the day after the contest.

From there I met up with my loyal friend, Gordon, and for a while we settled back in our comfortable routine. Where would I be without his steadiness and sheer common sense?

～ 13 ～
Monaco

The day dawned for my first flight on an aeroplane, as well as the first time my feet would walk on foreign soil. I was seen off by my dear landlady and her faithful gentleman friend, in a gleaming, chauffeur-driven limousine, on route to pick up the other four models, all based in Central London. I already knew one of them, a slender blonde beauty, Jean, the girlfriend of Stirling Moss, the great racing driver, who, sure enough, would be at the airport to see her off, and one of the first to pop up as soon as we arrived in Monte Carlo. The other three models were Jackie, a gorgeous redhead, and Eloise and Charlotte, both slender, high-fashion girls.

With more excitement than I'd experienced in my nineteen years, I stood in line on a breezy gangway, my attention drawn to the whirring of the four engines of the powerful beast preparing to transport its human cargo high above the scudding white clouds and into the blue beyond.

Finding myself separated from the others, I tucked myself away towards the back of the plane in my personal window seat. Eventually, the moment of take-off arrived, intense moments as we gathered speed, climbing higher and higher, until reaching the desired height, before quietly levelling out. I looked down on the map of London and surrounding green countryside, with its small towns and villages, the speed of their passing a reminder we were hurtling through the atmosphere. The blue sky took on a deeper hue than I was used to, a new moon flirted high in the heavens, and before long our captain announced we were flying over the Alps, the peak of Mont Blanc to our right.

Passing over Paris, I indulged in a hot meal, accompanied by a small bottle of champagne, causing me a few emotional tears, as I dwelt excitedly on my good fortune. Soon, we were passing over the city of Marseille, where we began our approach to the Côte d'Azur, following the coastline, its mountainous terrain littered with luxurious creamy white villas, rising high above sea level, each with its own palm-strewn garden hosting an elite blue swimming pool, with bikini-clad beauties making the most of their blessings.

In a short while we landed at Nice, where the runway edged alongside crashing breakers, almost scaring me to death, fearful of ending my days in a watery grave, but the captain of course avoided catastrophe, and I perked up no end, as I descended from the cool aeroplane into a blanket of intense heat, such as I had never experienced, before reuniting with my workmates.

We were to spend two nights in the celebrated Hotel de Paris in the tiny country of Monaco, before boarding the yacht *Bonaventure* in Monte Carlo Harbour.

In our air-conditioned limousine, we eased our way along the breathtaking coastline to the splendid city of Nice, where we drove through the elegant Promenade des Anglais, stretching for several miles alongside a pebbly beach crowded with sunbathers and swimmers. Leaving the city behind, we were soon passing roadside fish restaurants, their tables sheltered from the sun by huge conifers, as were crowds of oleander bushes, their rosy blossoms relishing the borrowed shade.

Local fish was prepared and grilled beside each table, making it impossible, as we passed by, not to catch a whiff of locally caught specialities enhanced by the herbs of Provence, whetting our appetites.

Monaco was still a relatively small place in 1955. The steep hills on which it was set, host to magnificent private villas with lovely grounds, tranquil reminders of the days when the Côte d'Azur was looked upon as a refuge from the harsh northern winters, due to the all-year clemency of its climate.

There were as yet no skyscrapers in Monaco. All that would change with the arrival of Princess Grace the following year. The Monaco Grand Prix was world-renowned for its annual car race, and to a lesser degree, The Monte Carlo Rally, but soon, peace would be shattered in the tiny principality by towering cranes constructing high-rise blocks of stylish apartments, shooting up into the sky seemingly overnight, as would acres of land reclaimed from the sea, on which to develop more apartments and hotels, completed by newly designated sandy beaches. I was fortunate to have experienced the charm and character of peaceful old Monaco before the bulldozers took over.

We girls were delivered to the sumptuous Hotel de Paris in the late afternoon, where we rested in the awesome reception, where obliging staff darted here and there with our luggage, referring to each of us as Madam. After being shown to our adjoining suites, we agreed to meet up in the bar later, before dining in the calm of the dining room.

After settling into my suite, I thought I'd enjoy a stroll. The hotel stood on one side of the central garden square of Monte

Pretty from the Outside

Carlo, its beautifully tended grass surrounded by borders of lush geraniums, alternating in shades of crimson and white, the official colours of Monaco. On the right of the square the casino ruled, a commanding sight, probably the most visited spot in the principality. I'd long known the song 'The man who broke the bank of Monte Carlo,' but I shouldn't think that occurred too often these days. From the casino I sauntered along a parade of splendid jewellery shops, every item in their windows the real McCoy. I stared in disbelief at the designs of Cartier, Van Cleef and Arpels, Tiffany, Harry Winston, names I'd heard of but never imagined I would see. A single solitaire of solid perfection set in a platinum ring, clusters of smaller stones reflecting from a dainty bracelet or brooch, all magnificent, designed, I imagine, to snare some lucky gambler wishing to impress the lovely lady on his arm.

Following such excitement, I took myself to the Café de Paris, opposite our hotel, known locally as the hub of the world, where I took a frothy coffee, before thoroughly spoiling myself by reading that very day's English newspaper, flown in specially. Returning to the hotel, I stood waiting for a lift, when, blow me down if I didn't spot more showcases displaying exquisite jewellery, placed either side of the two lifts? Indulging in my latest passion, I took longer than intended, almost making me late for my meeting with the girls.

I woke to a wet Sunday morning, the splendour of the previous day having departed overnight, leaving a murky morning of drizzle and low swirling mists. Unexpected as it was, it came as a hard lesson. Things aren't always as they seem, as the old saying goes, 'into each life some rain must fall,' but why must it arrive in Monte Carlo, today of all days? I might just as well be in Bognor. What a spoiled brat I was becoming. I must take myself in hand

and learn to count my many blessings.

We'd been expecting to visit the yacht prior to boarding it the following day, and relieved to find the meeting postponed, I thought I'd go sight-seeing. With no sign of the others, I draped myself in the slight item of protection I'd thought of packing.

Climbing the steepest steps upwards in the by now driving rain, the mountains above invisible, draped as they were in a cloak of fog enveloping all we stalwarts, working miracles on my complexion, it's an ill wind that blows nobody any good. It wasn't long before I found myself in Beausoleil, on the border of France, with its jostling street market.

I'd always loved street markets, and this one proved a treat, plump fruit and vegetables gleaming with drops of rain. Although food rationing had finally ended at home in 1954, there was nothing to compare with the quality of the produce of this French market.

My mouth watered at the thought of sinking my teeth into the luscious peaches, the size of which I'd never seen before, and shining rosy apples, the likes of which I'd last seen back in Gloucestershire, but who needs fine fruits when they're dwelling under the roof of Monte Carlo's Hotel de Paris? Entranced by the locals, happily ignoring the weather, outgoing and noisy, no cheeky stallholder could pull a fast one on them, being more streetwise than any buttoned-up Englishman. Back at the hotel, I dried myself off before meeting the rest of our team.

Apart from we five models, there was a charming if rather quiet man named Frederic Mullaly, in his forties, a journalist and public relations officer. Then there was Bert Hardy, the world-famous photographer; today, the top man of *Picture Post*'s photographic section, very much an easy-going person and one of the boys. The captain of the yacht was an attractive young man whose name I've forgotten, very much a hit with one of our ladies. I recall regular scuttling back and forth under the cover of night, but I won't snitch as to which lady it was. The remainder of the crew we would meet when boarding the next day.

~ 14 ~
Côte d'Azur

It was a mellow dawn, with no sign of yesterday's watery tantrums, a cloudless blue sky reflected by the calm of a still sea sparkling with a million winking diamonds. This was more like it. The rains of yesterday had served their purpose. Without the rain, where would we grow the delicious, squelchy figs, those run down your chin, and juicy peaches, one noisy slurp, then a hasty swallow, just the thing on a sweltering day.

Later that morning, we ladies were driven the short distance to the harbour where we boarded the vast, elegant sailing yacht, *Bonaventure*, where each girl claimed her allotted cabin below deck. As we arrived, I noticed a section of the deck set out for lunch. This would become the regular dining area for we girls to lunch, the boys joining us in the evenings.

We were to set sail the following morning, so until then we were free to relax on board. Our living quarters were comfortable, each of the main party having their own cabin. A fine chef lived on board to conjure up light lunches and dinners, it being essential not to be sleepy, with Bert always hovering somewhere in the background, ready to pounce with his handy camera hidden somewhere about him.

Thus began my first taste of 'Days of Wine and Roses.' Our first port of call would be Saint-Tropez, recently made popular by its links to film star Brigitte Bardot, the world's 'sex kitten.' A beautiful young girl with extraordinary sex appeal, she shot to fame for the way she wore a bikini. In 1966, she was to earn her place as a first-class actress in the film *And God Created Woman*, directed by her then husband, Roger Vadim. Brigitte would soon become as big a name as Marilyn Monroe, which was no mean feat at that time. What's more, Brigitte is still alive, doing good deeds, which is more than be said for poor Marilyn.

Our departure from Monte Carlo was something to behold. Our amazing crew manoeuvred the splendid *Bonaventure* from the security of its resting place, gently guiding her from the harbour of Monaco out to the open sea, where with sails aloft, I took in the true splendour of our home. Later, while lazing on deck, I daydreamed as to what it would be like to own such a yacht every day of the year. Draped in a glamourous caftan of silk, I'd waft from hammock to chaise longue, iced champagne in hand, pausing now and then to glance at the latest fashion magazines from Paris, featuring next season's, too divine, must-haves.

Saint-Tropez

On arrival at Saint-Tropez harbour, our crew worked their magic once more, making sure we were well tucked into our allotted position among the large boats, and we were then free to step on shore.

Saint-Tropez was fast becoming the jet set of the rich and famous, due to the presence of Brigitte and her entourage. The young, beautiful and wealthy flocked here in their desire to be in the swing of things. As we stepped ashore I couldn't help but notice the bikini-clad beauty of the young, both girls and boys were wearing what appeared to be a couple of mini handkerchiefs knotted together on their equally slender hips. The girls were without exception petite and perfectly formed, unlike we English girls who seemed to be naturally gigantic by comparison. The boys were all gorgeous, with their manly attributes barely hidden from view. Back on English beaches, it was still common to see youngsters in their old-fashioned, woollen, one-piece garments, guaranteed to sag unattractively the moment they entered the water.

By now desperate with hunger, we piled into a pleasing restaurant on the seafront, grouping ourselves in the shade, eating wisely, knowing we'd be having a first-rate meal later in the day, but I admit letting rip on the rosé wine. Meanwhile Bert inched his way around the tables with his camera so sneakily, we were hardly aware of his presence, although he refused, what he called, poncey wine, preferring to stick to a good old bottle of beer. In most ports of call, we girls set up a swimwear show in the late afternoon, but we missed out today, after overdoing it a bit on the rosé. Besides, there was hardly any point in a swimwear parade in Saint-Tropez, just like there's no point in taking coals to Newcastle. Exhausted after a most agreeable day, we meandered back to base where each of us took a timely doze, in preparation for dinner on deck.

The Cruise

We were soon off again, this time to Santa Margherita, a small Italian fishing port. I loved these mornings, when lost in my own company I relaxed on deck in the cooling breeze, marvelling at the splendour of the ever-changing coastline. Vibrant bougainvillea, in shades of deepest purple through to the palest pink, cascaded over the roofs of tiny white villas, protected from the elements by jutting rocks overhead, their vivid turquoise doors and shutters reflecting the blue of the sky.

Following a short walk around the town of Santa Margherita, we lunched in the central square, where I would happily have spent longer but Captain's timetable decreed we depart for the nearby fishing village of Portofino.

As early as 1955, Portofino had moved on from its humble beginnings and had become a fashionable retreat for the rich and famous. After docking in the pretty harbour, among a number of handsome yachts of varying sizes, we wandered to the piazza, a small cobbled square edged by an abundance of seafood restaurants and fashionable boutiques, all framed from above by a harmony of tall pastel-shaded houses towering against the skyline.

It was in the friendly atmosphere of the piazza that we girls set up our first outdoor fashion show, as directed by Freddy, the art director. It turned out to be a light-hearted affair, drawing interest from holidaymakers.

From Portofino, the *Bonaventure* sailed alongside the Italian Riviera, each port of call more stunning than the last. Sadly, all good things must come to an end, and soon we had to face reality. Our final stop would be the port of Sanremo, close to neighbouring Ventimiglia, with its Friday outdoor market, considered by authorities in such matters to be the market supreme. We girls thought we'd while away the day at this happy hunting ground, hoping to find special items for loved ones back home. Bert accompanied us, camera in hand, always on the lookout for something a bit different. While ambling towards the din of the market, we found ourselves almost swept off our feet, when out of nowhere the *carabinieri*, bells wildly clanging, pulled up beside us.

Côte d'Azur

It appeared that one of our number had broken the law. I could see no point in these chaps shrieking hysterically in a language we didn't understand, distraught as we clearly were. It took a passer-by who spoke both English and Italian to sort things out. The wrongdoer was me. Apparently, I was committing a gross offence in the eyes of the Italian law. By wearing shorts, I was exposing my legs to all and sundry on the open highway, would I cover myself immediately? Fortunately, we were about to enter the market, so I begged the officer in charge to allow me time to buy something suitable to cover my offending limbs. Feeling like a criminal, it had never crossed my mind, in the 1950s, that Italy was such a God-fearing country. How could they account for all those saucy films I'd seen back in Watford?

Deemed suitably attired by the *carabinieri* after buying a brilliantly patterned large scarf and knotting it daintily on one hip, I was allowed to enter the market, secretly thrilled to think my legs could cause such a kerfuffle.

Dealings with the police behind me, I was free to roam at will. We girls soon became separated in the hustle and bustle, as we were drawn towards our separate interests. Every corner exuded tons of *joie de vivre*. Whenever I find myself in the vicinity of an open market, my spirits soar. Even in murky old England I feel the same, as cheerful marketeers and customers alike forget their inhibitions, each one (as someone wiser than me once declared) playing their part as on a stage, for what else is life but a performance? Especially congenial when finding yourself in a lively open market on a glorious summer day in the company of friendly Italians.

Before long, I found myself in massive food halls, where hefty Parmesan cheeses were being rolled about, one cheese being enough to feed an army. Whole sides of smoked gammon swung from hooks above the customers' heads. Fortunately, shoppers weren't obliged to buy the whole animal, but could select a section according to their needs. It seemed a family would buy a six-month supply, returning to replenish when stocks ran low. Endless yards of pasta draped from above, and judging by the amount one family bought, they must gorge on pasta until it comes out of their ears. The soft fruits of the region were a delight, just looking at them was a pleasure. Mind you, our Cox's Orange Pippin back home take some beating, to say nothing of Bramley cooking apples, packed with Vitamin C, oven baked, before a tablespoon of golden syrup is poured over them, and what can be more enjoyable than a succulent Comice pear, come autumn?

It was time to think of presents. Back home, Gordon was a fine cook, but I didn't think he'd appreciate endless skeins of pasta, so I made my way to the other side of the market, but not before pausing at the treasure trove of colourful plants. Hydrangeas in heavenly colours from icy blue to deep purple, each plant expertly potted, waiting to be transported to someone's terrace.

After several more distractions, I finally reached the section of the market specialising in more expensive items. The first thing my sharp eyes hit on was a stall selling real leather handbags, the quality of which I'd never seen before other than in London's Bond Street. Having been warned to beware of market goods, I was on my guard, but on close examination the handbags bore the imprinted name of Gucci and were in the best of taste, so I succumbed. After all, I'd spent my money on an absolute classic which would take me anywhere, all the way to New York, then on to California. I found several ladies' items I knew Mum would love. She was so funny, her preference always being the clothes I chose for her, wearing them till they fell apart. For Gordon I chose a selection of Italian glamour wear for young ladies, as he could never have enough girls' bits and pieces for his work.

At last I made my way back to the harbour, making sure I was decently covered, delighted with my acquisitions, and looking forward to my last evening on board the *Bonaventure* in the company of the group.

London and then back to Cannes

As soon as I reached home, I excitedly recounted the exploits of the cruise to my lovely landlady and her gentleman friend, but was surprised when she told me that my agent was desperate to talk to me first thing on Monday morning about an urgent booking for the coming week.

It transpired I was to leave that evening for the South of France, with a master of beauty photography, Basil Sturgeon. Renowned the world over for the quality of his work, he was also well known in the gossip columns for his connections with several titled young ladies, debutantes, fresh from the season, on the brink of forging their way into the world of desirable society.

He was to pick me up at my home at 6.30 pm. The gentleman in question turned up in a tiny, open sports car, in which we were to drive through the night to Cannes, hopefully arriving in time to get some work in the next day. Basil turned out to be a long-haired hippy, well into his fifties, I should think, scruffily dressed in the briefest shorts, shabby, clumpy footwear, sporting a bandana around his long greasy hair. After depositing my suitcase in the back of the car, he started the car up, the exhaust delivering several unwilling explosions, before charging through London as if his life depended on it, aiming for a small airport on the south coast, where he'd booked a carrier flight to France at 9.30 that evening. A crazy driver in an open tin box, with no such thing as a seat belt, they hadn't been introduced yet, I took my life in my hands, as we tore through the streets of South London.

We made it to the airport, with just enough time to digest a sandwich and polish off a cup of coffee, before diving onto a small plane, where we remained seated for the short flight over the English Channel. Sitting in such close proximity, I was forced to recognise that Basil wasn't fresh about his person. On closer inspection of his features, it was clear to see his face hadn't seen a flannel for some time, and his rumpled shorts and grubby T-shirt indicated he'd left in a hurry. Pondering things for a while, I was well aware I was inclined to judge harshly; maybe circumstances had been against him.

Once we landed, we tore through northern France, our lives in his hands. I figured I might as well forget the forthcoming Miss Universe Contest. They'd be sending for my runner-up if things carried on the way they were going. Through the streets of Paris we careered until, without warning, we found ourselves stuck in a track in what appeared to be an isolated field. I froze, fearing the worst, when amazingly, he adjusted his thinking, and before long we were back on track, travelling at full speed on the main route to the south, when a sharp shriek rang through the night air, 'Take the wheel, take the wheel!' Having never had anything to do with a steering wheel, what on earth was I to do?

Still the cries rang through the darkness, 'For Christ's sake, take the bloody wheel!' In desperation I leaned across his body in an effort to stop this flying machine lurching from one side of the road to the other. After what seemed like an eternity, having adjusted his bandana to his satisfaction, he regained control and

Côte d'Azur

on we sped.

The sun was rising above the horizon as we neared the city of Aix-en-Provence, where even at this hour there was no mistaking the pungent odour of the Conifer Forests, for which the Alpes-Maritimes was famous. The last hour of our journey was a pleasure, with Basil, quite likely exhausted, travelling at a more reasonable speed. With any luck, he'd need to rest after our crazy journey. Our destination being Cannes, though just a short distance from Monte Carlo, couldn't have been more different in character. Even at this unearthly hour I couldn't miss the sense of youthful *joie de vivre* filling the air, quite unlike the regal solidity of wealthy Monte Carlo.

We were to stay at the famous Carlton Hotel on the popular La Croisette, where the 'in crowd' paraded day and night, their sole object being to see and to be seen. The sandy beach opposite our hotel was an equally favoured spot, much in demand for attracting names of consequence in the world of film.

Exhausted, on arrival, I was shown to a dazzling, en-suite apartment overlooking the sea, and Basil's suite was several doors down from mine. By promoting the hotel with his first-class photography at no charge, he and a guest were permitted to stay at the hotel for free, if rooms were available.

I didn't hear from Basil that first morning until lunchtime, when he called my room suggesting we meet up for a bite to eat. We sauntered along La Croisette with its many enticing eating places, alternating with high-quality shops, many selling ladies' beachwear and loungewear. The number of shops aimed at fashionable young men was an eye-opener for me, as back home in the 1950s, the male species was, by comparison to the female species, very much the underdog.

Pretty from the Outside

We settled on a welcoming restaurant where, after consuming a first-class meal accompanied by a glass or two of local wine, I relaxed, without a care in the world.

Basil suggested we take some shots on the beach, the light being perfect. I perked up no end, I loved my work, and that's what we were here for.

Time flew as we lost ourselves in our work. I, being a non-swimmer, was in no danger of drowning, the seawater being calm and with no tide to speak of. Revelling in the splendid conditions of that afternoon, I couldn't help but recall the icy blasts of England's east coast, always invigorating, but compared to the standards of the Côte d'Azur a true test of one's modelling skills.

The next morning, the weather still glorious, Basil decided we'd travel to a location familiar to him. After driving for some time up the slopes behind Cannes, we turned into the grounds of an uninhabited villa, with a picturesque but wildly overgrown garden. Seemingly familiar with the territory, Basil brought the car to a standstill next to a picturesque curving walled bridge, overlooking a neglected but pleasing garden. The idea was for Basil to position himself on the bridge, while he took shots of me from above, smiling with delight as I gaze at the exquisite crystal container to which I owe my flawless complexion. As he leapt along the wall above me, his aim being to find the most suitable angle, there was no mistaking the sight above me: the fellow was not wearing any underpants, his manly bits and pieces leaping around in harmony as he frolicked back and forth above my head, naked beneath his miniscule shorts.

I didn't have the confidence to confront him about it, but I can tell you, it took true acting ability to hold my concentration on the magic of Max Factor's Crème Puff powder with that sight directly in my line of vision. After making our way back to Cannes, with recent events dominating my mind, we lunched at what had quickly become our regular stopover. I'd always known the fellow was grubby, I couldn't imagine what his debutant friends would think of such behaviour, but, soothed by a comforting glass of wine, I erased the incident from my mind. Even so, you'd think a highly respected photographer would travel with spare underwear, especially when on an assignment for such an esteemed client as Max Factor.

Making our way along La Croisette later that afternoon, we were approached by a French man who'd seen us working on the beach the previous afternoon. He asked me if I was aware that the Miss Cannes 1955 Beauty Contest was taking place the following day, as in his opinion, I should take part. Having nothing else planned we thought we might as well have a go. We were to be at the Cannes Sporting Club the next day at 2.30 pm. Luckily, I had my favourite white swimsuit with me, so we wandered along to the Cannes Casino and Sporting Club at the appointed hour. The casino was set in a splendid setting on the seafront, right next to the harbour. I added my name to the list of about twenty girls, some having travelled from all over France, each one of them a beauty.

The routine was similar to back home. I was somewhat at a disadvantage by not being able to speak the language and having to rely on a friendly tap on the shoulder from other contestants to keep me in line. Blindly dependent on other entrants, all I could offer in gratitude was a beaming smile.

The commentator and Master of Ceremonies was the American George Jessel. In his younger days, George had been a successful Jewish actor in American films, before moving into the field of comedy, where he carved out a successful career on the stage until, with the arrival of television, he found success for his Jewish humour. He was now in his late fifties but looked much older due to the hideous ill-fitting dark wig he chose to wear. When the TV shows dried up, George, being addicted to stardom, popped up all over the place as a professional Master of Ceremonies, including Miss Cannes 1955.

The contest started with me in my allotted space, not understanding what was going on until, following the conclusion of several routine elements, I found myself being gently pushed to the rostrum by the girls next to me, then draped in a sash proclaiming me the winner, surrounded by enthusiastic photographers, who coaxed me outside to pose amid the attractive surroundings, including the swimming pool.

I was touched by the friendliness of the other contestants. My being a foreigner unable to speak the home language caused me a tinge of guilt, but thankfully, the girls insisted I was a worthy winner. Back home, those regulars making up the heats for Miss England would have had her guts for garters if a usurper had barged in, as I had done.

Escorted to the poolside, surrounded by photographers, including Basil, I was made a great fuss of, the whole thing turning into a happy experience. On returning to the hotel, I took a call from George Jessel asking a favour. The following Saturday was to be the biggest night of the year, The Monte Carlo Red Cross Ball, attended by the crème de la crème of Riviera Society. George had an old friend, an American widower of ninety-three who would dearly love to attend the ball, but was loath to do so without a partner. Would I accompany him?

My first thought was I had no suitable dress, but that proved no problem. George's friend, Sam Cotteslow, was extremely wealthy, and there was time to get a couture ballgown made to measure in Cannes the next day. The plan was to drive into Monte Carlo next Saturday, where we would stay at the Monte Carlo Beach Hotel. I was assured I would have my own suite. Sam would arrange my flight to London for the following day. Thankfully, I would be spared the hazardous drive with Basil, which would have quite likely turned me white-haired overnight. As luck would have it, he went along with the idea, saying that he'd already seen the results of our work and couldn't be more pleased. I knew he'd be equally thankful to see the back of me, as I would him; we'd never really hit it off.

Friday was taken up by fittings for my ballgown. I was picked up from my hotel and driven to the couture house who were to make my gown. Stunned to find myself in such a place of excellence, I was coaxed into sampling a glass of champagne, while discussing my needs for the grand occasion. After running through the highlights of the collection with a proud wafer-thin Madame, the leading light of the establishment, I was happy to go along with her suggestions.

Due to my youth, it was decided I should go with pure white, which happened to be the shade of the current season. By midafternoon, with the last stitch in place, I couldn't resist holding the breathtaking creation to my body as I regarded my reflection in a full-length mirror. Could it be possible, the steady look returning my gaze was really me?

The nipped-in bodice of the gown, a sparkling delight, made up of a thousand sequins, my breasts, the star of the show, permitting me to appear deliciously provocative. Madame sent out for the perfect shade of nylons, before my feet found themselves enclosed in the daintiest satin high-heeled slippers, in which I might dance the night away if called upon so to do, although hardly likely, considering the age of my escort.

My host turned out to be a most agreeable gentleman, one of those rare gifts that turn up when least expected. Although ninety-three years of age with a marked stoop, his cheeks were as rosy as ripe apples, his gait that of a much younger man.

We occupied identical suites on separate floors, each with its own terrace directly overlooking the sea, where the sound of waves gently lapping the pebbles directly below was soothing, but inclined to make me nod off at the most inappropriate moments.

Anxious to rescue my gown from the large cardboard box in which it was gently enclosed, I excused myself, arranging to meet up as soon as I'd unpacked. Once more I held the gown against my body, a quick glimpse at my reflection signalling a heavenly evening ahead of us.

I met up with Sam as arranged in the splendid reception where we decided to take a stroll before the sun became too hot to do anything other than laze. As we were close to the evening's venue, we made our way there to see how things were coming along. The place was alive with activity, workers heaving enormous props to form the background and setting for the star of the evening, Zizi Jeanmaire, ballet dancer and dancer extraordinaire, the toast of France, star of several major Hollywood musicals, who, for reasons unknown, never really made it big in England.

Hating the dust and din and not wishing to get under the feet of the workforce, we felt it best to head back to base for lunch, as the temperature was rapidly rising.

We spent the afternoon lazing in the shelter of the cypress trees in the cooling gardens of the hotel. Whiling away the hours, we got to know each other pretty well. Sam asked me about myself. I told him as much as I felt fit, skirting over things that were best left unsaid.

I learned that Sam had long been a widower, with married children and grandchildren, nevertheless, determined to hang on to his independence. Remarkably, a few months earlier he'd survived a dreadful plane crash, ending up in the Atlantic Ocean, floating for four hours in freezing conditions, before being rescued without so much as a scratch. What an ordeal, especially for a man in his nineties, but here he was, fit as a fiddle, about to attend a ball on the French Riviera with a nineteen-year-old, flibbertigibbet called Margaret. During that afternoon we formed an affinity. I filled him in on my love of Wordsworth's poetry, allowing him to see my tattered copy of 'The Prelude.' It happened, his favourite poet was the American, Walt Whitman, whose work I eventually grew to admire. We vowed to always be friends, to keep in touch by telephone, but the truth is, it wasn't long before I received word from his daughter telling me he'd died suddenly from a stroke. After surviving four hours in the freezing Atlantic, we'd been granted one brief moment to salute each other as time glided by.

Meanwhile, the Grand Ball lay ahead. It wasn't long before George Jessel arrived, sporting his usual bonhomie. I'm certain he had no dealings with the evening's entertainment, but judging from his actions, you'd have thought he was running the whole caboodle. Anyway, he enjoyed clucking around like a flummoxed pigeon.

Arriving for the ball that evening, it was hard to recognise the magnificence of the Sporting Club was the same shoddy workplace on which we'd encroached earlier in the day. Being early, we were lucky to watch the arrival of the Monaco Elite. I'd been curious as to who bought the priceless jewels I'd so admired in the jewellery shops of Monte Carlo. It didn't take me long to see that the whole of the Sporting Club was overflowing with customers. Never in my wildest dreams had I seen such polished women, it must have taken them all day to get ready. Radiant women, young and not so young, in glorious gowns flown in from Paris. The hairdressers of Monaco must have had their work cut out, manipulating locks, their sole purpose being to support the dazzling array of tiaras on show, while diamonds, emeralds, sapphires and rubies dripped from ears, throats and wrists, sparkling from every part of a woman it was possible to sparkle.

We were placed at a table close to the dance floor, with a group of George's special American acquaintances who were touring Europe. They were easy-going and friendly, as I've usually found Americans to be. The head table, always reserved for members of the Grimaldi family, usually headed by Prince Rainier III, who was at the time madly pursuing Grace Kelly, the lovely American film star he was to marry in the spring of the following year in Monaco's Cathedral, so he may well have had other things on his mind.

That evening I shone. Not from jewels, I didn't own the tiniest diamond, but I was happy. My skin glowed, my hair lustrous and bouncing, as I floated in my gown and satin slippers. Sam and I took several turns round the dance floor. He still had everything going for him. I couldn't help but notice a number of golden glints in his remaining fine hair. Perhaps in his younger days, he'd been fair-haired.

Our entertainer, Zizi Jeanmaire, turned out to be a gamine, short-haired, all-round entertainer, breathtaking in her ability to persuade her lithe body into athletic, sculptured shapes, double-jointed, I would imagine, how else was it possible for a human to tie herself in such knots? Apart from her physical prowess, she was a gifted singer, keeping the audience mesmerised for as long as she desired. Altogether a marvellous evening, never bettered, but all good things must come to an end. Back in the privacy of my room, I danced and pranced before my mirror admiring myself, hating to waste precious time with sleeping. In due course, overtaken by nature, I must have fallen asleep, still in my ballgown.

The following day I departed for the airport quite early, not wishing to make a song and dance about it. Sam liked to sleep in, and after the activity of yesterday, he needed to rest. As I was leaving, who should I bump into, but George. If only he wouldn't persist in wearing that ill-fitting wig, unable to withdraw my eyes from the dreadful join, I surely appeared as discourteous. He asked for my home phone number, saying he'd call me.

George called me at the start of the new week with a request. Would I be free to accompany him to a film on the coming Thursday evening, followed by dinner with a few friends?

Sounding good, I looked forward to catching up with him.

Meanwhile, I caught up with Mum, not having seen her since the early summer, but I'd been thinking of her, missing our secret giggles, understood by no one but we two. I put a call in to Dad and Edna, which I didn't fancy, but needs must.

As always, Dad was seeking the Lord's protection, praying ceaselessly for my safe return to the fold. Edna prayed for me every day, her dream being that I might meet a truly Christian young man and settle down happily with this gentleman. My reply, however misjudged, was to utter the words, 'Don't be disgusting.'

~ 15 ~
London

My evening with George arrived. I chose to wear a simple lilac taffeta dress, made by a handy dressmaker I'd been introduced to, ideal for an evening at the pictures before dining in a niche restaurant. He turned up, as usual in a chauffeur-driven car, taking us to the Empire Cinema in Leicester Square, where to my amazement, I saw crowds of enthusiastic fans, a good-tempered police force keeping them back.

George had omitted to mention we were attending the swanky premiere of a British film, the name of which I've long forgotten, but which appears to have sunk without trace over the years. It was too late to worry about my inappropriate dress. There was nothing I could do but brave it out, so I took up position in the foyer admiring the arrival of the beautifully clad, bejewelled ladies of the world of film. As soon as the picture ended George aimed for a quick getaway, and in a matter of minutes we entered the ballroom entrance of Claridge's Hotel, where we found ourselves being guided to the midst of a grand ballroom heaving with bigwigs from the film industry, all docked out in white tie and tails, their ladies resplendent in their finest gowns. Arriving at a large round table in the centre of the room, I was introduced to none other than film goddess Elizabeth Taylor, and her second husband, the British actor Michael Wilding. They were sharing the table with a young British actor, Anthony Steel, who'd made a name for himself in several British war films, accompanied by his fiancée Anita Ekberg, an up-and-coming Swedish actress, who was to establish herself some years later as the buxom blonde who threw herself fully dressed into the Trevi Fountain in Rome, in the Federico Fellini film *La Dolce Vita*.

I recall Anita as being statuesque, stunningly glamourous, her waist-length blonde tresses tumbling over her ample breasts, displayed for all to appreciate. As young as she was, I detected a discontent clouding her lovely features.

Elizabeth was petite, breathtakingly beautiful, her face glowing within its own aura, her hair cut extremely short in a style which could only be worn by a perfectly symmetrical head. Both ladies wore billowing white ballgowns, whereas I, frustrated at knowing the perfect gown was hanging in my wardrobe, wore my neat little dressmaker's dress. At that moment, I could have killed George for not making things clear, as he happily proceeded with his introductions. I knew I was being targeted, when Anita remarked, 'Is this a little English girl trying to get into films, George?' George's reply was,' No, only Swedish girls try to get into films.'

Elizabeth, sensing trouble, smiled at me as she patted the vacant chair beside her, signalling me to go and sit next to her, which I did. The first thing I noticed about her, apart from her beauty, was her facial expression. It was an open book, there was no hidden side to this lady. Her deep violet eyes with their double-layered silky eyelashes looked unwavering into mine, making me feel completely at ease, quite forgetting whose presence I was in, as we chatted over our meal, while enjoying the odd glass of champagne. Keen to know more about me, I recounted a number of my escapades over the recent summer season, causing a few chuckles. Elizabeth's husband, Michael, was charm itself, but I couldn't help noticing there were few exchanges with the other pair at our table. Naturally George kept things lively, in his own inimitable way.

I had dined with the most famous, most beautiful film star in the world. This lovely young woman, only a few years older than me, had reached out with compassion to a fellow human being who was about to be bullied. In Elizabeth's company, the evening flew by, proving to be an unforgettable experience. Maybe it was just as well I hadn't worn the correct dress. In all likelihood, Anita wouldn't have bothered me and I wouldn't have sat next to Elizabeth if I'd been wearing Sam's gown.

I have never forgotten Elizabeth Taylor. How could I?

Elizabeth Taylor died in 2011. It can't have been many months earlier, while watching the evening news on TV, that I caught a report on her latest happenings. Buckingham Palace had recently acquired a sculpture of her former husband, the love of her life, the actor Richard Burton.

Elizabeth, who was in London undergoing hospital treatment at the time, had been invited to view the work in situation. I watched the TV screen as she was pushed along a corridor in a wheelchair, in the company of three male escorts, one being The Prince of Wales. I was shocked to see a shadow of the girl I'd met all those years ago. She was podgy, her plump face heavily masked in unbecoming make-up. With her wheelchair positioned before the image of the young Richard, her escorts distanced themselves from the scene. Tears rolled helplessly down her cheeks, landing where they happened to fall, with no move on her part to reach for a handkerchief. Her attendants stayed put, looking decidedly sheepish, making no move towards her. A camera zoomed in on her distress, intent on grabbing the most saleable shots. Appalled at the intrusion into Elizabeth's privacy, I wept in anguish as I watched this inhuman bear-baiting, remembering the day all those years ago when this spiky lady offered the hand of friendship to a scared girl in danger of being bullied, at a time when she, the divine Elizabeth Taylor, ruled the world.

The night before I left for my greatest adventure to date, I lay in my bed dwelling on how I'd reached this point in my life. It all began in 1940, when Dad and his fellow firemen saved their cigarette cards for me, each adorned by the most glamourous of film stars, both male and female, leaving me entranced by beauty for the rest of my life.

My exclusive luggage stood in the hall, in readiness for Brian, the Mecca man, who was to pick us up in the morning, when once more, I'd fly away in a great silver bird, up and away, this time to the Great New World of America, where everything was shining and modern. The people who mattered most to me would be at the airport to see me off. The whole family, including the Aunties, who wouldn't dream of missing an outing, Gordon and Miriam, how I'd missed that man lately with his steadying wisdom. I glanced at my white travelling suit, which had taken weeks to construct, but so elegant, well worth the wait, and as for curves, move over Marilyn. A white suit was asking a lot, knowing me. I must be on my best behaviour with all those photographers buzzing around. One splash of frothy coffee on my immaculate jacket would crucify my image, but this was not the time to fill my head with inconsequential maybes, now is the hour for sleep.

London

Tomorrow will take care of itself.

www.ingramcontent.com/pod-product-compliance
Lightning Source LLC
Chambersburg PA
CBHW011944150426
43192CB00016B/2774